THE INDIANS OF CANADA
THEIR MANNERS AND CUSTOMS

THE INDIANS OF CANADA
THEIR MANNERS AND CUSTOMS

BY

JOHN McLEAN, M.A., Ph. D.
(ROBIN RUSTLER)

THIRD EDITION.

With Eighteen Full-page Illustrations

GYAN

Published by

GYAN

Gyan Publishing House
5, Ansari Road
Daryaganj, New Delhi-110002
Phone: 011-47034999, 9811692060
E-mail: books@gyanbooks.com

Distribution Network
gyanbooks.com
India, USA, Canada, UK, Australia, France

ISBN : 978-81-212-3623-2 (PB)
First Published, 1892

2nd Impression 2020

Printed at: Gyan Press, Delhi.

THE INDIANS

OF CANADA:

Their Manners and Customs.

BY

JOHN McLEAN, M.A., Ph.D.

(ROBIN RUSTLER.)

THIRD EDITION.

With Eighteen full-page Illustrations.

LONDON:

CHARLES H. KELLY, 2, CASTLE ST., CITY RD., E.C.;

AND 66, PATERNOSTER ROW, E.C.

1892.

American Indians.

TO

HORATIO HALE,

WHOSE EMINENT LABORS AS A

PHILOLOGIST AND ETHNOLOGIST

HAVE BEEN ADMIRED BY THE SCIENTIFIC WORLD, THE

FOLLOWING PAGES ARE

Dedicated by Permission,

WITH SINCERE AFFECTION AND RESPECT.

PREFACE.

NINE years spent among the Blood Indians of the Canadian North-West, studying their language, customs, mythology and traditions, have given me opportunities of learning much that may prove interesting to young and old. After three years' residence among the Indians, I was requested to send information on the North-West tribes to the British Association, the Smithsonian Institution, and other learned societies. I then began earnestly to collect a good library of books on the Indians, and to study with enthusiasm among the lodges everything pertaining to the life and labor of the Red Men of the West. I soon found that many of the books written were of a sensational character, and at once determined to try to write something that would be reliable and, at the same time, interesting to all. The strange life of the dwellers in the lodges, the wonderful mythology and traditions, and the peculiar customs which are essentially their own, reveal to us a civilization that is fascinating, and yet but little understood. As I sat in the wigwams and lodges of the Indians listening to their strange stories, I thought I could not do better than record them for the benefit of the young; and as tales of adventure among cowboys in the Far West were recited as we were camped upon the prairie, they were preserved for the good of young and old. Herein are written stories of missionary heroism, episodes of every-day life in the camps of the red men, records of life among the cowboys, and facts and fancies of the Bedouins of the Western Continent. May the readers of these pages have their ideas changed as mine have been, by coming into closer contact with our dusky brethren, through their languages, literature, native religion, folk-lore, and later Christian life.

JOHN McLEAN.

LONDON,
February, 1892.

CONTENTS.

CHAPTER I. PAGE

INDIAN CUSTOMS:—Potlaches — Indian Names — Indian Women—Indian Telegraphy—Indian Burial Customs—Superstitions of the Blackfeet—Indian Marriage Customs—The Red Orator—War Customs—The Peace-Pipe—Scalps and Scalping—Prisoners in the Camp—Indian Charms—Camp Socials 13-75

CHAPTER II.

CAMP AND WIGWAMS:—The White Savages—The Minnesota Massacre—Indian Paintings—Picture-Writing—Medicine-Men—The Home of the Red Men—Native Religions—An Indian Camp—Footprints of the Red Man—Asokinuki—Indians and Buffalo—Indian Oratory—Primitive People—Native Americans—The Blood Indians 77-135

CHAPTER III.

INDIAN HEROES:—Tecumseh—Glikkikan—Red Jacket—The Swarthy Hero—Button Chief—Captain Joseph Brant.. 137-163

CHAPTER IV.

INDIAN TRADITIONS:—Legends of the Red Men—Kutoyis—Traditions of the White Man's Superiority—Myth of the Pacific and Legend of Qu'Appelle—The White Stone Canoe—Indian Traditions—Legends of the Hydahs and Ottawas 165-187

CHAPTER V. PAGE

THE LAND OF THE RED MEN:—The Canadian Wonderland—Landmarks—Western Americanisms—The Iron Stone—The Chinook Winds—Frontier Religion—The Old-Timer 189-215

CHAPTER VI.

FRONTIER TALES:—The Three Captives—The Doctor's Ride—The Long Hair—The White Chief 217-233

CHAPTER VII.

INDIAN LANGUAGES AND LITERATURE:—American Indian Literature—Eskimo Literature—Indian Syllabics—The Cree Language 235-258

CHAPTER VIII.

THE INDIAN PROBLEM:—The Civilizing of the Indian—Move On—Bible and Plough—Red and White—Among the Lodges—The Lazy Indian 261-285

CHAPTER IX.

CHRISTIANITY AND THE RED RACE:—The Gospel in the Wigwams—Language-Study—The Antagonism of Races—Environment and Religion—Light on the Prairies.. 287-325

CHAPTER X.

DO INDIAN MISSIONS PAY:—The Church and the Indians—The Red Aliens—Success of Indian Missions—The Cross in the Camp—The Lord's Prayer in the Cree Syllabic Characters 327-351

LIST OF ILLUSTRATIONS.

	PAGE
American Indians	*Frontispiece*
Indian Woman and Child	25
An Indian Grave	34
An Arctic Funeral	72
Indians Drying Meat	76
Indian Chief	92
An Indian Village	116
An Eskimo Village	136
Captain Joseph Brant	154
Indian Warriors	164
Shooting the Rapids	184
Crossing the Rockies	188
Hunting in the West	200
A Red River Cart	208
A Pawnee Chief	216
Indian Woman Carrying Wood	228
Making a Portage	234
An Eskimo Traveller	246
Camping Out	260
An Indian Boy	266
Indians Fishing through the Ice	282
An Indian Missionary	286
Indian Brush Lodges	326

THE INDIANS

OF CANADA.

CHAPTER I.

INDIAN CUSTOMS.

POTLACHES.

AN Indian accepts and gives freely, he remembers a kindness and never forgets an injury. There has never existed a more hospitable race of people, when they had anything to grant, to the wayfarer on his journey. They gave without stint, and did not expect any thanks for extending their hospitality and friendship. When they received gifts from friends, they thanked them not for this display of friendship and love, and when they bestowed help on others, they waited not for any token of gratitude.

We are thus apt to speak of them as lacking in appreciation of what has been received, but though prizing the gifts, they bestow freely, and thus an equality is made. This seems strange to the members of civilized races, who are very profuse in giving thanks for favors, but with the Indian it is "give and take." In some Indian languages there is not a single expression for "I am grateful to you," but they will say, "You have a good heart." For all favors received, they expect to give as much in return. When this principle is applied to them in their relation to the white people, they accept without thanks and do not expect to pay again, as they think that the white people have received in land more than they can ever repay in gifts to their red brethren. Hence it savors of ingratitude to us, who do not expect anything in return, to see them accept benefits without a word of thanks. Among the Indians of the Pacific Coast, there exists a festival known as "Potlach." It is a Chinook word meaning "to give," from the fact that the chief object is to make a distribution of gifts to friends. A chief desiring honor, or an Indian wishing to obtain a good name for himself, will call the people of his own and other tribes to enjoy the abundant provision made for them. Many of the adult members of the tribes will spend years of hard toil, live in poverty, denying themselves the necessaries of life, that they may be able to save a sum sufficient to hold a Potlach.

At these festivals a single Indian has been known to distribute, in money and various kinds of articles, to the amount of fifteen hundred dollars. At the beginning of the Potlach, the names of the persons to receive the gifts are called aloud, and they come forward in a very indifferent manner to receive a blanket or a gun, but when nearing the end of the distribution there is a general scramble for the property to be given away.

The Canadian Government has very wisely prohibited these festivals, as they are the cause of retarding the progress of the Indians. The industrious and thrifty alone can hold them, because of their wealth; and the evil becomes a serious one, when such persons will labor for years that they may be honored with a Potlach. The same thing, in principle at least, is practised among other tribes. I have gone through the Blood Indian camps and listened to their chief, or a person wishing to be held in high esteem among his fellows, calling upon the male members of the lodges to come to his lodge to enjoy his hospitality and spend the evening with him. In some half-breed settlements, the aristocratic members will save their funds that they may purchase the good things of life, and enjoy a season of feasting, lasting several days. The Potlach is sometimes given by a few persons in combination, who will invite the members of other tribes to assemble and share in the distribution to the number of several thousand persons. Fortune or fame is not confined to the ambitious pale-face, and the desire for honor and a place among the illustrious ones of the camps dwells in the hearts of the red man.

WAMPUM.

Readers of Longfellow's "Hiawatha" will find many striking references to wampum, as when Hiawatha went forth from his lodge

> "Dressed in deerskin shirt and leggings,
> Richly wrought with quills and wampum,"

and old Nokomis spake unto him about

> "The great Pearl Feather,
> Megissogween, the magician,
> Manito of wealth and wampum,"

who was

> "Clad from head to foot in wampum,"

which protected him when he fought with Hiawatha, so that he would have proved to be invulnerable had not Hiawatha struck him upon the head with a stone as he stooped to the ground, and thus slew him. At Hiawatha's wedding with Minnehaha, the guests came clad in

> "Robes of fur and belts of wampum."

Oweenee, the youngest daughter of a hunter of the North-land, rejected all the

> "Handsome men with belts of wampum,"

and chose the

> "Son of the evening star, Osseo!"

Chibiabos sang of the maiden's love for an Algon-k-in who had given her

> "As a pledge, the snow-white wampum,"

and the ghosts pleaded with Hiawatha not to lay

"Such weight of furs and wampum"

upon those he buried.

Wampum was made in early times of wood and shells, of various colors, but similar in size. The white wampum was wrought from the great concho into the form of a bead, and the purple from the inside of the mussel shell. It is thought, by some writers, to have belonged solely to the Indian tribes, but it has been found in mounds, thus proving its use among the mound builders.

It was used as a kind of currency among the tribes, as an ornament of dress, a means of sending communications, a token of friendship or precursor of danger, a record of historical events, and a pledge at the making of treaties. The shells being made into the form of beads were perforated, strung on leather thongs, and used as wampum strings, or woven into belts of various sizes and designs. The peace belt given to individuals, and tribes, as a token of friendship, was made of white shells, and the war belts were woven with those of a dark color. When a war belt was sent to a tribe and accepted, it denoted that common cause in war was to be made by both. A curious custom prevailed among some tribes, of adoption by force. When a family had lost a son or daughter, the parents hired a captain with a black wampum belt to secure a substitute. Taking his band with him, he went out, as if going to war, and took a prisoner, who, if he were a white man, had his head shaved and painted. Whoever he might be, the belt was hung about his neck, and he was brought to the family, who received him with much affection.

Through the influence of Zeisberger, the Moravian missionary, and his colleagues, the Delawares, during one summer, three times rejected the war belt. When messages were sent, if they portended danger, black belts were sent, but if they betokened peace, they were white. Sir William Johnson, during the troublous times in Pennsylvania in 1768, sent runners out with peace belts, and kept the tribes from going to war. Belts were given as a pledge at treaties, some of which were received by Sir William Johnson. They were of several rows, black on the sides, and white in the middle.

Wampum strings, known as mourning wampum, were given to the friends of deceased persons as remembrances. The Indians who had been Christianized through the labors of the Moravian missionaries, prepared belts of a peculiar kind. The Christian Delawares sent belts to the Wyandots as an acknowledgment of lands ceded to them. These were half a fathom long, had no devices, except through the middle, and a white cross at one end. They denoted their national equality with the Delawares, and their religious distinction from them.

Wampum strings were given as pay to the performers at the Indian feasts. Among the Iroquois, wampum strings were employed for narrating historical records. They served as guides to each topic or subject of address. There was a keeper of these strings, who thus became the keeper of the Iroquois archives.

When Peter Jones had his audience with the Queen, he presented a petition and some wampum from the Ojibways of Canada. In speaking of Her Majesty in his journal, he records: "I then proceeded to give her the meaning of the wampum, and told her that the white wampum signified the loyal and good feeling which prevails amongst the Indians toward Her Majesty and her government; but that the black wampum was designed to tell Her Majesty that their hearts were troubled on account of their having no title-deeds to their lands; and that they had sent their petition and wampum that Her Majesty might be pleased to take out all the black wampum, so that the string might be all white."

Several belts have become notable, because of the perons and facts connected with them. When Count Zinzendorf was in America, he met a delegation of Iroquois Sachems, who gave him a fathom of wampum, consisting of one hundred and eighty-six pieces, which was taken to England, brought back to America by Bishop Spangenburg, and used oftentimes by the Moravian missionaries in their negotiations with the Iroquois.

After the treaty of Pittsburg between Congress and the Delawares, including some Senecas and Shawanese, a deputation of Americans went into the Indian country, bearing to the tribes the "Congress Belt," six feet long, and more than half a foot wide. Then there is the Penn treaty belt, supposed to have been given by the Leni-Lenape Sachems in 1682, at Shackamaxon. It is composed of eighteen strings of wampum, has in the centre white wampum, and the device of an Indian grasping in friendship the hand of a white man. The various designs have their own meaning known to the Indians, and interpreted by the wampum keepers of the tribes.

INDIAN NAMES.

It seems strange to a pale-face that when an Indian is asked his name, generally he will appeal to his Indian friend to answer for him. The reason for this lies either in shame or modesty, as the names given them relate to honor or dishonor. Some Indians have two or three names. Among some tribes the name of a deceased person is never mentioned.

The names of children are sometimes given by the mother, and at other times by other persons, from some strange circumstance that has happened in connection with the child, or from some peculiar characteristic. Some are very pretty and others detestable. A Dakota mother allowed her babe to lie with its head outside the tent when the rain was pouring down. She thought it was dead, but another woman saw that the rain had revived it, and the child was called "Rain in the Face." Indian names of persons sound strangely to civilized ears, as Eagle, Black Hawk, White Calf, Morning Star, Red Crow, Seeing Afar Off, Bull's Head, Old Sun, Three Suns, and White Antelope. Generally these names are changed at manhood for others more appropriate, and serve to remind the owner and his friends of some deeds of honor or shameful actions. Tall Man, Old Woman, Beggar and Thief, are names oftentimes given to men. Who does not remember the beautiful Winona and Minne-ha-ha—laughing water—immortalized by Longfellow in his poem upon Hiawatha.

Some of the names given to places in the Indian languages are very significant. Many, however, have lost their beauty in being translated. High River does not sound so well as Spitsi (pronounced Spitze). Montana is preferable to its Indian name of which it is a translation of Tayabeshockup, meaning the "country of the mountains." A better name has been found for the capital of the North-West than its former Indian one, "the Creek where the Bones Lie." Belly River received its name from the fact that the Gros Ventres at one time lived there, and Bow River from the wood found on its banks suitable for making bows.

Many of the Indian names of places have been retained, but these have oftentimes been sadly changed by persons entirely ignorant of Indian language as almost to lose their meaning. The first name that comes up is Canada, said to be from the Iroquois language, meaning a village of tents or huts; some think it comes from the Cree word Kanatan, which signifies something neat and clean. There is, however, another explanation that I have not yet seen proposed by any writer upon the subject, and which I think is worthy of consideration. The mountain gorges were called, by the emigrants to California in the famous '49,

Canadas, the canada or gorge being often spoken of, especially by the Mexicans who went to San Francisco at that time. Many places have been named after Indian tribes and bands, as Lakes Erie and Huron, the former after the Indians also known as the Chat or Cat tribe. Then we have Ottawa, Seneca, Onondaga, Cayuga, Kansas and Utah.

There are names made from Indian words relating to some characteristic of the places to which they are attached. The following will explain themselves: Miramichi, the Happy Retreat; Couchiching, the Lake of Many Winds; Muskoka, from Musquotah, the Red Ground; Maganetawan, the Smooth Flowing Water; Manitoulin, from Manito, the Ojibwa for a god, and L'ile, the French for island, hence the Island of the Spirit; Manitowaning, waning, signifying a cavern, thus it becomes the Cavern of the Spirit; and Manitoba from Manito, spirit, and waba, a strait, the Strait of the Spirit, so called from the many mysterious things seen and heard in the strait of Lake Manitoba by the Indians; Saskatchewan received its name from the Cree Kisiskatjiwan, the Swift Flowing River; Keewatin, the North Wind; and Assiniboine is an Ojibwa word meaning the Sioux of the Stones, from Assin a stone, and bwan, an Indian, hence we have the Stone or Stoney Indians, a tribe of the great Sioux or Dakota confederacy. These people used heated stones for cooking their food, and thus received their name, from which we have the district Assiniboia. Quebec is called by the Indians of the Gulf of St. Lawrence, Kepec, which means, being shut, from the fact that in looking up the river at some distance it appears as if it were closed; and Winnipeg is the term used by the Indians for Lake and the Sea, although it is properly unclean water. In Alberta we have Okotoks from the Blackfoot Oqkotokists, stones or rocks.

In the United States the Indian has left an indelible mark in the names given to places in his language. When Henry Hudson discovered the river which bears his name his men made the red men drunk, and this circumstance has been preserved in Manhattan, the place where they got drunk. Then we have Wilmette, from Ouilmette; Winnetka, the Dakota for Beautiful Land; Pewankeeweening, the Lake of Shells; Owatonna, from Ouitunya, Straight River, and Waseca, the Dakota for the Land of Plenty. From the Cree language there are such names as Michigan, from Mishigamaw, the big lake; and Chicago, from Chicag, a skunk. From the Ojibwa there are Milwaukee, from milo or mino, good, and akki, earth, the good land; Mississippi, from Mishisipi, the big river, and Nipissing, meaning in the leaves. There are many names even in our own North-West from different Indian languages, and these become transformed by the influence of the white man. As an illustration of this we have Minnedosa, from the Dakota word Minikaduza, which is sometimes contracted to Miniduza. From the language of the Indians we can learn much of their history, and many facts relating to their religious, social and political life are brought to view. In the desire for euphonious names for the new towns and villages that are certain in the near future to spring into existence, it would be well for those interested to obtain the exact pronunciation and accurate meaning of these, from Indian scholars well qualified to give such, and not to inflict upon the coming generations the hideous terms supposed to represent the languages of the red men. The native races may become extinct, but they will live again in our history, and the nomenclature of our country will reveal the trails of the red men.

INDIAN WOMEN.

Woman's position among the Indians is one that is supposed to be very degraded in all the tribes, and yet some of the native confederacies have given to her a position of equality, while she has become sole arbiter in those things belonging to her own sex and family.

Notably among the native races, in their treatment of women, is that of the Huron-Iroquois. There existed among the Indians a natural division of labor, different from that of the white races, owing to the fact that the red men were in general a hunting and stock-raising people, while the white people were devoted to agriculture. The men of the camps erected their houses, built their canoes and procured the food for the family, while the women attended to their domestic duties, performed the light farm work that was done, hauled the wood and brought in the water. The civilizing influences of the Gospel have wrought a change among some tribes, so that some now occupy an exalted position and enjoy the fruits of peace. Some, however, have not thus been favored. Although their lords and masters no longer pursue the labors of the chase, and dwell at ease in their changed mode of life, the women labor on in their former routine duties, which become degraded by comparison. Such is woman's position to-day among the Crees, Blackfeet,

Indian Woman and Child.

Sarcees, Sioux, and all other tribes who have not accepted the civilization resulting from the gospel of the Nazarene. Among these tribes are to be found maidens with comely appearance, neat in their dress and active in all their movements. Having crossed the threshold of womanhood, the maiden's hand is eagerly sought by means of courtship on the part of the young men, or by a speedy marriage, without her consent, to some old man, and she is taken to share his lodge with several other wives.

Amongst the Blackfeet, marriage is simply a bargain between the suitor and the young woman's father, for a certain number of horses. If she is fair and beautiful, a greater number of horses must be paid for the intended bride. From two to twenty horses have been paid for a wife by young men. In the good old days when the buffalo were abundant, the more wives a man possessed, the richer he became, as the greater number of robes dressed by them soon proved. When the husband became angry with his wife, he beat her with impunity; when he wished her no longer, he sold her, and when she was found guilty of adultery, her nose was cut off. A life of suffering is that experienced by women who dwell among the tribes degraded by the civilization of the pale-face. It is sad to be compelled to say that the settlement of the country in the vicinity of Indian Reserves by white men is injurious physically, mentally and spiritually to the members of the red race.

The happy, active life of Indian women, when game was abundant, has given place to one of idleness, filth and pain. The joyous hours are now filled with sorrow, as they see their homes becoming desolate by the ravages of disease. The primitive virtue of Indian womanhood has been destroyed, and immorality prevails amongst young and old. The respect and gallantry manifested by some tribes for the female sex has long since departed from the Indians of the plains, if, indeed, these ever existed. Life on a Reserve is very much different from the nomadic habits of former years. There is a change in all the domestic work. The house, the food, the methods of cooking, the arrangements of the home, and the new customs have all been influenced by the civilization of the white man, and what has first been learned has been of the very lowest type. The stealing of women by the male members of the camps constitutes one of the chief causes of excitement and trouble. A young man will elope with the young wife of an aged Indian, and then there is either pursuit and capture, or reparation demanded by the injured party. When death enters the family it is the women who suffer most. They are the chief mourners, as may be seen by the mutilated limbs, short hair and bloody hands. The aged medicine women are feared by the people, because of the power supposed to be possessed by them. The hard lot of the Indian mothers soon brings on premature old age, and the ruddy glow that lights up the countenance of the young wife or maiden is soon replaced by the saddened look and disproportioned form. The songs of the maidens are the benisons of God, that dwell among the lodges, cheering the sick and lonely in their hours of pain and grief.

INDIAN TELEGRAPHY.

It is a matter of surprise to those who know little or nothing of the war customs of the Indians, that despite the intelligence and activity of the white men, the native tribes are kept well informed of all those hostile to their interests. During the troubles in Colorado, between the American soldiers and the Indians, they were thoroughly conversant with the plans of the military, and wherever danger presented itself they were able to keep several miles in advance of their foes. Such apparent activity and keen sightedness was due to the telegraphic communication kept up between the tribes. The small looking-glass invariably carried by the Indian in his native state, is held toward the sun, and the reflection of the sun's rays is directed toward the persons intended to receive the communication. By this means a message can be sent from bluff to bluff, and the sentinels placed there can converse with each other. I have been aroused from my writing desk by the flash from a looking-glass carried by an Indian two miles distant. One day in camp, an Indian's presence was desired, but he was fully two miles away, riding on his horse. A man standing near, took out his glass and with a single movement of his hand the rider suddenly turned on his horse and after a moment's thought rode toward us. By means of fires lighted in prominent places, the light and also the smoke were used as means of signals which could be seen at long distances. Lighted arrows were projected into the air for the purpose of imparting information. When the red men came in contact with the white traders, they obtained from them telescopes and field-glasses of various kinds, which became very serviceable to them in hunting for lost horses, and discovering the near approach of intruders. These were called in to aid in signalling. When scouts were sent out to reconnoitre, their return was eagerly watched for by those in camp. Selecting a ridge from which they could be easily seen by the anxious warriors, they conveyed information by means of their blankets, or their peculiar movements in riding, and these could be understood perfectly, as they were accurately observed through the field-glasses owned by the chiefs and warriors. Due credit must, therefore, be given to the Indians for the intelligence, experience and sagacity displayed in all that belongs peculiarly to their native civilization. Ignorance of native customs and language, inability through lack of training to distinguish between what is exclusively Indian and that which has been introduced into their civilization by contact with talents and learning of a different kind from theirs, and prejudice arising from the fact that we belong to another race and have compelled ourselves to believe that the Indian stands in our way in securing our personal territorial success, are some of the reasons for our not appreciating the native talent shown by the Stoics of the plains. Justice demands an intelligent and impartial study of the Indians and of the Indian question.

INDIAN BURIAL CUSTOMS.

When Attila, the valiant leader of the Huns, suddenly died, his faithful warriors rode around his grave singing a funeral song. They cut off a part of their hair, gashed their faces with wounds, and then slew the captive who had dug the grave. The spoils taken in battle were thrown into the grave and then the barbarians engaged in excessive mirth. Had the name of a noble Indian chief been written instead of "Attila," the above would have been a true representation of burial customs among some Indian tribes. Several modes of burial have been practised by the native tribes. There are several kinds of mounds, descriptive of the customs of the mound builders of prehistoric America. The Tshimpsheans of British Columbia in former years, and the Apaches of to-day, practise cremation. The latter place the body on some sticks of wood, and it is there consumed. Should the person die in a hut, it is consumed with all that it contains. Some of the Alaskan Indians embalmed their dead, as the mummies are still to be found in the mummy caves. Some of the native tribes erect scaffolds or place their deceased relatives in the crotches of trees and on the top of some lofty rock. Sometimes an eminence is selected, and again a secluded spot where a lodge is pitched and the corpse placed within. Graves are also made on the top of the ground and small houses built over them. Bravery in death was one of the characteristics of the German Barbarians, as it is of the American Indians. A life spent in arms and a glorious death in battle were held to be the best preparation for a joyous immortality. Brebœuf, the Jesuit missionary, tells us of the tortures of an Iroquois prisoner. While his enemies feasted, and before he sang his death-song, he said to them, "My brothers, I am going to die, make merry around me with good heart; I am a man; I fear neither death nor your torments."

Some tribes killed two young men when a chief died, that their spirits might accompany him by the way. Wrapped in his buffalo robe or blanket the warrior is borne to his grave, generally accompanied by very few of his friends. Beside him in the lodge, grave or coffin, are placed the relics of the deceased, pipes, tobacco, and many things of greater or less value are deposited there. Various reasons have been given by students of American antiquities, all of which are of some value and have some truth in them. These things are placed there to avoid disputes among friends, to protect the bereaved from sadness at gazing upon the relics of the departed, and to keep the conscience clear from a charge of stealing from the dead. The best explanation is that found in the native religion of the Indians. They believe that everything in nature is possessed of a spirit, and that the spirits of the articles devoted to the deceased depart with him and are used in the spirit world. Thus when you point to the goods lying at the grave after many days, the natives will tell you that the substance remains, but the spirits live on the spirit of the things. The souls of hatchets and pipes, horses and dogs, go to the "happy hunting ground" for their master's use. We find this same idea of object souls amongst the Arabs and Gauls. The camel of the Arab was tied near the grave of his master, that he might there perish and follow him to the spirit world. The Gauls oftentimes contracted debts which were made payable in the state of future existence. When any person died, letters were thrown upon the funeral pile that the deceased might carry the wishes of the living to his relatives and friends in the world beyond. When a chief died, all his valuables, and sometimes his servants, were buried with him. When the daughter of Spotted Tail, head chief of the Brule Sioux, died, her two milk-white ponies were killed and their heads and tails nailed on the coffin. The Indians of our plains killed horses in like manner, but the advent of the whites has caused a change, and now along with the numerous things placed beside the deceased, part of the manes, tails and forelocks of his favorite horses is deposited there. As the Chippewa mother clipped a lock of hair from her departed daughter's head, she said: "I know my daughter will be restored to me, by this lock of hair I will discover her, for I shall take it with me." In this she referred to her own departure to the land of spirits. A striking peculiarity of some tribes is found in the existence of ossuaries, as amongst the Hurons, which were connected with the ceremony of the "Feast of the Dead," or the "Feast of Souls." At stated periods, every eight or ten years, all those who had died since the last performance of the feast were brought by friends and relations, in a very solemn manner, to the place of burial, a large circular pit or ossuary was dug, into which were cast all the bodies of the dead. Each person solemnly took up a handful of earth for preservation. After the moans and lacerations the time was spent in dancing and savage debauchery. Many of these burial pits or ossuaries are to be found around Lake Simcoe and Georgian Bay. The Indian brave sang his death-song preparatory to death. Upon the death of a chief among the Six Nation Indians, a song of condolence was sung, which "contains the names, laws and customs of their renowned ancestors, and praying to God that their deceased brother might be blessed with happiness in his other state." The Pawnee women, at sunrise and sunset, for three days, go to the graves singing the songs of the dead. The Puyallup women mourn for three or four months. Our Plain Indian women cut off their hair, one of their fingers by the first joint, and make bloody gashes on their legs. The male adults of the Apaches cut their hair short as a sign of mourning. Sad indeed is the wail of the Indian mother for the dear ones they have lost. When a chief dies among the Osages, a party of young men go out in search of hair. Formerly they sought for scalps, but when the whites became numerous in the country they became contented with taking the hair, finally they had to submit to buying it. On these occasions they were not allowed to touch food until they had returned successful from the expedition. The native tribes are very much afraid of the dead. In Siam the coffin containing the body of the deceased is taken out through a hole made specially in the wall for its exit, and it is carried thrice around the house at full speed that the spirit of the dead forgetting the place it passed through, may not return to injure the living. The Indians express a fear similar to this. They believe that the spirits go abroad at night and

An Indian Grave.

they are afraid to go out. When passing a grave in the darkness they will run or shout that the spirit may be driven away. Several Indian tribes burn down all the huts in the vicinity, and others remove them. This is done from a belief that the spirits will return to their former home, and if seen by any near relative, something serious will happen. They are afraid to reside in the neighborhood as the spirit will return and seek a companion among his relations, who will soon die. Superstition lingers around their belief. Upon removal to a new location, should a person die, it is attributed to something mysterious there, and they must speedily remove. Should any special medicine be given or any particular religious rite be performed, or the advent of a new class of people take place, a short time prior to an epidemic, these things are supposed to be the cause. There is an old legend of Devil's Lake (Minnewaukan—mysterious water) which states that many years ago a terrible battle was fought there. As the contending parties struggled they threw each other over the craggy walls into the deep water. The sight was so horrible, from the large number of bodies lying there, that the Indians gave it this particular name of Minnewaukan, and they said that they could hear the voices of the spirits as they passed by on the other side of the mountain. They believed that the water was possessed of a mysterious power, and they refused to eat the fish and drink the water. The name of a deceased relative is always mentioned with respect, some tribes never mentioning it and others only in a whisper. Totems and crest poles were erected over some graves showing the clan to which deceased belonged. In the temples of the Mexican Indians small images of the deceased were placed as their peculiar household gods. The influences of civilization are rapidly changing the customs of the Indians, and they will soon be things of the past.

SUPERSTITIONS OF THE BLACKFEET.

Mr. Frank H. Cushing, who was commissioned by the Smithsonian Institute at Washington, to investigate the history of the Zuni Indians, and who spent five years among them, becoming so influential as to be made second chief of the tribe, said to a friend, "If you are told that any primitive people is ignorant of its history, don't believe it. They know all about it."

In accordance with this statement we ask, "From what country came the Blackfeet?" Some of the aged Indians have stated that they remember when they were children hearing the old warriors tell how they came across the Rocky Mountains and were accustomed to engage in battle with flint-headed arrows. All their early history is shrouded with uncertainty. From their traditions it appears that the great ancestor of the Blackfoot nation dwelt on the eastern slope of the Rocky Mountains, that his children crossed the mountains and dwelt for a time on the Pacific Coast, where they mingled with other tribes and finally returned to the country in which they now live. That they must have associated with some other leading branches of the human family is evidenced by their language, religious ideas, customs and festivities. In the numerous Indian migrations that took place, probably they were driven by tribes stronger than themselves and compelled to seek an abiding home on the plains of the Canadian North-West.

Indians are strong believers in dreams. They attach a great deal of importance to the visions that pass in review during the silent watches of the night. They impart a reality to the object seen that oftentimes haunts them on their journeys over mountain and plain. They are afraid of their dead friends, and when they dream that they have seen them, they assert that the spirits of their dead friends have appeared unto them. An Indian chief died suddenly in one of the Blood Indian camps, and a few days afterwards two chiefs dreamt that they had seen him, and so great was their fear that they departed with all their people and sought another location several miles down the river.

Returning home one stormy wintry evening a Blood Indian friend desired me to stay with him, but I politely refused. As he persisted in his entreaties, I asked the cause, and he told me that I had to pass by two large trees, in the branches of which were two men buried, and that as I proceeded, the spirits of these men, which hover in the vicinity, would pursue me and try to carry me away to the land of the spirits. I inquired what he would do under the circumstances, and he replied that he would shoot his gun, shout several times and then run. As I smiled at his superstitious fears he sought to impress me with the advisability of whistling, that the noise made by this performance might drive the spirits away.

I sat in conversation with several Blood Indians, amongst whom were some chiefs, and directing my enquiries to the belief of spirits elicited some information on the subject. During our social gathering I learned that the spirits will linger for some time around the house of their friends and will then depart to the favorite haunts of the spirits. Some of the men solemnly asserted that they had seen the spirits of their deceased friends; several stated that they put out of their lodges pieces of bread with pipes and tobacco, and that the spirits fed on the soul of the thing and enjoyed the feast, although to our eyes they remained the same. This idea of object souls is a prevalent one between Indian and savage tribes in the first periods of their existence. The dead feed on the souls of the things while the objects still remained the same.

While distributing Sunday-school papers among some children, I gave away a copy with an illustration of the raising of Lazarus. On my departure a boy came running after me, stating that the paper was bad, because it had the picture of a ghost on it and he could not keep it. Some Indian nationalities ascribe to inanimate things the thoughts and feelings of intelligent beings. The Blackfoot nation possesses ideas akin to these. Winds are said to result from the flapping of the wings of a great bird in the mountains, and other phenomena are said to arise from the influences of inanimate things, or because the dead objects inherit the powers of living things. These Indians have, like many others, a superstitious dread about portraits. They seemed to feel that part of their personality left them and was reproduced in the photograph. It is only within the past few years that the fear so prevalent has begun to subside. Superstition is interwoven in many of their customs and also in their religious worship. When a person is lying sick, and the medicine-man is praying preparatory to performing his incantations and dispensing his medicine, no one is allowed to enter the lodge. The strange mysteries that enshrouded these superstitions of the past are losing their power, and the Indian mind, groping in the darkness for the light to direct, is gradually assuming an attitude of independence that will ultimately bring success.

INDIAN MARRIAGE CUSTOMS.

Various customs relating to courtship and marriage exist among the Indian tribes. Some have definite ceremonies and others are devoid of any religious ceremonial. Some of the Algon-k-in youths, charmed with the lovely countenance of a dusky maiden, seek to win her good graces by acts of kindness and bravery which are easily interpreted, and the way is made smooth for interceding with the parents by means of gifts for her heart and hand. In some tribes, courtship is not once thought of, and the marriage ceremony is a simple bargain between the young man and the parents of the maiden, or between the parents of both. It is simply marriage by purchase, the amount given being according to the abilities and personal accomplishments of the lady. A gun or horse will buy one, and others will not sell for less than five horses. As marriage is thus easily arranged for, so divorce is easily accomplished.

A singular and interesting ceremony exists among the Piute Indians. When a young lady reaches a marriageable age, she is placed in charge of two elderly women, in whose lodge she stays for a period of twenty-five days. Three times a day during this period she piles three large loads of wood, and every evening, under the guidance of her attendants, she goes to the river to bathe. At the end of the period she presents her wardrobe, which is oftentimes very expensive, to her attendants who prize it highly, and then returns to her father's lodge. She is now eligible for marriage, and becomes an object of attention on the part of young and old of the male portion of the camp. The young men vie with each other in exhibiting their skill and bravery, and the maiden naturally falls in love. None of the young people speak to each other save by the language of the heart and eyes. When a young man has determined to make her his wife, he repairs to the lodge of the maiden's father after all the occupants have gone to sleep, and entering quietly goes to the place where the girl is sleeping and sits down beside her. Being under the particular care of her grandmother, who sleeps lightly, keeping watch over her charge, and beside whom she is sleeping, the old lady speaks to her and she moves over to where her mother is sleeping and lies down at her side. The young man arises and goes out, without having spoken a word. This is continued for a long time, and constitutes the period of courtship. Never a word passes between the young man and maiden. Previous to this, he may have been on intimate terms with the members of the family, but from this time they cease to have anything to do with him. They hunt no longer together, and he is almost avoided. Should the young lady not wish to become his wife, her grandmother takes up a handful of ashes, and as he sits in the lodge, throws them in his face. Should he persist in his attentions, the other members of the family join in the persecution by throwing ashes and water upon him, and beating him with sticks. Despite all this, the enthusiastic lover is sometimes successful in gaining his prize. If the young lady is favorably impressed with the young man, she tells her grandmother, who informs the father of the maiden. The young people are brought together, and asked if they love each other. Should the reply be in the affirmative, the wedding day is fixed, and a feast prepared. At the feast, where are assembled many of their friends, the young people to be married sit side by side. The girl has a basket of food which she has cooked for her husband's use, and when handing it to him he seizes the basket with one hand and with the other grasps her left hand. The father then pronounces them man and wife, and the marriage ceremony is concluded.

THE RED ORATOR.

Native eloquence in the camps and lodges is not a

fiction, but sterling reality. Good voices, keen intellects, independence of spirit, and love of liberty, characterize many of the speakers among the Indian tribes. They are not accustomed to our modes of thought, different questions occupy their attention than those discussed in the councils of the white men, and they are not trained by the same methods as we employ. Life in the camp exerts an influence upon the minds of these men, which is felt in their treatment of subjects and their elocution.

When important questions relating to peace or war, hunting and other social, political and civil matters are to be discussed, they are talked over individually and in small groups in the homes of the people, and then a council is called that these may be studied from the different standpoints of the speakers, and a decision arrived at.

There is generally one leading speaker who has thought well over the matters in hand, and he introduces these in a speech, which the lesser orators support or dissent from in their addresses. Not possessing the ability to write in their own languages, or of even having such a grand medium as the syllabic system of the Crees and Cherokees, they do not write out their speeches, hence they are not memorized. Some of the young men among the Delawares were allowed to attend the councils to listen to the deliberations of the chiefs, and were instructed in the art of public speaking by some of these, after which they were employed as ambassadors to other Indian tribes before they took part in the proceedings of the councils.

The council was comprised of the chiefs, councillors and middle-aged men of the tribes. Women were not allowed to attend the meetings, but the young men assembled outside and listened to the addresses of their superiors. Visitors from among the white people were occasionally permitted to be present.

Seated on the ground, or on low benches, the peace-chief, who was generally the best speaker, presided and opened the proceedings by stating the object of the gathering, and then in a neat address expressed his views upon the question introduced. Profound silence ensued, the closest attention was paid, and no one interrupted any of the speakers. The assemblage indulged in smoking, as the speakers proceeded, and at the end of each address applause was given verbally. Voting on a question was done by the Yeas and Nays of the assemblage.

When a government official or representative of any leading institution is one of the parties to any agreement, or subject investigated, the Indian speaker will now step forward, uncover his head, shake hands, and then address the officer. During his address, if asking for concessions, occasionally he will shake hands, and when he is finished he goes through the same performance before retiring.

The orator stands erect with his blanket over his left shoulder, his right hand being free to use in suitable gestures. Dignified in his bearing, his eye lights up as he speaks; slow in utterance at the beginning, he argues, persuades and declaims in a rapid manner as he waxes warm with his subject, and then, with bursts of eloquence which moves the audience, he finishes in a strain of polished diction, that only those who understand the Indian language can appreciate. Judge him not by the careless and loose translations of illiterate men. Do we accept the translation of a French or German classic made by a bold incompetent pedagogue? If not, why should we receive the frivolous interpretations of men lacking the genius to seize the beauties of the Indian tongues and express them in acceptable Queen's English? We cannot appreciate fully the beauty of the expressions, nor the grandeur of the eloquence when the Indian is discussing a question that is specially and purely English, but when the orator has a native theme, he shows himself a master, and we must accord him the praise. The language of oratory is full of expression, clear, concise and dignified in tone. There is also an ambiguous method of expression employed by some Indian speakers for the purpose of delaying questions until events are such as will suit deliberate statements. The language of the councils is that of nature, figurative and more exalted than what is employed in common conversation. Red Jacket, Cornplanter, Netawatwees, Tecumseh, and Joseph Brant were famous orators, and amongst us to-day Crowfoot and several others are noted for their strength of intellect, shrewdness and eloquence of speech. When the Cherokees wished to renew their alliance with the Delawares they sent their ambassadors with wampum, which was to be delivered, and speeches made relating to the treaty. When the ambassadors arrived, they learned that one of the

Delaware chiefs was dead, and they had to wait until a suitable time came for their reception. The following is a part of the speech they made:

"We extract the thorns from your feet which you have got upon your journey, we take away the sand and gravel between your toes, and the wounds and bruises made by the briars and brushwood, we anoint with balsamic oil; we wipe the sweat off your faces, the dust off your eyes, and cleanse your ears, throats and hearts from all evil which you have seen or heard by the way or which has entered into your hearts."

When expressing their wish to re-establish peace between two nations, they said:

"We make a road extending above five hundred miles through the wood, we root out the thorns and bushes, remove all the trees, rocks and stones out of the way, transplant the mountains, strew the road with sand, and make everything so clear and light that one nation may look toward the other without any interception."—*(Laskiel.)*

The tongue of eloquence still lives in the Indian camps, and we shall rejoice in its strength when we draw closer together, so that the shadows of antagonistic customs may flee away.

WAR CUSTOMS.

The Indian's glory consists in being honored as a warrior. His ability as a hunter, medicine-man or orator is nothing compared to the esteem in which he is held by his tribe as a successful soldier. The training of the male portions of the tribes from infancy to manhood lies in that direction. Even in these times of peace, the boys and youths on the North-West reservations naturally carry their bows and arrows, as the city youths their marbles and balls, and practise continually with them. Living as the Indians have done for a long period in a state of warfare, tribe against tribe, and man against man, there have sprung up many customs, similar to each other in the majority of the tribes. These are singularly at variance with the military customs of white civilized nations, and the dissimilarity incites us to study them, that we may at any rate have something to create an interest for us amid the monotony of daily life. Indian wars generally arise from selfishness, a desire for military glory, revenge, or the attempt to secure captives. The members of one tribe enter the territory of another, for the purpose of hunting; depredations are committed and a war ensues. Some of the young men may go out to steal horses and women, or the stronger tribe may desire the land of the weaker, and one of the Indians is then killed as a mere pretext to start hostilities. Many of the petty things that originate contentions between civilized nations, beget strife among Indian tribes, spreading bloodshed and terror wherever they go. The Huron-Iroquois made war for the purpose of securing captives or slaves for adoption into some family or gens, that had from some cause been weakened. In this manner there was given strength to the tribe, by means of the foreign elements introduced. War was also made to propitiate the *manes* of deceased friends.

The spirits of the dead cried out for vengeance, and would not be appeased until some one was slain. When there has arisen any provocation, a council was held for the purpose of determining what was to be done. It may happen that an attack had been made, and the necessity for defence or revenge became so apparent that no council was held. The chiefs attended these councils, and urged, persuaded or opposed the warriors. Amongst the Huron-Iroquois the women had the power to command or prohibit a war. When anything concerned the women of the camps, they repaired to the councils, and made their demands in an authoritative manner. Such was their influence, that the noblest warriors and orators were compelled to submit to their demands. When the dull routine of camp life had become irksome during the winter months, and the young men became desirous of enriching themselves at the expense of their neighbors, they began to "make medicine."

Some of the Indian tribes rely upon the medicine-men or soothsayers, who consult the flights of the birds, and then make predictions. Some of the most notable Indian warriors have assumed the *role* of prophets. They dreamed dreams, and saw visions, and upon the strength of these they went to war. These seers were shrewd men, with much force of character, enabling them after having made the prophecy, to carry through all their plans to a successful issue. There is no doubt that the concentration of the minds of the warriors upon the prediction, with the faith and enthusiasm of the prophet, contributed greatly to produce successful results, as most of the prophecies were fulfilled. Prayers are made by the Choctaws and the Blackfoot confederacy to the sun before starting on a military expedition, that success may follow them. Should the answers given to their prayers be unpropitious, the war is deferred.

When the "making medicine" has been "strong" and everything bids fair to end in victory, a period of dancing and feasting follows. War-songs and war-dances are indulged in, the brave deeds of their ancestors are recited, and there, amid the excitement, vows are made of what shall be done when the enemy is found. The Sioux and other Indian tribes engage in the "no-flight dance," which means that they will not flee, but fight until they have taken some scalps, no matter how large the numbers opposing them. They vow to devote themselves to death rather than return unsuccessful.

The excitement becomes intense during these preparatory arrangements, which are exhibitions of cruelty and debauchery. Thirsting for blood, they are ready to go on the war-path. When there is an expectation of a general Indian war, it is necessary to secure the assistance of friendly tribes. This was formerly done by means of wampum and war symbols, such as a hatchet painted red. When the leader of a deputation presented the wampum to the chief of a friendly tribe, he delivered a speech upon the subject of the war. If the wampum was accepted, the cause was made a common one. In later times, tobacco has been freely used in making treaties and in seeking to enlist the help of allies. Bull Shield, a Blood Indian chief, told me that when out on the prairie alone, should he meet an enemy, and wished him to be on friendly terms, he would light his pipe, hold it to the sun, and then present it to his enemy. Holding the long stem of his pipe toward the unfriendly Indian, if it were refused they were still enemies, but if a few "whiffs" were taken from it, all animosity ceased. Amongst the Indians there are chiefs and captains, called by some of the tribes of the plains the peace-chiefs and the war-chiefs. In times of peace the peace-chiefs were supreme, and cared for the people, protecting, guiding and imparting counsel; but in times of war, the war-chiefs became dominant.

When a messenger was sent bearing wampum and a hatchet to secure the assistance of a neighboring tribe, he gave a speech, called upon the captain of the tribe to take up the hatchet and delivered the wampum. The lifting up of the hatchet and acceptance of the war-belt meant a declaration of war, the refusal of such was a "declaration of peace or neutrality." Thus arose the terms to "dig up the hatchet" and to "bury the hatchet," which became very significant terms in the early part of the present century in many new settlements in the United States. We oftentimes hear and read of putting on the war-paint. This referred to the habit the Indians had of painting their bodies in the most hideous colors when starting on the war-path, that they might appear formidable to their enemies.

The Omahas on going to war wore white blankets,

had their hair concealed under a white cloth, and their faces whitened with clay. They were thus enabled more stealthily to avoid their enemies and suddenly pounce upon them, by the colors blending with the prairie grass. The colors of other Plain tribes differ from each other, the most hideous being chosen.

The night previous to the departure of a war party, the Iroquois spent in feasting and dancing. Pork and dog's flesh were eaten, the latter to give courage to the warriors. The chiefs and the wives of the warriors were present. After the feast the captain led the dance, and throughout the whole night, until daybreak, the dancing and war-songs were kept up. A line was then formed and the war party marched through the camp or village until the last hut or lodge was reached, when the captain, followed by his men, discharged their guns and then marched into the forest singing war-songs. The wives of the warriors and the guests spent the second night in the forest camp in riotous carnival. After they had all become excited for action, and had boldly declared what they would do, they departed for the field of plunder, blood and scalps. Sometimes war parties were absent for years, and sad, indeed, was the return, though crowned with victory, for some had fallen in battle, and the camp had also been visited by death.

Some of the Plain tribes west of the sources of the Mississippi chew a bitter root called Zhigowak before going to battle, believing that it will give them courage and make them insensible to pain. A hideous-looking spectacle is that of a party painted and feathered from head to feet. Some of these I have seen, and it is impossible to forget them. The Indian warriors of the Eastern States stamped their mouths with the symbol of a red hand, signifying that they had drunk an enemy's blood.

When the Moravian missionaries were attacked at Gnadenhutten, there was found the remains of George Fabricus guarded by his faithful dog. Upon the stump of a tree lay a blanket and hat with a knife stuck through them, which signified, "Thus much have we done, and are able to do more!"

A message was once sent to the Muncey Indians against Zeisberger with the accompanying war symbols, a string of wampum, stick painted red with several prongs, and a leaden bullet.

Sometimes, by stratagem, the Indians will have their plans so fully developed and carefully managed, that the white settlers will not suspect an outbreak, but this is rarely so. In times of peace friendly Indians will be found with their families congregated at the towns and villages, but when they intend to attack the unwary, they will remove their wives and children to some safe place, that their lives may not be endangered.

Spring and summer is the time chosen for engaging in warfare, for at those seasons of the year there is good grass for the horses, and these are in good condition.

Just before sunrise, or after sunset, an attack is made, as travellers are tired at night and drowsy in the morning, consequently not able successfully to resist the enemy. The Moravian Mission at Gnadenhutten was attacked at night, just as they had finished supper. Very rarely do the Indians make an attack during the day or night, or engage in war in the winter. They generally steal horses and get ready to fight when the grass is good enough for their horses.

The fighting men of the camps consist of the able-bodied men, many of whom are quite young. Some of the tribes have peace-chiefs, but amongst the Delawares there were no regular war-chiefs. A sachem on going to war was reckoned only as a common soldier.

Any warrior could form and lead a band to war, but when a general war took place there were two supreme military chiefs, who directed the campaign, and whose office was hereditary.

The warrior may throw a buffalo skin over his right shoulder and a quiver of arrows over the left, but invariably he goes forth naked and painted, wearing a head-dress of swan's feathers, or those of the most sacred bird of the Indians, the black eagle. The Delawares had trinkets dangling from the ears and nose, and tatooed their chests, arms and legs with the most fantastic figures. The Blackfeet painted their horses as well as themselves, and their war-bonnets carried the charms which were to protect them. These were the skins of the animals seen in visions, and the visible representations of the Indian's Spirit Guide. These were supposed to ensure success in war and were only worn at that time, or in times of great necessity and extreme scarcity of game. They were held to be very sacred by the Indians. The arms used in battle were bows and arrows, spears, war-clubs; and for defensive armor, round shields made of buffalo skin, painted with various devices, such as the Arickarees carried. A corselet made of pieces of hard wood fastened together with bear-grass, which fitted the body and was pliant, and a kind of casque of cedar bark, leather and bear-grass, which protected the head from an arrow or war-club; or a very thick shirt made of elk skin of several thicknesses, which reached from head to feet, and was arrow-proof, such as was worn by the Flathead Indians.

The Indians do not fight as the white men, but resort to stratagem. Instead of meeting in a body and opposing the enemy, they contend singly, without any order—running, shouting and fighting, each on his own account, and all under the direction of the war-chief. It was because of this mode of fighting that oftentimes more white soldiers than Indians were killed in battle. The solid ranks of the white regiments present a fine target for the Indians.

During our late rebellion this was not seen, as the Indians were Forest Indians, but had the Plain tribes risen there would have been different modes of fighting, a larger number of warriors, stronger physically, better equipped, with Winchester rifles, and horses, and accustomed to war. We must feel grateful for the fact that they remained loyal during the rebellion.

Sometimes pitched battles are engaged in between the tribes. The Flatheads of the Pacific Coast frequently engaged in pitched battles on opposite banks of small streams. Not many of the people were killed, although they fought for several days. When one party lost more than the other, compensation was made in slaves or some other kind of property.

In making an attack upon the foe, the warriors always tried to surprise or confuse their opponents by a sudden rush, shouting their war-whoop.

Selecting a good location, they rushed suddenly upon the cavalry, throwing their blankets in the air and shouting, which startled the horses of their opponents, throwing their riders, and leaving many of them at the mercy of the red men.

When desiring to attack a coach or train upon the prairie, they never did so without counting accurately every man and gun in the party.

The striking contrast between the customs of the red and white men in war are evident, but these will be still further seen when we come to study their modes of making peace, the war-whoop, and treatment of prisoners.

THE PEACE-PIPE.

When the Sioux Indians met a party showing hostile intentions, and they desired a parley, they took their buffalo skins, raised them with both hands above their heads, and then spread them on the ground. When the parley was agreed to, the principal chiefs separated themselves from the tribe, when a short distance apart, and sat down, a few chiefs of the other party came out and, sitting down, completed the circle. The calumet, or peace-pipe, was then brought out.

This was generally made of red clay or stone, the long stem of the pipe beautifully ornamented with symbolic feathers, skins and paint. Many an old legend lingers around these calumets, and many wonderful stories are told about the battles and treaties when these are shown to the visitor at the lodge. One of these in my possession is an old one, smoked by the chiefs of the Blackfoot confederacy at the making of the treaty with the Government at Blackfoot Crossing in Alberta.

In the song of Hiawatha, Kitcimunitu, the Great Spirit, addressing the red men as his children, directs them to—

> "Bathe now in the stream before you,
> Wash the war-paint from your faces,
> Wash the blood-stains from your fingers,
> Bury your war-clubs, and your weapons,
> Break the red stone from this quarry,
> Mould and make it into peace-pipes,
> Take the reeds that grow beside you,
> Deck them with your brightest feathers,
> Smoke the calumet together,
> And as brothers live henceforward."

The stem of the peace-pipe was about four feet in length, beautifully decorated with horse-hair dyed in various colors, feathers, and the white skins of the weasel.

The entire party seated in a circle, a fire was lighted in the centre, the pipe-bearer stepped within the circle, lighted the pipe, held it toward the sun, then toward the four points of the compass, gave it to the principal chief, who took a few "whiffs;" holding the head of the pipe toward himself, he gave it, stem forward, to the head chief of the other party. It then passed successively around the entire circle, each one smoking, after which friendship was established, and negotiations entered into.

Sometimes the pipe-bearer, after lighting the pipe, inhaled the smoke, gave one puff toward the sun, another toward the earth, and another toward the east, afterward handing it successively to each of the party. There may not seem to be much importance attached to the acceptance of a piece of tobacco, or smoking out of the same pipe, but it meant a great deal to us during the Rebellion, when these acts implied the agreement of the persons in the disloyalty of the rebels. When the air was filled with reports of battles, and strange Indians visited the reserves to converse with our Indians, we felt very anxious to know whether they had accepted the bonds of union or not. Significant, indeed, are these customs of the red men, but they are devoid of meaning to those who care not to make any inquiries into the native civilization of the Indian race. Travelling on the prairie, the weaker tribe desiring leniency at the hands of the stronger, sent some of their number to an eminence, where they spread their arms toward the foe, beseeching them by this action to show clemency toward them. Meeting those whom they knew to be friends, or, at least, thought so, they shook hands with them profusely. There is not the least doubt but they learned this from the white men. In times of war they signalled to each other by means of their sign language, as they rode upon the bluffs. By the use of looking-glasses, they could telegraph to each other for miles, and at night they shot lighted arrows into the air, which could be seen for twenty miles.

By these means, during the Indian wars in the Western States, they were able to keep ahead of the troops for twenty miles, and always be conversant with the movements of the enemy.

Runners were employed by our Indians who, in some mysterious manner, kept themselves posted as to the progress of our troops, and the events of the half-breed insurrection. My own suspicions were that, independently of the telegraphic system, they were supplied with information by white men in the country.

The days of peace have come, and again are we rejoicing in the friendship of the dwellers in the lodges, under the shadow of our Rocky Mountain home.

SCALPS AND SCALPING.

War-whoop and scalps are associated in our minds with the cruel warfare of the red men. The thrilling stories of painted Indians shouting the scalp-yell, and carrying the scalps of their victims as they dashed into the forest, or sped swiftly over the plains, have impressed us so deeply, when we read them in the days of our youth, that the pictures which rose before our imaginations are as vivid to-day as when first they were read. When prisoners were taken in battle, and the successful party returned, the whole party shouted the war-whoop as many times as there were prisoners.

Heckewelder, the famous Moravian missionary and Indian scholar, says in his writings, that the war-whoop or scalp-yell consists of the sounds of *aw* and *oh* uttered in succession. The last syllable was prolonged until the breath was expended, and was raised an octave higher than the first. It was a terrible yell, which, when heard for the first time, made such an impression that language fails to describe it.

Captain Pipe, a famous Delaware chief, was unfriendly to the Moravian missionaries and their work, and sought to frustrate all their efforts made for giving the Gospel to the Indians. He seized the missionaries and took them to Detroit to the commandant, who had instructed him to take them there. When he entered the fort, he and his Indians shouted their war-whoop for some time. At the council held there, he made a speech and presented the commandant with a stick, on which were fastened seven scalps. He was followed by others, who presented sticks having scalps on them. The artists of the olden time, including Benjamin West and his successors, invariably painted the Indian with his traditional scalp-lock, and yet few, if any, of the present generation have seen amongst the Indians of the Dominion and the United States a single red man with his head bereft of hair, save the scalp-lock. But it is not a fiction, it is a reality. The Delawares tattooed their chests, arms and legs with fantastic figures, and the head was bald except a circle at the crown, and two twists hanging down on each side, ornamented with beads and various trinkets. Now, the Indians did not use razors for this purpose, but followed, no doubt, the practice now in use among the Crees, Sarcees, Bloods, Piegans and Blackfeet of our Western plains. These Indians carry a small pair of tweezers fastened by a string around the neck, and with these they pluck the hair from their faces, until not a vestige of a beard is seen. By the aid of their small looking-glasses, which they always carry in a small bag, hanging from their necks, for the purposes of signalling on the prairie, according to their system of telegraphy, and for arranging their toilet, they will spend hours performing the process of depilation, which, though very painful, they would rather endure, than have their faces covered with hair.

The Indians were always anxious to secure scalps, as the warrior who had the greatest number was held in the highest estimation by the members of his tribe, and feared by his enemies. It was impossible for a warrior to carry the body of his victim to prove his valor to his fellows, so he took the scalp, and showing it to the warriors and people of his tribe, he vaunted his courage and received their applause. The victorious Indian having thrown his victim, put his foot upon his neck, twisted the scalp-lock with his left hand, pulling it lightly to detach the skin, then cutting the skin around the crown of the head, tore the scalp off. This was done quickly, and then fastening it to his belt, or carrying it in his hand, he hastened to join his comrades or make his escape. After the expedition was over, scalp dances and scalp processions were held. When an Iroquois war party returned with success, they gave scalps to friends to supply the lack of prisoners. These scalps were worn on days of rejoicing, and at other times hung at their cabin doors. Many scalp-locks have I seen in the years gone by hanging outside the lodges of the Blood Indians, but to-day not a single one is to be seen in all the camp. The scalps and trophies of war were placed on poles, and paraded among the lodges, followed by the warriors decked in savage finery, and hideously painted as for war. We shudder when we read of the cruel warfare and the deeds of blood.

The reeking scalp and the wild war-whoop seem to belong to savage tribes, and still, during the early years in New England, the colonists and soldiers took the scalps of the Indians, and the officers of justice in America, acting under the British Government, offered large bounties for Indian scalps.

Governor Morris declared war against the Shawanese and Delawares, and offered large rewards for scalps and prisoners.

Hannah Dustin, in 1698, took ten scalps with her own hand, and received a bounty for them. Captain Lovewell and his party surprised ten Indians, killed and scalped them, and was paid in Boston a thousand pounds for them.

The colonists who attacked Zeisberger's mission, scalped the Christian Indians, and bore their scalps with them.

Dr. Ellis states that Wm. Penn declared the person of an Indian to be sacred, but his grandson, in 1764, offered one hundred and thirty-four dollars for the scalp of an Indian man, one hundred and thirty dollars for that of a boy under ten years of age, and fifty dollars for that of a woman or girl. The excitement and cruelty of the period of colonial warfare aroused the people to commit these horrible depredations, but allowing every reasonable excuse for the angry passions of those who had lost friends and relatives, the superior intelligence of the white race should always be sufficient guarantee for the prohibition of cruel and savage rites.

Many persons have been scalped and still have lived. Washington Irving, in "Astoria," mentions the Kentuckian Robinson, who had been scalped and lived for years afterward.

Jacob, one of the members of the Mission at Gnadenhutten, was scalped by the soldiers and left for dead. He became subject to fits, and in one of these fell into a creek and was drowned. He was known for years as the "Scalped boy of Gnadenhutten." This subject is a very unsavory one for the pen of a writer who believes that great injury is done to the youthful mind by the reading of sensational Indian stories, and by putting into the hands of our youth the records of crime. I have placed the matter before you, free from the spurious tales and horrible details of savage life, which profit nothing, but leave behind them sad impressions, injurious to young and old.

PRISONERS IN THE CAMP.

The battle is over; men, women and children are flying in every direction, and the victorious tribe has taken a large number of prisoners. It is difficult to keep the male prisoners in subjection, so they are slain, and the women and children preserved. Out on the battle-field the dead are strewn, the bodies of the enemy are scalped and perhaps mutilated; but the victors take their dead friends and bury them. Conquerors and conquered look well after the dead. The Indians are always careful not to allow their dead to fall into the hands of their enemies. Sometimes a grave is dug in the forest, and so carefully covered that none, save those who know the spot, can ever find it. Thus Tecumseh, the famous Shawnee leader, was hidden from his enemies when he fell in battle. They may take their dead friends and fasten stones to the bodies, place them in running streams where they are never found by the foe. They will brave the greatest danger to remove the dead and wounded from the field of battle.

A war party having returned, and being successful, waited outside the camp or village until their comrades came out to meet them, to conduct them to the camp, to give them a grand triumphant entry. The procession divided into its separate bands, each under a leader. Each band had its own standard, a spear or bow decorated with beads, porcupine quills and painted feathers. Native bands of music played, old men and women went out to meet the returned warriors with expressions of joy and sorrow. Mothers and children shouted for joy when they beheld their husbands, fathers, sons and brothers; and loud wails rent the air when those whom they sought returned not, or were borne sorely wounded into the camp. Then began the scalp procession and scalp-dances, the singing of war-songs and feasting. Criers went around among the lodges, shouting aloud the chief events of the battles, and the various exploits of the warriors.

Should the party be unsuccessful in war, the prairie was burned to conceal the traces of their retreat, as they were afraid of being pursued by their enemies.

The first thing to be done, upon the return of a war party having prisoners, was to decide as to the manner of their disposal.

The Iroquois generally burned two or three of them, and then distributed the others—men, women and children—among several households for adoption. By this means the Iroquois kept up their strength. A council was called to discuss the question of distribution, and when a decision had been arrived at, the result was made known by a crier, and the distribution made in the public square. When a son or daughter died, the parents engaged a captain to procure someone to fill the place of the deceased. A woman having lost a husband, did in like manner.

A belt or collar of black wampum was presented to the person intrusted with this duty. If the prisoners were secured, and the women were satisfied with them, they were adopted into the family; but if rejected, they were burned. White prisoners had their heads shaved and painted. The belt or collar of wampum was fastened around the neck of the prisoner, and in this manner he was taken to the bereaved family.

When sufficient prisoners were not secured to fill up all the vacancies, scalps were given to complete the number. When a larger number of prisoners were taken than were needed, they were distributed amongst the allies of the Iroquois. The place of a deceased chief was never filled by any but a chief, or by two or three slaves, who were always burned. The custom of adoption is practised amongst the Cree Indians, though not in the same manner, nor to such an extent as amongst the Iroquois.

Many years ago, an Indian missionary amongst the Crees was travelling with his interpreter, a fine young native. They were together in their canoe, and were engaged shooting wild fowl as they journeyed on their mission of peace. The missionary's gun accidentally went off, killing his companion. Some of the people advised him to flee, but he determined to trust in God and the justice of the Indians. He repaired to the lodge of the young man's friends, narrated the sad tale, and offered himself to fill the place of the deceased. His proposition was accepted, and he was adopted into the family.

Amongst some of the tribes, the prisoners were subjected to severe torture. They were handed over to the women, who mocked and spat upon them, calling them hard names, and severely taunting and jeering at them. The brave warrior suffered in silence, or returned scoff for scoff, urging them to go on with their cruelty, that he was a man with a brave heart, and heeded them not. The Blackfeet placed their prisoners as a mark, and shot at them with their arrows.

Prisoners amongst the Indians were sometimes led out in advance of the party, and given a chance to run for their lives. The entire party of warriors would then pursue them, and if overtaken they were killed.

A white man taken prisoner was allowed this privilege. When he saw that it was a race for life, he darted forward, pursued by the warriors, shouting madly. Being a good runner, and knowing that his life depended upon his legs and courage, he fled with wondrous speed, leaving the main body of his pursuers far behind. Fainter became the sounds of their voices, and venturing to look behind, he saw that two Indians only were close behind him. Turning suddenly upon the one nearest to him, he quickly surprised him, and slew him with his own weapon. Onward again he sped, and the yells of the main party, when they discovered their comrade dead, reached his ears, and gave fresh impetus to his courage and speed. Bounding into the strip of timber that lined the river, and dashing into the water, he soon reached a place of safety, far from the deadly weapons and tortures of his pursuers.

Sometimes the prisoners were compelled to dance for the amusement of the people. You may have read of the custom of running the gauntlet. A place of safety was shown to the prisoner, and toward this he was directed to run. The Indians formed two rows, between which the prisoner had to run. He started, and ran with all possible speed, for the Indians were armed with sticks, with which they beat the runner as he passed. If he became discouraged, he was certain to receive more stripes, and very likely would be beat to death, but should he be anxious to escape the blows of his enemies, he ran quickly, and thus many failed to strike him. When an inveterate enemy of the tribe was taken, he was subjected to greater tortures than the other prisoners. Col. Crawford was taken by the Delawares, stripped naked, first beaten with sticks, and then tied to a post fifteen feet high, which was surrounded by a large fire of hickory poles, distant from the post six yards. The rope by which he was fastened was long enough to allow him to walk around the post two or three times. They burned him with brands, coals and hot ashes, and discharged gunpowder at him. The space between the fire and post was soon filled with hot coals, and upon these the Colonel was compelled to walk. He suffered these terrible tortures for three hours, while the Indians were making sport of him, and then death gave to him a glad release. The Indians excused themselves for thus treating him, by saying that he had fought against the Indians, and committed many inhuman deeds on their friends, so that they were but repaying him for the evil he had done.

The Iroquois sometimes feasted on the bodies of the prisoners whom they had tortured to death. They gave pieces of their roasted hearts to the boys and youths of the tribe, to give them courage to fight against their enemies.

Female prisoners amongst the Indians were handed over to the women who took care of them, but they were generally given to the Indians to become their wives. Captivity in an Indian camp for white women is terrible, but still a few instances are on record where girls taken in infancy, when found in womanhood as mistresses in the Indian lodge, have preferred to remain with their Indian husbands and children, rather than return with their parents and friends of their youth, to happy homes. Great excitement prevailed in the North-West Territories during the late Rebellion, when it became known that there were female captives in the camps of the rebels. Members of the mounted police force, cow-boys, ranchers and others were loud in their denunciations against those who had the prisoners; and often during those exciting times did I hear vows of vengeance against any who should do any harm to the white women.

The massacres of whites and Indians that have taken place during the past one hundred years, have generally been caused by the carelessness of persons breaking the Indian laws, neglecting to fulfil promises, or the precipitancy of the colonists in attacking the Indians, because of reports which have been grossly exaggerated.

The young men of the camps, in their love of adventure, have committed depredations which brought down upon the whole tribe or confederacy the wrath of the white men. There have been faults on both sides, and many useful lives have been taken away through a few hasty words. We read of many massacres of white people by the Indians, but we hear little of the massacres of the red people by the white men. And why is this? Because the Indians are not blessed with historians to record their exploits and berate their enemies, and they have not many newspapers; and in the days of colonial warfare they had none to detail their grievances, and preserve them for posterity. Besides, the white men's ignorance of Indian customs causes them to make mistakes, and begets prejudices in their own favor, but against the Indian.

Here is one only of the horrid deeds committed by the soldiers against the red man. On March 8th, 1782, the militia under Colonel David Williamson attacked the Moravian Mission at Gnadenhutten, where the Indians were all members of the Christian Church. The young men in the militia sported with the Indian youths, the men conversed with the Indians on religion, and for a few days they lived together as friends. The Indians and the militia slept side by side, when, at a given signal, the white men arose and slew those who had trusted in them for protection.

They killed and scalped ninety of the Indians, and returned to the rendezvous with ninety-six scalps. Is it any wonder that hatred of the white man has dwelt for years in the breasts of the Indians? During the early years, when travellers were going to California and Colorado, many of the helpless Indians were shot down in sport, and the Indians, without any guns, were taken by surprise.

But the day of retribution came, and many innocent men and women were killed because of the cruel sport of desperadoes in former years.

It is estimated that every Indian warrior killed on

the plains by the military has cost the United States Government one hundred and fifteen thousand dollars. It pays to treat the Indians in accordance with the principles of justice.

Canada may justly feel proud of the position she occupies as guide and friend of the Indian race. Deal honorably with the red men and they will abide by the treaties, as evidenced by the treaties made between tribes, and the codes of honor in war, which are strictly adhered to.

A brave man is the Indian on approaching death. No craven fear possesses him when his enemies scoff at him and exercise their ingenuity in torture. He gives scoff for scoff, and urges them to do their utmost to injure him. When death is inevitable, he sings his death-song, which Loskiel says is translated into these words:

"I go to death, and shall suffer great torture; but I will endure the greatest torments inflicted by my enemies with becoming courage. I will die like a valiant man, and go to those heroes who have died in the same manner."

The warrior who killed an enemy in his own land was entitled to drag at his heels a fox-skin fastened to each moccasin, and he who had killed a grizzly bear could wear a necklace of bear's-claws. Rewards of valor in war were not the same in all the tribes, and a different signification is given to some customs by each tribe or confederacy. The little children in the Blood Indian camps wear necklaces made of bird and bear's claws, so that we can easily see how these have not the same meaning as when worn by an Indian warrior of another tribe. The scalp-locks and dress adornments of the Indian warrior are the medals betokening valor, which are the same amongst the soldiers of the white race, only expressed in a different way.

INDIAN CHARMS.

I sat one evening in the lodge of an Indian chief receiving notes from him on customs relating to the people amongst whom I labored. Taking up his war-bonnet he placed it on my head, and then put in front of it the head of a squirrel, saying: "Now you can go to fight your enemies, and they will not be able to harm you. When I go to fight I wear this bonnet with this charm in front of it, which, when I am not using, I keep in my medicine-bag. My enemies shoot at me, but the bullets fly all around me. They are not able to harm me when I wear this charm." When a young man intends to become a medicine-man, he fasts and prays until in a vision there is revealed to him his god in the shape of a bird or animal which he seeks, and carries with him as his protector and guide.

Every young man must seek a god to protect him. The representation of this god he carries at all times as a charm. Sometimes old men and women prepare charms and sell them to the Indians. War charms were borne upon poles as standards, and these were held to be sacred in war. Such was the faith of the people in the potency of these charms, that, when the standard-bearer was slain, their courage departed, and they were easily defeated by the enemy. The Indian, stimulated by his belief in the virtue of his charm, became almost invincible in war. The Sioux Indians had strong faith in their gods, but when they were severely punished for the Minnesota massacre, they lost faith in their deities and charms, and sought the protecting power of the Christian's God.

The skins of animals and birds seen in visions are stuffed and worn on the person. Sometimes deer-skin and cow-hide are cut into strips and made into snakes, toads and various reptiles, ornamented with beads and carried about on the person or in the medicine-bag.

The native women of British Columbia wear charms on their person. Different kinds of potions are drunk by women to ensure the love and faithfulness of their husbands. Then the hunter and warrior carry with them representations of their guardian spirits to secure game in times of scarcity and success in hunting, and to give victory on the field of battle.

During a time of severe sickness in one of our Blood Indian camps, the medicine-men were performing their incantations in one of the lodges where I was visiting. The patient was treated, and then each individual was brought forward to the medicine-man, who had in his hands a piece of a lady's dress. He prayed and then stroked the arms, legs and body of each with the garment, shaking it as the mesmerist does, to throw away the baneful influence that may have fastened upon the person. As he performed this operation, he muttered some words in the native tongue which I could not hear, and consequently could not know their

An Arctic Funeral.

meaning. The Sioux Indians kept secret the animal revealed to them in a vision, and the amulet was kept in a bag, so that no one was ever permitted to see it.

Animal societies sometimes originate from these amulets. The charms are worn by some Indians on sacred festivals and only when they are needed, and are regarded with great veneration.

With all the superstitious reverence for these things, they are only doing what many persons of culture have done, although surrounded by all the blessings of a higher civilization and sustained by a nobler faith.

When the Indian wears a charm as a protection against witchcraft, he is doing exactly the same thing as our ancestors did one hundred years ago.

CAMP SOCIALS.

Amid the hum of voices ascending from a large assemblage of lodges, there fell upon our ears an invitation in the native tongue, illustrating one of the customs of the red men of the plains. The crier was an old man, bent with years, supporting himself with a long stick, resembling the historical shepherd's crook.

The burden of his message was an invitation given to the chiefs and male friends of "mine host" to repair to the lodge of one of the leading personages in the camp, there to eat, drink, smoke and talk.

The name of the person was mentioned in whose lodge the feast was to be held.

The crier had gone throughout the camp, and then from several directions we saw the chosen ones solitarily wending their way to the feast. There were the halt and the maimed, and the blind, but not a child or woman was found amongst the favored ones. At different times during the day, and on toward the evening, we heard similar invitations for like purposes for other lodges in the camp. "Without money and without price" was the principle acted upon: but there was in these Camp Socials a resemblance to the Potlach of the Indians of the Pacific Coast, viz., a giving away of their possessions, that they might be accounted great and honorable among their fellows, whilst another principle was at work, which virtually meant pay, in that these socials were held again in the lodges of the invited guests, who were wealthy enough to make a feast for their friends. Let us enter the lodge where the people were assembled. The beds were arranged on the floor close to the walls of the lodge, and upon these the people sat or reclined. Different kinds of Indian food were brought in by women on plates, and in pans, pots and kettles, which were handed around to the guests. Large pails of tea were placed in readiness to supply the demands of the party. The pipes were rapidly filled with tobacco and "*kinni-kinnick*," and the owner of the lodge, and his *best wife*, presided over the ceremonies.

Every man, woman and child in an Indian camp drinks tea and smokes tobacco, therefore at all these feasts a large quantity is provided for the persons assembled. The tea is generally drunk without sugar, and it is not an unusual thing for a single individual to drink ten and twenty cups of tea at one of these feasts. As the people drank freely, the pipes were passed along, each guest taking a few "whiffs," and passing to his neighbor, until they had reached the end of the line or semi-circle, when they were re-passed, without smoking, to the first member of the group. The stimulating properties of the tea began to act as an intoxicant, until the entire party seemed to be under the influence of strong drink. An old man rehearsed the "twice-told tales" of the camp, living over again the happy days of his youth, and fighting anew the battles of former years. Jokes were cracked, thrilling stories of love and war were told, until the stolid faces of the braves relaxed, and peal upon peal of laughter followed each other in rapid succession, filling the lodge. Our early-formed opinions received from books on the Indians, respecting the lack of humor, and inability to appreciate a pun as inherent in the Indian nature, passed away as the morning mist, when we saw with our eyes the stalwart braves convulsed with laughter, and heard the humorous tales, illustrating the comical side of the red man's life. The simpleton became a target for the puns of the party, and the hero of a late contest with the Indians of the south was lauded for his courage and success. Serious matters relating to the welfare of the whole tribe were discussed, and the general affairs of the camp were passed in review.

Sunday has found us at one of these feasts, where, as usual, at the lodge of some important personage, service was to be held. The pots, pans, cups and pipes were laid aside, until the missionary conducted a religious service, when back to their cups they went, seeking peace amid their sorrows, and joy in each other's companionship and love.

Indians Drying Meat.

CHAPTER II.

CAMP AND WIGWAMS.

THE WHITE SAVAGES.

A FEW years ago, a Piegan youth went east to Ontario with a friend. After he returned, he came to the Blood Reserve, and word was sent around the camp about his arrival. The chiefs and people were anxious to learn all they could about the white people who dwelt in that far-off land. The young man was to them a great traveller, who had made discoveries, and they were so filled with the love of adventure, that they longed to hear of the wonderful land, and the inhabitants of that country. The people gathered in a lodge, and listened to the thrilling account of the young man's travels. He began, after a few preliminaries, in a series of short stories relating to the things he had seen. After stating the length of time it had taken them to go to Ottawa, where the white chiefs lived, he said that the big white chief gave him a paper, and whenever he felt hungry he went into a trading post, and showed the paper to the chief, who gave him all he could eat for nothing. He saw a great many houses standing on the top of each other, and the people were living on the heads of their friends. He then took his paper whenever he wished to go to any of the camps or towns of the white men, and gave it to a man who stood at the door of a house which rested on wheels. When he got inside the door, the house ran over the prairie very quickly. Two birds came along and tried them a race. Away they went, the birds and the house together, each trying to beat the other, but after a sharp contest, the birds were left behind.

All over the white men's land he travelled, and saw many strange things, and said he, "There are more white men than there are blades of grass upon the prairie." "Stop!" cried the Blood Indian chiefs, as they gazed in astonishment upon the young man, "the white medicine-men have been making strong medicine, and have blinded your eyes that you could not see straight. We do not believe you!" And they believed him not.

The stories told them of the wealth and strength of the white race were so strange that they would not give them credit, and they believed that the trappers and traders were making proud boasts about the white tribe to which they belonged. The white people were to them the same as any of the Indian tribes that lived on the prairie, and they believed that all the white men they had seen belonged to the same tribe. That was the reason why they punished one white man for the depredations committed by his white brother, although the two men lived thousands of miles apart, and had never heard or seen each other. Not more strange is this than the abuse heaped upon a Blood, Blackfoot or Cree, because some member of these tribes was guilty of a misdemeanor.

Red Crow, head chief of the Bloods, and North Axe, chief of the Piegans, went east two years ago, and the sights witnessed by them revolutionized their ideas, and consequently those of their people.

Day after day they related what they had seen, and the people believed them. The strange ways of the white men were amusing to them, and they agreed that in many things the white men were inferior to the Indians, and that they were white savages.

When in one of the cities of the east, some of their white friends took them to a large trading post. They went all through the place, admiring many of the things for sale, and then they went into a small room which had an iron door. At once the whole room began to move upward, and away it went, as if it were going to the sky. Suddenly it stopped, the door was opened, and they went through a large number of other rooms, where there were many people. After they had spent some time there, they opened a door and went into a small apartment, when it began to descend, and it seemed to them as if they were going to the place where the white men say the Great Evil Spirit dwells. It stopped descending, the door opened and they came out at the same place where they had started from. The Indians study the customs of the white race, as the white men the ways of the Indians, and their observations upon the life of the white men are not more strange than what has been often written, and what is spoken of every day in the towns and cities of Canada and the United States, about the Indians.

Eagle Arrow, Running Wolf, and some more of my Indian friends were telling me some of the customs of the red men, and amongst these they related the marriage customs of the Blood Indians. Now and again I laughed at the strange things which were connected with courtship and marriage, but presently it was the Indian's turn to laugh.

"How many horses did you give for your wife?" said Eagle Arrow to me.

"I did not give any," said I. So I had to tell to them the old story of how I got my wife. They listened very attentively, occasionally nudging each other, and laughing at the strange customs of the white man. Again I related the story of the years of courtship, the struggles of the youthful heart in mustering courage to ask the young lady's consent, the seeking of the approval of the young lady's father and mother, the marriage ceremony, presents given by friends, the feast, and last, but not least, the bridal gifts of household articles, given by the young lady's mother. When I had reached this part of my story, they lost control of themselves, and roared with laughter. Eagle Arrow was able, after a moment, to ejaculate, "Her mother paid you for taking her!" and again were they convulsed with laughter.

The Indian paid his father-in-law for his wife, by giving him several horses, and the white man received pay from his mother-in-law, for taking her daughter, in the goods which were given with which to begin housekeeping.

"Where do the orphan children go to when their parents are dead?" said one of my friends.

I explained to him our custom of providing for the care of such by sending them to institutions where they will be fed, clothed and educated.

He turned upon me with a sneer on his countenance, and said, "The white men are fools. They are savage people, and do not love their children. They pay men and women to love them, to save them the trouble. We take our orphans into our own homes, and become fathers and mothers unto them when their own are dead."

I lent some money to some of the Indian chiefs, who promised to return it when the annual treaty payments were made. Before that time came one of the chiefs died, and when his widows and children received their annuity, I ventured to ask payment of the debt. With a look of astonishment, the eldest widow, whom I addressed, said to me, "He is dead. We cannot pay you. If you want your money returned, you will have to go to him to get it."

Debts, therefore, die with the Indian, and I have had to exercise great care in lending to the Indians. When first the missionaries went amongst the tribes of the Blackfoot confederacy they baptized some children, and unfortunately some of them died, which was attributed to the anger of the Great Spirit, for allowing such a ceremony to be performed. The death of the older persons, and the diseases prevalent in the camps, were said to have been caused by the native deities, for permitting the white men to settle in the country, and for listening to the teachers of other religions.

We may laugh at the strange ideas entertained by the Indians about the white people, and yet they are as favorable to the white race as are the opinions held by the white men about the savages of the west. Underlying the blanket of the red man beats a noble heart, that shows true affection for his own kin, can be moved deeply by a brave action, and is true to the principles of honor, justice and truth. Under the war-cap there exists a keen intellect, educated in the arts and sciences of the native civilization. Red Jacket, the last of the Senecas; Joseph Brant, the Mohawk leader; Tecumseh, the Shawnee; Glikkikan, the Delaware; Poundmaker, the Cree; Crowfoot, the Blackfoot, and Red Crow and Button Chief, the Blood Indian chiefs, are striking examples of the intellectual power and native dignity inherent in the Indian race.

The beauty of their mythology, which has many things in common with the Hindoo and Scandinavian mythologies, reveals the strength of their intellect and imagination, and the religious sentiments that pervade the whole of their lives. All of the customs of the Indians have been different from ours, and yet we have been guilty of judging these people in the light of our own customs, and not estimating them from their own standpoint. Foreigners entertain peculiar ideas of the British race, which may be seen and read in books, but were we to visit the people of France and Germany in their own homes, we should learn that in many things they are ignorant of us, and judge us wrongly; but to a very slight degree can even this mistake be compared with our ignorance of the thoughts, feelings, customs and life of the Indians. We might learn many lessons from the native dignity and independence of the red men. They are studying our customs and adopting many of them, and alas! to their sorrow, they are imitating many of the vices of the white men. The nobler civilization of which we are the inheritors demands of us sweeter spirits, and more refined intellects, and commands us to go forth to the forests and prairies of our land to compel the red men, by the power of love, to accept the blessings of peace and grace, and enjoy the advantages of education, with the results of a more remunerative kind of toil.

THE MINNESOTA MASSACRE.

In the summer of 1862 the Sioux Indians of Minnesota and Dakota manifested a spirit of dissatisfaction, bordering on rebellion, on account of promises made to them by Government officials which had not been fulfilled. Many of the white people had hoped for a change for the better in the management of affairs when the Republican administration was in power, but they were doomed to disappointment, as subsequent events speedily showed. Some of the Indian agents informed the Indians that the Great Father at

Washington was going to make them a large present, and accordingly they were full of expectation. Some whites had expressed their belief that Canada became interested in the approaching contest, and Britain was likely to aid those who were sending emissaries amongst the Indians to stir them up against the Government. This, however, has not been proven. There are strong suspicions, however, that there were many persons in the United States who expressed their hatred toward the Republican administration by arousing a spirit of discontent amongst the Indians. Tampering thus with the savage feelings of the red man, the rebellion was precipitated, and sad consequences followed.

About four thousand of the Upper Sioux Indians were assembled at the Yellow Medicine Agency for the purpose of receiving their annual payments, but the money did not arrive. They were told to return to their homes, but they were one hundred miles distant, and should they start on the buffalo hunt the payments might be made, and they would lose their money. The Government had begun to pay them in goods instead of gold, and this made the Indians dissatisfied.

Real and apparent grievances increased as they talked over these matters in the lodges. Some of the Indians returned home, but over one thousand were fed at the agency during the winter of 1861. The treaty payments were delayed six weeks after the appointed time, and during this interim the outbreak commenced. The match that lighted the smouldering embers of rebellion was the killing of some white men by four or five drunken Indians who were refused liquor at Acton, Minnesota, on the 17th of August, 1862. These fled to the Lower Sioux, and reported what they had done. After a council had been held, early the following morning the stores were sacked and many white people killed. There is no doubt that the Indians intended to attack the villages, but the outbreak had been hastened by the deed of the drunken men. Captain Marsh, with fifty men, was sent against them, but half of these were killed. Little Crow, the leader of the Sioux, saw that they had subjected themselves to threats of punishment, and he determined to carry on the war. Yellow Medicine Agency was attacked and the stores sacked. The settlers all over the country became alarmed as the news spread, and they fled to Fort Ridgley and other forts and towns for safety. New Ulm was attacked and many of the whites killed, but the people defended themselves nobly until relieved by the military. Fort Ridgley was besieged for nine days by the Indians, but on August 26th the soldiers brought relief. General H. H. Sibley was dispatched with soldiers to chastise the Indians. He defeated them at different points, and learning by sad experience that the forces against them were too strong, they moved northward, spreading desolation on their trail. Governor Ramsay called a session of the Minnesota Legislature, and an appeal was made to the Government for help. In response to this, General Pope was sent with United States troops from several points. The Indians attacked Fort Abercrombie, but were twice repulsed with heavy losses. The whole country was thoroughly aroused. Many of the relatives of the first families of Minnesota had been slain. The settlers had abandoned their homes, and much property had been destroyed. Some of the rebels fled to Manitoba, and in the Indian camps were large numbers of white women and children. The soldiers burned with indignation, and vowed vengeance upon the heads of the Sioux.

On September 22nd General Sibley was encamped at Wood Lake, near Yellow Medicine Agency, and the Sioux were in the vicinity, determined on taking a last stand. Two of Sibley's soldiers were killed in a waggon early in the morning by some Indians concealed in a ravine. A battle ensued, which lasted for two or three hours, and resulted in the defeat of the Sioux and the end of the rebellion. Little Crow and the remaining Indians fled to the Yankton Sioux in Dakota. The captives were then brought in day after day by the Indians. Many of the white women were dressed as the Indians, and a few had white women's garments to wear. Nearly a hundred white captives were taken from Little Crow, besides many half-breeds. It was a time of rejoicing, and the place was appropriately named "Camp Release." Reports of cruelty and abuse against the white women and murders by the Indians having been made, an investigation was held which resulted in over four hundred Sioux being sent to prison. Thirty-eight were hanged, on December 26th, at Mankato, and the rest were doomed to spend a winter in the prison at the same place, while the wives and children of the prisoners were detained at Fort Snelling. Subsequently the prisoners were kept for three years at Davenport, and then sent to their homes. Many died in prison from confinement, changed diet and disease. It is estimated that five hundred people were killed by Indians, or died from exposure and excitement, and the loss of property amounted to about three million dollars. Between twenty and thirty thousand people fled from their homes, many of whom never returned. The suffering subsequent to the outbreak was very great, but the people of Minnesota and other States assisted the sufferers nobly, and thus peace and comfort returned to the happy homes made desolate by war.

INDIAN PAINTINGS.

Indian life and customs have proved to be, in the hands of some artists, a fascinating study, profitable and interesting to teacher and taught. In the art exhibitions of Canada and the United States there have appeared some notable paintings illustrating the history and character of the Indians; but there remains for us, as prominent persons worthy to be kept in remembrance on account of their work, the artistic trio, Catlin, Kane and King. A few years ago there was presented to the Peabody Museum a gift of rare value, consisting of one hundred and five oil paintings of American Indians of life size, executed by C. B. King. Sixty-eight of these were the originals of what appeared in McKenny & Hall's "Indian Tribes of North America," which was published in 1836, and gave letter-press sketches of the persons represented.

Paul Kane, a native of Toronto, spent three years travelling among the Indians with pencil and note-book in hand, gathering materials, which he expanded into hundreds of paintings. He travelled from Toronto to Vancouver and Oregon, and away in the north in the Hudson's Bay country, living with different Indian tribes, and obtaining sketches for his future work. But we must let him tell the story of his beginnings:

"On my return to Canada from the continent of Europe, where I had passed nearly four years in studying my profession as a painter, I determined to devote whatever talents and proficiency I possessed to the painting of a series of pictures illustrative of the North American Indians and scenery. The subject was one in which I felt a deep interest in my boyhood. I had been accustomed to see hundreds of Indians about my native village, then Little York, muddy and dirty, just struggling into existence, now the city of Toronto, bursting forth in all its energy and commercial strength. But the face of the red man is now no longer seen. All traces of his footsteps are fast being obliterated from his once favorite haunts, and those who would see the aborigines of this country in their original state, or seek to study their native manners and customs, must travel far through the pathless forest to find them."

He returned from his wanderings as an artist among the Crees, Eskimo, Flatheads and numerous other tribes, to spend several years in completing his paintings, which were varied in their character, and of great service to the ethnologist. The name of Paul Kane, the Indian painter, is still mentioned with enthusiasm by writers upon Indian subjects as a man of ability and energy, which were fully displayed in his work.

There has ever existed amongst the Indians a superstitious dread connected with the art of the photographer and painter. The people think that some virtue goes from the person into the picture, and henceforth the benighted red man is at the mercy of the operator. Even at the present day it is a very difficult matter to induce some Indians to have their photos taken, and indeed many positively decline. Paul Kane found it hard, and sometimes dangerous, to carry on his work successfully. Several times did he narrowly escape with his life. His reputation as a great medicine-man increased his influence and saved his scalp.

The prince of Indian artists is George Catlin, who spent eight years among the Indians, visiting forty-eight tribes in Canada, the United States and Mexico, and painting several hundred pictures. Having abandoned the practice of law, he became a portrait painter; and having seen a delegation of Indians gaily dressed in their native costume, he was seized with a passion for depicting the various phases of aboriginal life, which would soon pass away. He went into the Yellowstone country, and met in his travels chiefs and famous medicine-men of the Cree, Blackfoot, Sioux, Crow, Mandan, Flathead and other Indian tribes, whose features and dress were painted on the canvas for the pale-faced tribes to gaze upon with astonishment. Having finished his first set of paintings, he became a travelling showman, exhibiting his pictures, with numerous dresses, ornaments and weapons of warfare, which he had collected during his residence among the red men. Thousands of people visited his entertainments, and were highly delighted and instructed. Having spent some time in Philadelphia, Boston and New York, he went to Europe with his collection. His lectures and entertainments were exceedingly popular in England, Scotland, France and Germany, insomuch that he spent eight years in giving exhibitions in Europe. He wrote during this time his "Manners, Customs and Condition of the North American Indian," and other works illustrating Indian life, and notes on his Indian collection. Financial embarrassment compelled him to mortgage his collection, which eventually found its way to Washington, and thence to the Philadelphia Exposition. The work that has been accomplished by these delineations of Indian life will never need to be repeated. The scenes, costumes and customs are rapidly passing away under the overpowering influence of the race of whiteskins, and other thoughts belonging to a nobler life will be the heritage of the red men of mountain, forest and plain.

PICTURE-WRITING.

The Indians of the American Continent have three distinct forms of speech: spoken, written, and sign language. The languages and dialects are numerous, differing according to the tribes. Sometimes a band becoming detached from the tribe, as exemplified in the Siouan or Dakota family, will generate a dialect containing many features distinct from the parent form of speech. The sign language is universally employed by the red man, and such is its adaptation to the needs of this people, that, though ignorant of the spoken languages of their respective tribes, they can by means of signs converse intelligently together.

Some mode of communication was necessary, however, for conveying thoughts to persons at a distance. This was done by means of messengers, bearing wampum belts, who spoke the thoughts of their fellows. The Indian's system of telegraphy was also very successfully employed. Written communications were also necessary, and the red man employed what is called picture-writing. . The language of color was very significant, and helped to express ideas. Around the lodges ran the historical record of the exploits of the owner of the lodge. Oftentimes have I gazed on the strange figures on the buffalo-skin lodges, and with the help of the Indians received a fair idea of the history they contained. Some Indians made fantastic pictures upon rocks. Historical records were sometimes written upon the insides of buffalo robes. A few days ago, a young man brought to me a paper containing a sketch of an Indian camp, detailing the different kinds of lodges, with the ceremonies going on at the time represented. Picture-writing is the lowest stage of writing in use amongst men. It is crude and cumbersome, when compared with the hieroglyphic and phonetic systems in use. An Indian desirous of writing "Red Crow," the name of a Blood Indian chief, would draw the head of a man, place on the

Indian Chief.

crown the drawing of a piece of wood, upon which a crow is sitting, and this bird would be painted red.

Many tribes of Indians still use this method of conveying their ideas, though many others have learned the language of their conquerors, or have relied upon the syllabic systems, with their strange characters, and the native language, with its modified Roman alphabet, devised by the missionaries for the instruction of those under their care.

Conversing with some of the Blood Indians about the pictured rocks of the Missouri, they said: "We have seen them, and we know that the spirits have made them, for no man could climb high enough to do that work." They are very superstitious about writing of any kind.

Sometimes a letter will be sent me by a friend from town, through an Indian, and a month or so after it is written, it will be handed to me. An old lady brought my rubber coat across the river from home whilst I was in the Indian camp. She saw me pass along the road on foot, and ran after me with the coat. She told me that she had brought a letter for me from *Apauakas* (Mrs. McLean). On asking her for it, she said that it was in her lodge. I then inquired why she did not bring it, and she said, "I did not know what was in it, so I did not bring it."

An officer of the Mounted Police told me that, when on duty near the International Boundary Line, he had heard that there was a wonderful cave some miles distant, containing Indian pictures. This he visited, accompanied by one or two friends, and found within stone couches raised above the ground, and drawings upon the walls. When conversing with some Indians about the two young men who were killed by the Gros Ventres Indians two years ago, they said that the young men had gazed upon the writing on the rocks, and consequently they were killed.

Picture-writing has many disadvantages, and whilst becoming the first step toward civilization, it clogs the intellect by its laborious mode of execution, and lacks the ingenuity and expressiveness of the cultured systems of hieroglyphics and phonetics.

MEDICINE-MEN.

The medicine-men of the Indian tribes are designated by several names, as Shamans, Sorcerers and Conjurers. The Eskimo call them Angekoks, which is, wise men. The Indians are subjected, like other races, to the ills of body and mind, and are therefore dependent upon medical practitioners to help them in their hours of pain. Blindness, arising from the smoke of the lodges, uncleanness, the habitual use of paint, and hereditary diseases, are very prevalent among the tribes. Sitting in a lodge a short time ago with twelve persons, young and old, I counted five blind individuals. There are numerous cases of scrofula, consumption, rheumatism, immoral diseases, bronchitis, and chronic constipation. Toothache is rare amongst them, their food, no doubt, conducing to the preservation of their teeth.

The medicine-men are the priests and doctors of the camp, uniting religion and medicine in their practice.

Generally there are grades of distinction, the lower resorting to the use of herbs and other medicines only, and the higher relying upon supernatural influences to aid them with the dispensing of their *materia medica.* Shrewd and intelligent, they are revered by the occupants of the lodges, and become instructors of the youth and the guardians of the sacred legends. Occasionally medicine-women are found, generally aged persons, who become famous through the numerous cures wrought by their skill. "Medicine" has a two-fold meaning—the one referring to the charms and incantations, the supernatural part of the work; and the other to the use of physic, the natural part.

In some tribes there exist secret societies and organizations of medicine-men, who keep sacredly their medical lore and mysterious rites, thus creating superstitious fears among the people, and enhancing the value of their services. According to the statement of F. Assikinack, a warrior of the Ottawas, there were secret societies among the Ottawas, one of which was called "Wahbahnoowin," signifying the east. It has been asserted that those who were fully instructed in all the mysteries of this society could hold a burning coal in their hands, or thrust their fingers into boiling water, without receiving any injury. They had a very strong preference for the pleasures of the sweat lodge, and were able to endure a greater amount of heat than any other persons. Another society, named "Medaowin," had several sections, each of which consisted of eight members. They had secret signs and passwords, which enabled them easily to get rid of their enemies, and to exercise a commanding influence in the tribes. Nothing was positively known of their private meetings, but their public meetings were held in a large wigwam or in the open air, where the people assembled in large numbers to witness the ceremonies. Within the enclosure the members sat, each holding a stuffed bird or animal in his hand, which seemed to revive from the sounds uttered, as some of the members danced in the open space, or ran around holding a bird or animal in front of them. Placing small bones in the mouths of the animals, these were thrown into the mouths of the persons standing near, and caused in them superstitious fears, believing that the members used some powerful medicine for accomplishing their purpose. It was believed that when an enemy was disposed of, one of the members, disguised as a wolf or bear, went on the eighth night, dug up the body, cut off one of the little toes, the little fingers, and cut out the heart and tongue. These were taken to the next meeting, where the tongue, being divided into eight shares, was eaten, and the other parts of the body used in the preparation of their medicines. Wherever the secret fraternities of medicine-men existed, there were initiatory rites which the candidates for the profession had to undergo to fit them for their duties. In some tribes this consisted merely in passing successfully through a period of fasting, until the guardian spirit had been found. Some held that from birth a supernatural influence rested upon a person designated for the office, and in due course, he entered upon the career marked out for him by the gods. The Eskimo taught that death and resurrection were necessary in every candidate for the sacred office. A keen intellect and dignified bearing, or a tinge of madness, betokening the prophetic vision, were held by others to constitute the necessary qualifications of a candidate. Paul Kane states that among the Chinook Indians, the aspirant for medical honors prepares a feast, which is free to all, and bestows gifts upon the medicine-men. A lodge is prepared for him, wherein he fasts three days and nights, while the initiated dance and sing around it during the whole period. The fast ended, he is taken up apparently lifeless, and the ceremony of washing the dead is performed, which implies plunging the candidate into the nearest cold water, and rubbing him briskly until he recovers from the effects of his fast. He now rushes into the woods, and returns dressed as a medicine-man, and then, relying upon the dignity of his profession, and the influence attending it, for his support, with his medicine rattle in his hand, he collects all his property and divides it amongst his friends. The singing and dancing are kept up during the distribution, after which the ceremony of initiation ends with a general feast.

Among the Crees there are four grades leading to the highest position. The first grade is "Wapunu," conjurer of the morning, the members of which have the power of extinguishing fire; the second is "Miteo," the man who uses the bone or shell in killing, and the "birdskins," who has an extensive knowledge of healing remedies, and possessing mesmeric power. The third is " Kesikowejineo, the man of the day," who is the revealer of secrets, and the fourth is called "Tipiskoweyineo," who has the power to nullify the evil influence of the Miteo, and even to heal those who have been affected by him.

The initiatory rites among the Crees consist in physical torture, to test the power of endurance, this being a necessity in the profession, as the novitiate will be prepared for stolidly witnessing suffering in others, and a fast of ten days' duration. The candidate's first degree is obtained by undergoing this period of fasting in accordance with the customs of the medical priesthood. He leaves the habitations of his people, repairs to a lonely spot and takes up his residence in the branches of a tree, where he fasts and meditates, holding converse with the spirits who visit him and become his guardians and friends through life. The Great Evil Spirit visits him, and takes him under his care, and the lesser spirits that abound in the animals, and in all the wonderful things of nature, become his servants. He prays for the impartation of supernatural powers, and this mysterious agency becomes his source of strength and success in his work. Subsequent training under a medicine-man qualifies him for all the grades of his profession, entrance into each of these orders being under the direction of the chief medicine-man.

Celibacy is held by the medical priests of some tribes as a necessity for ensuring success in the healing art.

Their dress is generally the most hideous and grotesque that can be conceived. The skin of a bear or other wild animal is wrapped around the body, encircling the limbs, the claws reaching to the tips of the fingers, and the head being so closely fastened that a part only of the hideously painted face is seen.

Medicine-men belonging to the Blackfeet wear a peculiar head gear, made of the skins of animals and eagle's feathers. The eagle is the sacred bird of the Indians, and a young man will keep watch a long time that he may obtain some of the tail feathers, which are believed to possess the power to ward off disease. The skins worn on the head-dress are also believed to have inherent in them virtuous properties. The Chinook medicine-men daub their bodies with thick grease, and then cover themselves with the soft down of a goose, over which they wear a cloak of friezed cedar bark. Every member of the medical fraternity possesses the indispensable medicine-bag, the contents of which are various.

I have been deeply interested in examining some of these, and strange thoughts have passed through my mind as I gazed on them. The bags are made of the skins of animals taken off whole, and the contents are wrapped in separate parcels. These consist of herbs of various kinds, the heads and claws, feathers and teeth of birds and animals, the skins of animals, dressed and stuffed, human finger and toe nails, a small bone whistle used in their incantations and at the Sun-dance, and the totem of the owner of the bag. Whilst examining the contents of one of these bags, the owner held up his charm and informed me, that should he be attacked by enemies, he would fasten this on his head, and then would he prove invincible to every foe. Some of their medicines are excellent, from what I have seen of their effects among the Blood Indians. Dr. Robert Bell, senior assistant director of the Geological Survey, in a very interesting paper on "Indian and Eskimo Notions of Medicine," mentions the following plants used among the Crees as medicines, namely: sweet flag, yellow pond lily, spruce, balsam, willow bark, honeysuckle, juniper, dogwood, blue flag, pigeon cherry, mountain ash, wild mint and snake root. The methods of procedure in treating a patient are similar among the Chinook, Nooksachk, Cree, Blackfoot, and many other Indian tribes. Entering a lodge, there is seen one or more medicine-men sitting near the sick person, singing, praying, and swaying their bodies energetically until the perspiration flows freely. One of the medicine men blows continuously a whistle, as he sways to and fro. The friends of the sick person beat on small Indian drums and sing while the medicine-man is performing. These incantations are for the purpose of driving away the evil spirits that are afflicting the patient. While these songs are being sung, the medicine-man may fall down in a trance, or he may resort to the use of his *materia medica.* The excitement may be so great, that the performer will be exhausted, and then another takes his place. One of the doctors shakes vigorously his medicine-rattle, while one of the others is treating the patient.

Deceit is practised to gain their ends, as they will show the people in the lodge the bugs and venomous reptiles they have extracted, which have been the cause of the disease. The mouth is used as a leech for sucking blood, and cleansing wounds. Suddenly the performer, in the midst of his gesticulations, will seize a part of the patient's body with his teeth, while he is trembling violently, and after much exertion, will shout that he has found the disease. Holding his hands to his mouth he will plunge them into water, and pretend that he is keeping the disease from returning to the patient. He will then show the disease in the shape of a piece of flesh or a reptile, and declare his work well done. A piece of glass, stone, or iron is used as a lance. Hot stones are employed as a remedy for dilatation of the stomach. In cases of rheumatism, the affected parts are burned with a stick thrust into the fire; the same remedy being used for biliousness. In severe headache, an herb is chewed and the saliva injected into the nostrils by means of a small tube. Charms and amulets are worn to protect the person against disease. Sick persons were often brought by the Eskimo to Hans Egede, that he might cure them by blowing upon them, the people saying that was the method by which their Angekoks cured the sick.

The sweat lodge is one of the most frequent resorts of the Indians when they are sick, and is productive of great benefit, and harm. Properly used, it is an efficient remedy in colds, but when the patient exposes himself to the cold air, there is great danger to his enfeebled frame. A sweat lodge among the people of the plains consists of the supple branches of tender trees, such as the willow, fastened in the ground in a circular form, about four or six feet in diameter, resembling a bee-hive, and about four feet in height. This is covered with blankets until every aperture is completely closed, and no air can come in to cause a draught. The patient goes inside, and if in a weak state of body, a friend goes with him. Hot stones and water are placed within, and the water poured upon the stones. In a very short time the entire person is in a state of profuse perspiration, beneficial in certain stages of a disease.

Among some of the California tribes of Indians, an underground dwelling was made, to the depth of six or eight feet, the roof covered with slabs and several feet of earth. Shelves were made on the walls for the Indians to lie. A small door opened into the dwelling, and a single aperture in the top permitted the smoke to escape. The Indians entered, lay down on the shelves; a fire was kindled in the middle of the room, and in a few minutes the patients were sweating profusely.

Some of the medicine men are possessed of ability, have a good knowledge of the human system, have a very fair list of remedies, some of which are excellent, judging from the effects produced, and perform, by means of their herbs and incantations, some wonderful cures. Some of these have been very striking. The power of the will, the magnetic influence, has been such, that even the conjurations of the medicine-men have been at times productive of much good. Although I can point to famous cures of gun-shot wounds, dog-bites, rheumatism, and other diseases by these men, their system, taken as a whole, is injurious and distasteful.

Their knowledge of poisons, which in some instances is quite extensive, and the power possessed by them of inflicting injury to any persons in the camps, make them feared by the people, and their influence is thereby increased. There are numerous instances of injuries inflicted by these medicine-men by some mysterious power, and when some of these men have become converts to Christianity, they have stated that some mysterious influence accompanied their incantations, which they had not now in their new religious state.

Believing that the laborer is worthy of his hire, they take good care that they are well paid for their services. The patient's friends will take the last garment they own and give it to the medicine-men, as they dread their anger, and are afraid lest they inflict evil upon them by means of the spirits, who are their servants. Blankets, food, horses, and other kinds of Indian property, are freely given to reward the practitioner for his toil. It matters not how poor the people are, they will make strenuous efforts to obtain something to give him. The sick will sell their dearest treasures to pay their doctor, for they are afraid of his vengeance when the day of settlement comes. They will beg, borrow or steal to pay this debt. The medicine-man keeps no books, does not issue any statements of accounts of long standing, and is not troubled by resorting to a lawyer to collect old debts. The mystery of his profession, and the terror he inspires by means of his superior knowledge, are sufficient to insure a speedy settlement. As to the amount given, that depends upon the wealth of the patient, and the length of time necessary to effect a cure. They are, however, well paid.

The conjuring practices of these medical experts are sometimes very effective. Many of them perform clever sleight-of-hand tricks that would have done credit to the Wizard of the North. Christian missionaries have become their enemies, through exposing the falsity of their tricks. They practise mesmerism, spiritualism and clairvoyance. Entering a lodge, one of these medicine-men, as he prays, will cause the lodge to tremble, as if shaken by a violent wind, strange, rumbling voices will be heard as he is communing with the spirits, and he will foretell the advent of a stranger, the decease of a friend or foe, the prospects of the weather, and make rain.

Among some tribes failure to cure means death for the medicine-man or severe punishment. The Papagos of Arizona punish the unsuccessful medicine-man with death. When he fails to cure one of the Sachems of the tribe, he is led forth after the burial, and is instantly shot. Failure to effect a cure means, at least, a loss of prestige. So strongly attached are the Indians to all their native ceremonials, and especially to the rites of the medical priesthood, that it is very difficult for them to give them up. The last custom rejected by the civilized Indian is his appeal for assistance to the medicine-men in his hours of pain and grief.

THE HOME OF THE RED MEN.

Who are the red men? and whence came they? are questions at once full of interest and prolific in their suggestiveness. The origin of the Red Race is a theme that has attracted the attention of the most eminent anthropologists of the Old and New Worlds. The opinion held by some that the terms Adam and Eve are merely representations of races and not individuals, conflicts with the prevailing theories of the unity of the human family, and our cherished beliefs of religion. Several books have been written to prove that the Indians are the descendants of the "ten lost tribes." Catlin, during his eight years' sojourn among the tribes of the Missouri and Yellowstone, thought that he had discovered in the Mandans the descendants of the lost Welsh colony.

One thing is evident, they are the result of an evolution, or rather of a series of evolutions. The geographical position of the country in which individual tribes are located, the influences of climate, isolation, food, labor, intermarriages, social, religious, and war customs, have all aided in producing new types of men, and new languages. During the existence of slavery on the American continent there were two kinds of slaves, the house slaves and the field slaves. The latter were subjected to coarser food and clothing, heavier labor and less refined associations. The two classes were distinct in features, intellectual ability and manner. When the field-slaves were dissociated from their fellows, and placed among the house-slaves, the descendants of these in the third and fourth generations became similar in every respect to the house-slaves, and thus a new class was formed. Education and labor are important factors in moulding the destinies of men. It is an established fact that persons of fair complexion are more subject to the diseases prevalent in malarial districts than those of dark complexion. Hence a greater mortality amongst these persons. The survivors in those districts during epidemics would be similar, or nearly so, in color. By intermarriage a new class would ultimately be evolved. Draw an ethnographical map of the world, study the various localities suitable for creating new races of men, and you may account for the origin of some of the varieties now in existence. Horatio Hale, eminent as a philologist, has shown clearly and conclusively how dialects and languages are generated in his "Origin of Languages and Antiquity of Speaking Man."

Various have been the conjectures as to the time and manner by which the continent of America became peopled. There is historical evidence to prove that the Norsemen visited America in the tenth century, thus wresting this honor from Columbus. There is not the least doubt that there have been chance wanderers eastward, from the islands of the Pacific, China and Japan. May there not also have been migrations? The crossing of Behring's Straits would present little difficulty to the hardy adventurer, and there are some who maintain that at one time the land at that locality was united. Short, in his volume, "North Americans of Antiquity," gives proofs of the discovery of "junks" on the Pacific coast, and if a few, why not many, with the inhabitants of islands, wafted thither against their will, or voluntarily seeking new lands. Travellers from British Columbia have informed me that the resemblance in features of the Chinese and Indians on the coast is very striking. Let both assume the same kind of garment, and the resemblance is almost complete. "Westward" has, in general, been the motto of the nations. After the period of the establishment of the Greek and Roman colonies, or rather from the invasion of the Goths and Huns, the tendency of migration has been westward, and to-day the direction is the same. The lost Atlantis theory of peopling the New World, has very many attractions for the student of ethnology. Ignatius Donnelly is enthusiastic in his belief of the reality of this island world, and Dr. Daniel Wilson as strongly declares that its existence is mythical. There are differences of opinion among philologists as to the Basque language of France being the foundation language for the numerous languages and dialects of the New World. The Basque people are the descendants of the primitive Eskuarians, who dwelt in Europe. If this affinity, then, of language can be fully established, it will be a strong factor in solving the problem of the relation of the Indians to the people of Europe. Much has been written on the origin of the Red Race, but it still remains an unsettled question. Some plodding genius may, in the near future, stumble upon evidence sufficient to unravel the mystery, and then will there be one less incentive toward enthusiastic culture in the intellectual world.

NATIVE RELIGIONS.

The Indians are an eminently religious people, strong evidence of which is seen in the elaborate religious systems existing amongst them. Their superstitious fears arise from the belief of spiritual forces surrounding them, and influencing their lives. The devotional spirit is manifested daily, in their customs, and in all the routine of life. Many of their traditions are of a religious character, and the mythology is moulded by their ideas of the spiritual world. In their social and political organization, and in their war customs, the spirit of piety is manifested. In the "medicine-men" we recognize the medical priesthood, the members of which are the priests and doctors of the camps. The majority of the Indian tribes believe in the existence of a Great Spirit, who may, or may not be the creator. He is not the same Supreme Being as that believed in by the white man, although the influences of Christianity oftentimes exert such a power over the theological opinions of the Indians as to cause them to accept the Christians' God as the same. To some he is the Sun, and to others, the Old Man, the Man Above, the Great Spirit, the First Cause, and the Captain of Heaven.

Besides the Great Manitou, there are lesser Manitous, lesser spirits, and secondary creators. These reside in the rapids of rivers, and in the strange things resulting from freaks of nature. A peculiarly shaped stone, contorted tree or lonely cave, are recognized as the stopping places of the spirits, hence the sacrifices made, and the presence of trinkets at these places. In the mortuary customs of these people, there is immanent the doctrine of the immortality of the soul. The widely prevailing custom of burying articles necessary for travelling with the dead, to assist the spirits on their journey to their future abode, and to be of service to them during their residence there, is begotten of this doctrine. Some believe, that as the things deposited in the graves decay, the spirits will take them away, to be again united, and used in the spirit world, but the more general opinion is, that the spirits being immaterial, must use spiritual things, and they take, therefore, the soul of the articles and leave the matter behind. Creation and providence are prominent doctrines in their theological system. The latter is to them a powerful reality. Though not taught explicitly, there is betokened in the recognition of sin the existence of a law, which belongs to the Supreme Being, and which, when broken, constitutes sin, and man is punished by the infliction of disease for his disobedience. The soul of the red man cries out for forgiveness of sin, and this finds its highest expression in sacrifice. Sacrifices are made by some tribes of Indians to the evil spirits to propitiate them, that their favor may be gained, and evil warded off.

Prayer is offered to the Sun, the Great Spirit, and to the lesser spirits at the stopping-places of the gods. I have oftentimes seen the red men reverently pray to the Supreme Being for help in their seasons of distress. At the Sun-dance the ideas of sacrifice and prayer are very prominent. The medicine-man in the sick lodge prays for the spiritual power to help him in healing the sick. The floating garment at the top of the lodge is placed there to attract the lesser divinity as he is passing by, that he may lend aid. The piece of tobacco thrown into the rapids is to propitiate the spirit that presides over the place. Prayers are offered, and songs sung when crossing dangerous streams, to seek the favor, divert the attention, or drive away the spirits that haunt the waters in their rapid course. The Mexican Indians possess elaborate forms of prayer, rites of baptism and purification.

Traditions of the flood, and several narratives of Scripture are found amongst the Indians, but it is difficult to learn correctly whether these belong to their native religion, or result from contact with Christian teaching. The souls of the dead go to the sand hills and the happy hunting grounds, a sensual heaven suited to the ideas of the people, whose minds are more firmly concentrated on the concrete things of life than on the abstract.

An inferior place is allotted to the existence of hell and a personal devil, the native intellect being more apt to dwell on the prospect of pleasure than pain, in the future. Invariably they are non-believers in evolution, the idea of a primal creation being more consonant with their views, as to their relation to the great First Cause. There is inherent in the nature of the red man a strong love for his own system of religion, which prevents the acceptance of any other form of doctrine from that in which he is trained. He will adopt more readily the mode of life of the white race, as he sees the benefits that will accrue from this, but his long-cherished beliefs are dear to him, and it is difficult to tear the mind and heart away from the religions of the forest and plain. As the boy grew up to manhood, he went out into the forest or mountain to wait for the vision that should reveal to him the animal whose spirit was to be the guardian angel of his life, and when found he returned with support for the duties and struggles that lay in his path through this world. To accept another religion without experiencing the power of the spiritual forces that lay within it was to deprive him of the strength, hopes and joys that dwelt in his own. There is sunshine and shadow in this native religion, yet there are features of interest, many of which we admire; and some exist that claim a kinship to the superior system of the Carpenter's Son.

AN INDIAN CAMP.

Entering a store we saw an Indian war-cap hanging, and after making some inquiries from an old Indian trader, got the following information:—" Four years ago our informant was an Indian trader two hundred miles further up the Missouri river. He was the only white man in the Indian camp. There were some horses belonging to his band grazing outside the camp. During the night news came to the camp that some Sioux Indians were stealing their horses, and at once the young men seized their guns, jumped on what horses were left, and pursued the enemy. After following for two days, some of the enemy were killed and the property recovered. One old Sioux had his horse shot under him, and being run down, threw up his hands and pleaded for mercy. One of the party stepped up to him, and drawing a large knife cut his nose off. Seeing by this that there was no hope, he told his name, where he came from, and why he stole the horses. He stated that his band were almost on the point of starvation, and they only came to take a few horses. His story being told, one of the Mandan Indians walked up behind him and cut off his head. After severing the different parts of the body, the head was fastened to the top of a pole, while the other parts were tied by ropes, and kept dangling to long poles which the riders carried. Returning to the camp, the poles were staked in a central spot, and around these they danced and feasted for a whole week." It was the war-cap of this old Sioux that we saw. It was sold to the Indian trader for one dollar, as the Mandan who had it was afraid of the spirit of the Sioux. So superstitious were they, that when the night was stormy the Mandans would go to the graveyard and shoot their guns to keep away the spirits of those whom they had killed. The cap had a long piece of leather attached to it, which hung down the back of the wearer, and this was full of black and white feathers. The black feathers denoted the number of ponies the wearer had stolen, and the white ones represented the number of persons scalped. This cap had twenty-eight black feathers and seven white ones. Happy were we that those days had passed away when deeds such as these were delighted in, and scenes of blood and cruelty the order of the day. During our stay in this city (Bismarck, Dakota), we had an interview with an Indian interpreter, who had just arrived with four chiefs of the Gros Ventre and Mandan tribes from Washington. The chiefs appeared very well satisfied with the results of their meeting at Washington. We were informed that one of these chiefs was the man who killed the Sioux, and that he ran a great risk, when returning from Washington, of being killed by some Sioux Indians who were there, as the murdered man's brother was amongst the number. Some Ree Indians are camped upon the plains, and we are anxious to see how Indians live amongst themselves. A lively walk through the heavy prairie grass, and we stand in front of a few canvas tents. We notice by the tents and the wearing apparel that these Indians have seen something of civilization. At the doors of the tents two or three Indians are reclining on the ground. Strong, able-bodied men they are, and well calculated to do efficient work on the farm ; but there is the want of training. Men and women wear their hair long, and were it nicely arranged would appear beautiful, being of a jet-black color. You can only distinguish the men and women by the peculiarity of dress. The men wore pants made of common blankets, with the seam about two inches wide on the outside. They had very large ear-rings, wore shawls or long white or black sheets, thrown over them, and one fine-looking fellow, who showed his beautiful white teeth to advantage when he laughed at us, had pieces of tin about three inches wide bound round his arms as ornaments. The women were dressed like our Canadian ladies, only not according to the fashions of the day. Shawls of a red or tartan color seemed to be their preference. A dog or two lay in the tents. Outside, the horses were roaming, while some young Rees were busily engaged training colts in a style differing from Canadian farmers. A Ree got upon the back of the colt, and having placed a bridle on its head, had a long rope trailing on the ground, so that if he were to fall off he could catch it before the colt got away from him. In front of the colt rode another Ree upon a spirited pony, and he carried a rope in his hand, which was attached to the colt's bridle, thus the untrained was drawn along when he became stubborn. Behind the animal being "broken in" ran a lad with a whip, to remind the young invincible that he must plod on. A good way of training, perhaps, but I should think a very laborious one. A little wooden cart stood between the tents, having a rack which was all covered with buffalo meat, put there to dry in the sun. An old woman with very coarse features was employed boiling some buffalo meat, the smell and color of which was not very enticing, even to a man with an earnest longing to satisfy the cravings of nature. The bones of the buffalo were strewn along the ground, looking very bare after having undergone the operation of passing between the teeth of a hungry dog or two. With the salutation of "Hi, hi," we approached the chief, who sat upon the ground, and he, answering with "Hi, hi," held out his hand, which we shook heartily. Not understanding their language, and they being just as deficient in English, we were about to leave when the chief handed us a paper, which was to the effect that his name was Black Fox. He was a tall, fine-looking man, and appeared to be very intelligent. For eight years he had acted as a scout, and served under Generals Custer and Miles. Thankful for the information, invigorated by the walk, and rejoicing in the fact that our early advantages were very much superior to such as these, we retraced our steps, perfectly satisfied with our first visit to an Indian camp.

FOOT-PRINTS OF THE RED MAN.

A feeling of sadness creeps over our hearts as we gaze upon the lingering traces of a civilization supplanted by a nobler system of morality and religion. Here and there along the rivers, on the prairies, in the forests, and on the mountains, the pioneers of this continent have left impressions of their customs, and reveal their hidden lore to those trained to listen to and interpret the language of the inanimate things that surround us in life. In former years the old trees that skirted the rivers were the resting-places of the dead, but the strong winds, and the decay of natural things have destroyed them, and few of these receptacles containing an Indian chief or famous warrior now exist. Sometimes small circles of stones may be seen on the prairie which were used to keep in position the bottom of the lodges, but these are becoming scattered, and even where they remain as they were left, few persons can tell the cause of this peculiarity. The sacrificial offerings surrounding strangely shaped rocks and trees

An Indian Village.

have been seized by vandals and cast away, betokening a different kind of training, and a lack of appreciation of the religious customs of the red man. Cairns of stones sometimes mark the spot where famous battles had been fought between hostile tribes, and could they but speak, strange narratives would they tell of horse-stealing, cruel torture, and scalping. A few of these cairns are still in existence, but most of the actors in these bloody scenes have gone to the land beyond, and the history of these strifes will soon be sunk in depths of oblivion.

Long years before the advent of the white man upon the continent, the highways of the New World were the trails of the red men. The rivers were the highways for those who travelled by canoe, and many scenes, strange and sad, were enacted on these waters. Over the mountains and prairies these singular pathways led to distant camp-fires, and the homes of hostile tribes. Through the forest they led, unmarked by tree, mound or stone, the keen eye of the red man, and the instinct of the race easily guiding safely toward his destination. These constituted a singular network over the continent, and many started on their journey from their camp-fires and lodges who were destined never to return.

Could these scenes of former years be revived, what strange emotions would thrill our hearts. The men have gone, and much of their history has died with them. The fires that burned, the tales of adventure that were told, are things of the past. The railroads follow the old trails, and the remnant of the red race have receded from the haunts of modern civilization. The well-beaten paths are almost obliterated, and a sigh escapes from our lips at the thought of the decay of the civilization of the pioneers of the white men.

ASOKINUKI.

A few days ago I passed by a stone resting under the brow of a hill. It was cone-shaped, of a peculiar color, about three hundred pounds weight, and held by the Indians in great reverence. A circle was made in the earth around it, and there lay articles of clothing and ornaments of various kinds. This was one of the famous "medicine" stones of the Blackfeet Indians. As the Indians passed to and fro, they knelt beside it and made offerings of berries, buffalo meat, or anything they might possess suitable for a sacrifice. Visiting one of the Indian camps some time ago, I met my old friend, Apoqkina, the medicine-man, and had a long conversation with him. Going through the camp I saw a man building his house, and I said to him, "My friend, this is Sunday; why are you building your house to-day?" He replied, "I prayed this morning, and now I can go to work." After talking with him a little, he promised he would not work on Sunday, and accordingly he left off building his house. I heard the medicine-man's drum beating, and inquiring who was sick, was informed that a little girl—one of our scholars—was ill. I went to the lodge where she was, and there saw two blind old medicine-men, who ceased beating their drums when I entered, and shook hands with me. Soon they began their incantations, which consisted in beating their drums, singing Indian songs, and shaking their bodies, keeping time with the tune. All the inmates of the lodge joined in the singing, and even the sick girl was compelled to join the rest of the company. The drums ceased beating and the chief medicine-man told the mother to lay the girl on her back and hold her hands. She screamed loudly, but the drums beat still louder, and the singing continued. The old man put a small piece of glass in his mouth, and then began to feel all over the body of the girl with his fingers. Taking the piece of glass between his finger and thumb he inserted it in the flesh as a doctor's lance, and then stooping caught the flesh between the teeth and very roughly and cruelly began pulling and sucking the blood. I felt sickened at the sight of his horrible roughness and felt indignant, but prudence suggested that I had better not interfere until the ceremony was over, and then try afterwards to prevent the continuance of such loathsome practices. After a great deal of exertion, the Asokinuki (medicine-man) spat out a few drops of blood. He was going to repeat the operation, but through the intervention of my school teacher he ceased. Taking an old wooden basin he poured into it some water, and putting in it two hot stones, he dipped his hands in the water, and, after spitting on them, bathed the girl's body and wiped it with a dirty brush made of feathers. The ceremony ended, he called for his pipe and had a smoke, evidently feeling that he had performed a wonderful operation.

INDIANS AND BUFFALO.

Schoolcraft was one of the most prolific writers on the Indians, and he is regarded by those who read only popular Indian literature as the most proficient author on this subject. He has, however, been surpassed by later writers, who have discovered very many inaccuracies in his writings, and the scientific student has been compelled to reject many of his theories and follow the teachings of better trained anthropologists. The investigations of these special students have revealed myths and traditions that increase our admiration for the native religion and literature of the American Indians. Amongst this race there have existed animal societies, having special forms for admission and a definite object in view.

Amongst the Omaha Indians there is a buffalo society, which is medical in its character. The members of this society attend to wounds and injuries. They possess the knowledge of a root, which they keep secret, and when attending a wounded person chew this root and inject the saliva into the wound. Fractures are bound with splints, but they never amputate a limb. They continue their services for four days, at the end of which time the patient is placed upon his feet, urged to walk a few steps, and then declared cured. Enforced rest completes the cure.

The buffalo occupies a prominent place in the legends of the Indians, and consequently a certain degree of veneration is given to this animal.

When a man among the Santee Indians dreamt of buffalo, he took the head of a buffalo which he had killed, removed the skin, restored it to its natural shape and allowed it to cure. He then removed the sods from a few square of feet of earth behind a lodge, worked the exposed earth very fine, took a new blanket or robe, which must not have belonged to a woman, and placed it over this prepared soil, which was called the "Umane." The skin of the buffalo head having retained its natural shape was painted blue on one side and red on the other, and then placed in the centre of the blanket. Upon the blue side tufts of white swan's down or small eagle feathers were tied to the hair, and upon the red side tufts of down painted red were tied. When this part of the ceremony was completed, a pipe was filled, the feast kettle hung over the fire, and after presenting the pipe to the head, the dreamer addressed the head as follows: "Grandfather! Venerable man! Your children have made this feast for you, may the food thus taken cause them to live, and bring them good fortune."

The superstitious fears of the Indians arise generally from their religious beliefs, in which fear and veneration of certain animals are incorporated. The native religion of these people is the expression of divinity inherent in their natures. When we can examine these from an Indian's standpoint, and interpret them fully, a higher appreciation of native civilization will result.

INDIAN ORATORY.

Much have I learned from listening to the lectures of famous English and American orators, and many lessons have I received from a close attention to the style exhibited in the speeches of our Indian orators. A commanding presence is not at all necessary to give a man influence in the Indian camp. To gain superiority, there must be the keen eye, dignified bearing, honest principles, intelligence, and a courageous heart. Tecumseh, the famous Shawnee chief, was physically and mentally a giant among his Indian followers. He was noted for his industry, wisdom, courage and military genius. His words were clothed with fire. When he addressed his dusky warriors, or spake to the white man in behalf of his people, he exhibited a vehemence of manner, and a power attended his words that aroused his followers to enthusiasm and sent a thrill through the hearts of his enemies. His life was eloquent, and his words were strong. I have been charmed by the utterance of Indian speakers among the Pottowattamies and the Chippewas, and the power possessed by such for swaying their audiences seemed wonderful. There was no studied manner, and no gigantic physical form, but the language was that of the heart, and it touched the souls of the hearers, producing the effect desired. There is manifest in the examples of true Indian oratory extant, what Goethe has well said:

> "If from the soul the language does not come,
> By its own impulse to impel the hearts
> Of hearers with communicated power,
> In vain you strive, in vain you study earnestly.

* * * * * * * * *

* * Never hope to stir the hearts of men,
And mould the souls of many into one,
By words which come not native from the heart!"

The eloquence of the Indian orators is unstudied, yet what added power would they possess, and what majestic eloquence would be theirs were they to enjoy some training in the art of true speech! Some of the most eloquent speakers among the Blackfeet Indians are men of low stature, but none of them are mean and base. They are intelligent, possess good principles, and are brave of heart. There is an excitability in the Indian temperament that is more easily roused by the manly words of their leaders than is experienced among their white brethren; yet the warrior who does not act well in times of peace will soon realize that when he calls to action those who should follow him, though he speak never so eloquently, his words will fall lifeless, and few will respond. The life must correspond to the words in order to insure success. Indian eloquence, then, has its source in the heart, is illuminated by the imagination, strengthened by intelligence, guided by reason, and gains its greatest success by the eloquent life. Practice brings perfection to it, and cultivation is going on continually. Blest is the man who has the commanding presence to prepare the way for the powerful speech, and who can, by his manner, keep the attention of his audience while he gives them words of wisdom to cheer and guide. The true method of English, American and Indian oratory is well expressed by a lady writer:

"There's a charm in delivery, a magical art,
That thrills like a kiss from the lips of the heart;
'Tis the glance—the expression—the well-chosen word,
By whose magic the depths of the spirit are stirred,
The lip's soft persuasion—its musical tone;
Oh! such were the charms of that eloquent One."

PRIMITIVE PEOPLE.

"The proper study of mankind is man."

This is true as related to the knowledge of human nature, and equally so, as applied to the information received concerning the physical and mental characteristics of the human race. Deeply interesting is the study of the ten thousand objects in the Smithsonian Institution, illustrating the life of prehistoric man in western Europe. The chipped stone implements of the people who lived in the dim past of the world's history, and the peculiarly shaped skulls, which anthropologists say belonged to a race lacking the power of speech, or, if possessing this faculty, having few ideas worthy of expression, excite our curiosity and awaken our interest. The relics of the cave-dwellers and the men of succeeding generations, reveal the progressive development of man, and indicate the fact that the Divine Intellect is educating the human race which shall receive its full complement in the future, when the ideal race shall be the result of a union of nationalities speaking a universal language, and accepting a common faith.

The shadow of mystery hovers over the races of mound-builders and cliff-dwellers, only to pass away when we read the history of the Indians of the New

World. In Europe and America remnants of primitive people still exist, and the customs of these and extinct races, although savage and strange, are deeply interesting and instructive to the people of the present century. The intrepid traveller, Baron Von Humboldt, states that the natives of tropical countries show an irresistible desire to eat earth. When the women of Magdalena river were fashioning their earthen vessels, they would take large pieces of clay and eat them. When descending the Orinoco, he spent a day with an earth-eating tribe of Indians called Otomacs, and thus describes the habits of these people:

"The earth which the Otomases eat is a soft, unctious clay, a true potter's clay of a yellowish-gray color, due to a little oxide of iron. They seek for it on the banks of the Orinoco and Meta, and select it with care, as they do not consider all clays agreeable to eat. They knead the earth into balls of from five to six inches in diameter, which they burn or roast by a weak fire until the outside assumes a reddish tint. The balls are re-moistened when about to be eaten. A very intelligent monk, who had lived twelve years among the Indians, assured us that one of them would eat from three-quarters of a pound to a pound and a quarter in a day. If you inquire of an Otomac about his winter provision, he will point to the heap of clay balls stored in his hut." Regarding other peoples who practise this custom, Humboldt says: "We find the practice of eating earth diffused throughout the torrid zone, but accounts have also come from the north, according to which hundreds of cartloads of earth containing infusoria, are said to be annually consumed by the country people in the most remote parts of Sweden, and that in Finland a kind of earth is occasionally mixed with bread."

The ancestors of a tribe of Indians in Ecuador had a strange custom of preserving the heads of their deceased friends. By some strange process, now unknown, they removed the bony substance from the skull, and then compressed the fleshy part to the smallest possible dimensions, still retaining the features to a remarkable degree, although the head was not much larger than the bowl of a pipe. Very few of these heads have been taken away, as the Indians preserve them sacredly. They have been so completely hardened and kept from decay, that although supposed to be three hundred years old, they are in an excellent state of preservation. The cavities of the eyes, the cheeks, mouth and ears are much shrunken, and the matted, coarse black hair remains.

Strange barbaric customs still exist among the Svans of the Transcaucasian valleys. The people of the province of Svanetia leave a piece of waste land between themselves and their nearest neighbors, and the wanderer who treads this debatable border is liable to be shot. In the villages are innumerable towers with narrow slits instead of windows, arranged for defence. Among the Svans may be seen the chieftain supported by the gifts of his people, and surrounded by a motley band of idle fellows as a body-guard, a transposition of the feudal system. Cattle-stealing is to them refined sport, and occasionally they indulge in a raid upon the neighboring tribes to capture women for wives. When a female child is born in the community, any young man may claim betrothal by simply hanging a figured bullet around its neck. Should the parents or the girl refuse when she reaches marriageable age, that she become his wife, the young man or his friends may engage in deadly combat with the members of the family.

The striking contrast between the barbaric civilization of primitive people, and that of the people enjoying the benefits of modern refinement, creates ideas of increased responsibility and contentment with our lot. There is a continual evolution in the intellectual, moral and spiritual natures of man, and we are made partakers of the blessings resulting from the toils and trials, successes and mistakes of the men of yore.

NATIVE AMERICANS.

The natives of the American continent have been called the Red Man, as if they were distinctively of that color, and yet there are to be found tribes that are red, white, brown and black. Why they should be denominated Indians at all, may have puzzled the brain of many an honest inquirer; but the fact is of historical importance, that when Columbus discovered the New World, he thought he had reached India, hence the name given to the inhabitants. Although the error was subsequently corrected, the name clung to the people, which was finally qualified by writers on the subject by calling them American Indians.

In stature, there are striking differences among the

tribes, but there are similarities peculiar to the race, such as the square head, high cheek bones, sunken, dark eyes, and long, jet-black hair. There is a similarity in the construction of their language that points to a common origin. Their mythology, social, political and religious customs have a common source, and their mental characteristics are apparently evolved from the same germ.

There is a strange contrast between the refined civilization of the Mexicans and Peruvians, and the degradation of the northern tribes. There are some writers on Indian history, who teach that these people are not in the early stages of primitive barbarism, but have descended from a highly civilized position to the last stage of an effete civilization. It does seem strange to read and think of the Aztec architecture and literature as belonging to a people isolated and free from contact with the thought and works of the civilized world. Sad and wonderful is it to read the story of fallen greatness, and to gaze upon the descendants of the former rulers of the New World.

A new era has opened up for those who have accepted the civilization of their conquerors, and the prospect for the complete emancipation of the body, mind and spirit is bright indeed. Hope and industry are paving the way for abundant success in all that tends to their mental and moral welfare. The hope of the race lies in the infusion of holy principles that will arouse their dormant energies, and create a new era of independence. These principles are found in the gospel of the man of Nazareth, and their efficiency for this work is shown in the results so well illustrated in Miss Tucker's "Rainbow of the North," and Welcome's "Story of Metlakahtla."

THE BLOOD INDIANS.

The land of the Red Men is fast becoming the home of the pale-face. Much of the history of the aborigines of the west is shrouded in mystery, the aged historians of the tribes passing gradually to the land beyond, and the younger generations failing to grasp intelligently the interpretations of mythology, and the full meaning of the traditions related to them by their worthy ancestors. There still linger amongst us a few of the heroes of the olden times, who treasure the only remaining data of the early history and migrations of the people. It is a fascinating duty to sit in the lodges and listen to the brief biographies of haughty war-chiefs, the eloquent descriptions of famous battles, or the plaintive and pathetic stories of holy men, who dreamed dreams and saw visions until, on the lonely mountain or in the deep and rugged canyon, they contended with the spirits of darkness, and victory was ultimately gained. The land is dotted with places of historical interest to the red men, but the busy farmer and the earnest student, alike in their ignorance, pass them by, for they speak a language strange to their ears, and the sacred trees and rocks make unto them no new revelation.

The land occupied in past ages by the Shoshonees and Flathead Indians is now the home of the Blackfeet confederacy, known by the distinctive names of the three tribes which constitute the confederacy, namely: the Blackfeet proper, Bloods and Piegans.

The Indians speak of themselves by the name of the tribe to which they individually belong, but when referring to their confederacy, they call themselves by two distinct appellations, Sâketûpiks, *i.e.*, the people of the plains; and Netsepoye, *i.e.*, the people that speak the same language.

There are two thousand Blood Indians located on a fine reserve south of Macleod. The Blood agency is distant from the town about fourteen miles, the southern portion of the reserve, however, is about seven miles from Lethbridge.

There are nine hundred Piegan Indians on their own reserve, which is about twelve miles from Macleod. There are portions of both of these reserves which are nearer to Macleod than the distances given, but as the agencies are the central places, and the general rendezvous of the natives, these are chosen as the best adapted to give the reader an idea of the vicinity of the red men. The advent of the white men, and the influences of the encroaching civilization of the white race have wrought many changes upon the natives, so that no longer can we gaze upon the ideal Indian, as depicted for us in the pages of Fennimore Cooper and Catlin. The days of the bow and arrow, buffalo skin lodges, and ornamented native dresses are past, and in their stead there are plain matter-of-fact Indians, facing the stern reality that soon, very soon, they will be doomed to earn their bread by the sweat of the brow.

A few years ago the buffalo lodges were decorated with scalp-locks and picture-writing, but these are gone. Yet we need not despair of finding much that is interesting in their language, mythology, traditions, native religion, and customs. The student will find much to excite his enthusiasm in the study of comparative philology. The beautiful symmetry of the native language, its wonderful grammatical construction, the hundreds of forms into which a single verb may be arranged to do duty in the expression of thoughts, will reveal a few of the interesting features that will present themselves to the man of intelligence. The mythology of the natives is nothing but a heterogeneous mass of silly stories to the general reader, but when there is a competent guide to instruct those who are unlearned in the civilization of this people, there will follow new revelations of the unity of their mythology, and its influence upon the education of the race. There is a native civilization that will repay earnest study, and enlighten our sympathies toward this fallen race. There exists a native religion, with its priesthood, deities, sacrifices and doctrines. Oftentimes have I stood entranced as some aged chief has emerged from his lodge, and reverently gazing upon the sun, prayed sincerely for its smiles to rest upon himself and his people. The medical priesthood still directs the devotions of the pious few, and the lingering traces of their religion are annually seen in their Sun-dance. The customs of the people are changing, as evidenced by the decay of the practice of polygamy, the adoption of the ways of the white men in burying their dead, and in the new methods employed by them in their domestic affairs, and in social life. The continual strife between different tribes has no longer an existence, as the representatives of law and order settle these questions, and while protecting the Indians, prevent disturbance and ensure peace. Occasionally some young men may cross the International boundary line to steal horses, but they seldom enjoy their booty, as they are quickly tracked, and they do not care to risk spending three years in prison for the sake of a few head of horses. When the buffalo left the plains, the Indians were reduced to starvation, but the Government stepped in to save them, by supplying them with food.

Since that period they have been fed regularly by the Indian agents, under instruction from the Indian Department authorities. Twice a week they receive their rations, at their respective agencies, and they are well cared for in all that pertains to their temporal welfare. Farm instructors are sent to teach them farming, and these, residing continuously with them, exert a wholesome influence in the camps.

During the past two years, progress has been shown in teaching them how to work. The advancement is slow, but it must be remembered that hunting was formerly their occupation, and now having to discard the means whereby they gained a living, they have to begin anew, to toil, and there is much to learn. The young men are learning to work, and especially in the summer, many of them hire themselves to farmers to work in the fields. Some of the Indians raise good crops; others are lazy and careless, and work very little.

Medical attendance is supplied to the Indians, and by this means the medicine-men of the camps are losing their hold upon the people. Schools are in operation on the Blood and Piegan reserves, sustained by the Government and the churches. Biscuits are regularly supplied to the scholars, so that they may not have to repair to the lodges for their mid-day meal. As the Indians know little of the value of education, the attendance of the children is irregular, and the work difficult. Some of the boys and girls are apt scholars, but in judging of their progress, there is little allowance made for the fact that they are studying a new language, that at the schools they are taught English, while all the rest of the day is spent in camp, where they employ their native tongue. How to successfully civilize the Indian is a vexed question, yet we do not need to despair, for there are hopeful signs, and success will ultimately come.

Missionary work has been carried on for nearly a decade amongst these Indians. On the Piegan reserve, the English and Roman Catholic Churches have representatives at work, and on the Blood reserve the Methodist, English Church and Roman Catholic missionaries are instructing the natives in the precepts and doctrines of the Christian religion. These different agencies have thus far been engaged in preparatory labor, as much of their time and energy have been expended upon the language, thus fitting themselves for more permanent and promising results, than have yet been seen. Annually the Indians receive their treaty-money from the Government, as the price of the lands they have surrendered. At such times they repair to the towns to make purchases. The merchants are kept busy for a few days supplying the wants of the red men. They do not indulge their childish propensities, as in former years, in buying trinkets, or whatever pleased their fancy, whether they needed it or not. Useful articles of clothing and furniture are sought, with a feast of good things agreeable to their palates, as a kind of remembrancer of the good time that comes once a year. During the late Rebellion, all of these Indians proved loyal to the Government, and although the white people had their anxieties from reports of Indian uprisings, they were spared the desolation of their homes, and loss of life. The red and white people are on good terms, so far as it is possible for different races to be. Differences of language, customs, and religion beget antagonisms that are evident. Different nations and races fiercely criticise each other's works and ways, and seldom can they see any good but in themselves, and still there exists between them a kindly reciprocity and sympathy for one another in trial and pain. The antagonism of race is natural, but despite this barrier, there are many evidences of union in matters affecting the common weal. Some of the Indians are inclined to ramble to the towns, but the majority prefer staying on their reserves. When a few Indians become obnoxious by their presence to the citizens, they are ordered to their reserves by the protectors of the peace. The days of

Indian scares are gone. The people are gradually settling down to an agricultural life, and in the near future there will be seen the results of civilization, namely, decrease of the red men, and the elevation of the survivals of the fittest. When the crisis is past, and the influences of the Christian religion have fully exerted their power, and these have been accepted and experienced by the red men, the descendants of the ancient lords of Canada will become recognized as agents fitted for aiding in the development of the country, and giving unity to our race.

An Eskimo Village.

CHAPTER III.

INDIAN HEROES.

TECUMSEH.

ON the banks of the River Sasta, near Chillicothe, Ohio, about the year 1770, Tecumseh was born. He was a Shawanese Indian, and his name signified *The Crouching Panther*.

Little or nothing is known concerning his early years, but in early manhood he possessed great muscular strength, and became noted for his integrity, good judgment, dignified bearing, and courage. He was tall of stature, the faculties of his mind were of a high order, and he was able to conduct himself with propriety among men of rank and intelligence in the American and British armies. He had a twin brother, called Ollinachia, who was held in high esteem among the Indians as a prophet.

The brothers conceived the idea of uniting the scattered tribes of Indians in one grand confederacy, whereby they might more effectively contend for their rights against the intrusion of pale-faced adventurers. They may have borrowed this idea from Hiawatha's labors amongst the Iroquois. Hiawatha sought to combine the Indians in this way, and he so far succeeded as to unite those now known as *The Six Nations.*

Several attempts were made by the Americans to punish the Indians by killing them and destroying their villages, and these measures were at times skilfully met by Tecumseh and his followers; but when the Indians were defeated it only tended to exasperate them and make them more expeditious in securing union.

Tecumseh, therefore, travelled among the tribes urging the claims of an organized confederacy. He had all the qualities necessary for making him a great leader and warrior, and consequently he had many followers who had implicit faith in his abilities and in his devotion to their cause.

In 1811, while on one of his tours among the Indian tribes, he had an interview with Major-General Harrison, after which he continued his journey to the Creek Nation.

During his absence, General Harrison attacked his people at Tippecanoe, and killed several of his warriors. His spirit rose indignant within him when he found that his people had suffered much in his absence.

When the war of 1812 broke out, General Hull's messengers besought him to join the Americans against the British, and on refusing to do so, asked him to remain neutral. He would have nothing to do with the *Big Knives,* but cast in his lot with the British. His enthusiasm and courage infused life into his followers, and they gained several victories. When the British troops would be repulsed, he has charged with his men and won the day.

He had, however, to share the reverses with those whose cause he had espoused. His eloquent appeals to his warriors showed him to have been a true orator. When General Proctor—of whom he entertained a very low opinion—was preparing to retreat into Canada, and had purposely concealed from Tecumseh and his followers the defeat of the British on Lake Erie by Perry, lest it might have an injurious effect upon the Indian allies, he addressed the General in a council held at Amherstburgh, with great power. He said: "Father, listen! Our fleet has gone out; we know they have fought; we have heard the great guns; but we know nothing of what has happened to our father with the one arm (Captain Barclay). Our ships have gone one way, and we are much astonished to see our father tying up everything and preparing to run the other way, without letting his red children know what his intentions are. You always told us to remain here to take care of the lands. You always told us you would never draw your foot off British ground; but now, father, we see you drawing back, and we are sorry to see our father do so without seeing the enemy. We must compare our father's conduct to a fat dog that carries its tail upon its back, but when affrighted it drops it between its legs and runs off.

"Father, listen! The Americans have not defeated us by land, neither are we sure that they have done so by water; we, therefore, wish to remain here and fight our enemy, should he make his appearance. If they defeat us, then we will retreat with our father. . . . You have got the arms and ammunition which our great father, the king, sent for his red children. If you have any idea of going away, give them to us, and you may go, and welcome, for us. Our lives are in the hands of the Great Spirit. We are determined to defend our lands, and if it be His will, we wish to leave our bones upon them."

Such was the oratorical effect of this speech that Tecumseh's warriors sprang to their feet and brandished their tomahawks.

On October 5th, 1813, a battle was fought at Moravian Town, on the Thames. Just before the battle Tecumseh said to General Proctor: "Father, tell your young men to be firm, and all will be well."

The Americans had with them a party of Kentucky Rangers, who were accustomed to fighting like Indians in the bush. The British troops were repulsed, and in the contest that ensued between the Rangers and the Indians, Tecumseh was killed. His warriors took his body from the field of battle, and during the night they buried him where the white man should never find his grave. After his death his followers gave up the contest, and the great aim of Tecumseh was never realized. A few years ago, Moses Stonefish, the *last* of Tecumseh's warriors, died at the Moravian Reserve.

General Brock held Tecumseh very high in his estimation. Concerning this courageous and faithful Shawanese chief, he said: "He was the admiration of every one who conversed with him. From a life of dissipation he has not only become, in every respect, abstemious, but he has likewise prevailed on all his native, and many of the other tribes, to follow his example."

GLIKKIKAN.

Glikkikan was a famous Delaware Indian. He was a dignified war captain, who had gained many friends by his illustrious victories over his Indian foes. His fame, however, rested not altogether on his bravery and success as a warrior, for he was also the speaker in the council of Kas-kas-kunkes, and the leading counsellor of his tribe. He was shrewd and intelligent. As an orator he excelled. Oftentimes before his assembled countrymen has he stood denouncing wrong and proclaiming justice to the oppressed. Such was the power of his intellect, and so great was his command of language, that when the Jesuits sought to convert his countrymen they were compelled to desist, being unable to withstand the influence of his arguments and eloquence among his people. Frederick Post, a Moravian missionary, had to give up his mission also on account of Glikkikan's opposition. In 1769 he visited the Indian missionaries on the Alleghany, determined to frustrate their efforts in striving to save the souls of the Indians. Accompanied by several members of his tribe, who had implicit confidence in his abilities, and were already rejoicing in the anticipated victory of heathenism over Christianity, he set out on his journey. His speech was well prepared. The various arguments were properly arranged, and some of the language to be used was memorized. They reached the mission settlement, and found a native assistant named Anthony glad to receive them.

This converted Indian had a passion for saving the souls of the red men. He set food before his guests and then began in the style and phraseology peculiar to Indian speakers, to relate the wonders of God's creation, the fall of man, the sinfulness of man's heart, the inability of man to save himself, and the grief and glory of the atoning sacrifices of Christ. The missionary corroborated the statements of the native preacher. Glikkikan listened, his fine speech had fled from his memory, and he was convinced that the Christian religion was the true one.

Instead of the glowing vindication of heathenism, he humbly said, "I have nothing to say, I believe your words." He was a conscientious man; and while convinced that the native religion of the Indians was right, opposed with strong determination the efforts of the missionaries to convert his people. When the truth of God reached his heart he gave up the contest, and sought earnestly the way of peace. He returned to his people repentant. His glory as the champion of heathenism had gone, and his followers were now without a leader to guide them in their efforts against the Christian religion. In a short time he returned to the mission to say that he had embraced Christianity, and he then made an offer to the missionary, in the name of the head chief, to come and settle amongst them, and that a piece of land had been set apart for the use of the mission. This request had been sent before by some members of the tribe, but being opposed to the religion of Christ, they had failed to deliver their message. Glikkikan sat and listened to the gospel preached by the missionary, and the Spirit touched his heart. The proud Indian war captain bowed his head and wept. His sighs were changed to songs, and from being the persecuting Saul in his tribe, he became the devoted Paul. The teachers of righteousness went and settled among his people, and many were led to devote their lives to God.

Glikkikan was persecuted by the heathen section of his people. The head chief bitterly reproached him. He said, "And have you gone to the Christian teachers from our very council? What do you want of them? Do you hope to get a white skin? Not so much as one of your feet will turn white; how then can your whole skin be changed? Were you not a brave man? Were you not an honorable counsellor? Did you not sit at my side in this house, with a blanket before you and a pile of wampum-belts on it, and help me direct the affairs of our nation? And now you despise all this? You think you have found something better. Wait! In good time you will discover how miserably you have been deceived." In a Christian spirit, Glikkikan replied, "You are right. I have joined the brethren. Where they go, I will go; where they lodge, I will lodge. Nothing shall separate me from them. This people shall be my people, and their God shall be my God." The missionaries in their labors among the

Delaware Indians had to contend against the strong opposition of heathen priests, some of whom believed that they were possessors of the true religion, and they alone could grant salvation to men. These Indian preachers taught that sin must be purged out of the body by vomiting; and many, obeying them, were thereby ruining their health.

Glikkikan now became intensely in earnest for the salvation of men. He stood up in defence of the Christian religion in the grand council of the Delawares. He accompanied the missionaries on expeditions to the Shawanese, Wyandots, and other Indian tribes. He was instant in season in preaching to his fellow-chiefs and men of influence among the Indians. Once, when falsely accused, he was taken prisoner, bound and about to be killed. Boldly he stood up before his captors, who were afraid of him when they remembered his former glory in war, and with true Christian dignity, he said, "There was a time when I would never have yielded myself prisoner to any man; but that was the time when I lived in heathenish darkness and knew not God. Now that I am converted to Him, I suffer willingly for Christ's sake." Nothing was too great for him to do for Christ. Genuine piety adorned his life, and noble Christian courage made his name a power in the Indian councils and in the lodges of the people.

The country was plunged in deep distress by an Indian war—Indians and whites had been unmercifully slain. The Christian Indians were blamed with the others. A party of militia set out for the Christian

Indian villages with the resolve to slay every Indian. The Indians heard of this, but they relied upon their innocence for their safety. They worked at their grain, and were thus engaged when the troops arrived. The militia professed great friendship for the Indians, and told them that they had come to take them to a place of safety. They enjoyed the hospitality of the Indians. A day was set for killing the entire community. The day before the cruel deed was committed the young soldiers sported with the Indian youth. Evening came, and friend and foe lay peacefully, side by side. The hour arrived, and the Indians were bound. They were laughed at for asserting their innocence. Their last hours were spent in prayer and praise. The men were taken to one large house, and the women to another. There they were slain, and their scalps taken by the militia as trophies of their disgraceful victory. The militia returned with ninety-six scalps. The facts of history proclaim the innocence of these Christian Indians. Glikkikan was amongst the number. Trusting in God, he found at last a resting-place where all are equal as sons and daughters of the Almighty Father.

RED JACKET.

The remains of Red Jacket and of several other notable Indians have been reinterred in Forest Lawn Cemetery, Buffalo.

The Indian graveyard had not only been neglected, but the rights of the Senecas had been invaded, hence there arose the necessity for guarding and preserving the remains of those who were once great in their nation, and respected by the Government.

Red Jacket was born in 1752, and has been called the last of the Senecas. He was a pure Indian, dignified in his manner, and keenly alive to the interests of his fellows in the Five Nations. Sometimes it is said that there are no Indians capable of having their intellects developed, and worthy the lasting friendship of the white man—especially at the present time. Many of those who have suffered through the rebellion in the North-West are crying out that there are very few good Indians, and that, as a race, it is time wasted to spend years amongst them trying to lead them to Christ and civilization.

Red Jacket was not a Christian Indian, and though lacking the aid of those who were desirous to help him, he exhibited the influence of an untaught genius whilst striving to help those of his own race. He had a powerful intellect, a very tenacious memory, and when he addressed his people assembled in council, the convincing power of his logic was overmastering. The Huron-Iroquois sedulously studied the art of oratory, and many of their councillors excelled in it. Amongst them all, there was none equal to Red Jacket. He was one of the greatest Indian orators that ever lived on the American continent. He felt deeply for his people. He saw the warriors, the aged and the young, passing away. The nation that had once been so powerful was fast dwindling into insignificance, and his heart was sad at the gloomy prospects of being left alone—the last of his race. He beheld with indignation the encroachment of the white men. He saw land speculators and others taking away the land that belonged to his people. He heard fair promises made to them by those in authority, and these never fulfilled. He saw the missionary carry the Bible in his hand to tell the red men of Christ and salvation, but he looked around and saw hundreds of those who called themselves Christians who were more vicious than the Indians. The white man had given his Indians whisky to destroy their bodies, minds, and souls—ammunition and guns they had furnished by which they killed each other, diseases they introduced which carried away many of his people, and, as he thought of these things, his soul burned within him at the wrongs inflicted on them. Thus it was that he watched jealously the white man, and was unfriendly to the missionary. Yet in his last hours he was heard to say, ere he left this earth, "Where is the missionary?" He had been called "Always Ready" when, as a bearer of despatches during the war of 1812-14, he could ever be relied on, and was always found at his post. Then he was called "He Keeps Them Awake." When the remnant of his people were disconsolate, he cheered them. His voice asserted their rights, and he was ever their friend.

The noble Seneca passed away at Seneca village, near Buffalo, New York, in 1830, mourning the sad condition of his people. What might he not have been had he yielded to the holy influence of the Gospel, which becomes the savor of life unto the Indian, and lifts him nearer to God.

THE SWARTHY HERO.

The years are not far distant when a band of warriors belonging to the Blackfoot nation started on the war-path, determined to add to their wealth and reputation by deeds of valor and the ownership of a few head of horses. The number amounted not to a score, and already they had formed the foolhardy resolve of entering the Sioux camp amid the darkness of the night, and, with bold and reckless daring, making themselves masters of the finest chargers to be found. In those days the Sioux nation had some of the finest horses to be seen in the great Territories of the West. The buoyant spirits of the youthful warriors found expression in the gayest songs of the Indian tongue. There was no cause for fear during the first days of the journey, as the camp of the enemy was distant fully ten days' ride. Each of the braves carried a Winchester rifle, which he took the precaution to have well loaded, lest in an untimely moment the terrible war-whoop of a few stray foes might be heard in the rear. The painted bodies of the members of the war party were exposed to the cold, piercing winds; but they heeded not the intensity of the elements, as the red clay and paint which had been used to beautify became a preservative against heat and cold. The monotony of the prairie was enlivened by a recital of the heroic deeds of each.

Onward they pursued their course, their senses of seeing and hearing becoming intensified as they drew near to the country in which the enemy was supposed to be encamped. No longer in the shades of the evening did they light the camp fire and make merry among themselves. Wrapped up in their blankets, with one hand on their rifles and their horses picketed near by, they lay half-asleep while one of their number scanned the prairie during the silent watches of the night. Sleeping and watching as only Indians can, the few midnight hours passed, and ere the sun rose they were stealthily wending their way to the goal of their hopes. Before the shades of evening gathered around them, they descried in the distance the camp of the enemy pitched on a lovely plain. Circling on the prairie they sought a favorable position for seeing the plan of the camp and the movements of the stalwart braves. The horses were fastened inside the camp enclosure, every man with his favorite horse drawn up at his lodge. A determined look sat upon each countenance as they stood gazing at the treasures for which they had come.

Such was the strength of the Sioux camp that none of them dared attack it. Five days were thus spent alternating with hope and fear. At length, wearied with waiting and afraid to attempt such a foolhardy experiment, they all made up their minds to return home without having secured their object. No, not all; for there was a brave young heart that determined to do or die. The possessor of this courageous spirit was a young man of nineteen years. Persuasion failed to induce him to accompany his companions, so, scolding him for his foolishness, they left him to accomplish that which he desired.

Night gathered around the Sioux camp, and no eye

remained unclosed save that of the lonely watcher on the hill. Still and silent as death, the youthful avenger of the wrongs perpetrated on his forefathers crept among the lodges, until courage begetting courage, he raised the buffalo-skin door of a lodge, and, after gazing a few moments upon the sleeping occupants, entered. Around, on the floor, in the embrace of "nature's sweet restorer," lay three chiefs and five women. The fire burned dimly in the centre, and the curling smoke escaped between the lodge poles at the top. A small kettle of meat, the remnant of the evening's repast, stood by the fire.

Our young hero, with all the quietness and alacrity possible, soon satisfied the urgent demands of his appetite, and left an empty vessel to declare that he had done justice to the supper prepared for him. Slipping off one of his moccasins, he laid it beside the empty kettle, a silent declaration that an enemy had been in the camp. Departing without any ceremony, he unloosed the finest horse that stood near, and a few minutes sufficed to leave the camp and his enemies far behind. His companions were filled with wonder at his daring and were angry at themselves.

Judge of the consternation in the Sioux camp when it became known that a Blackfoot youth had performed such a brave deed. They knew as they looked upon the moccasin that a bloodthirsty Blackfoot had been there. Anger filled not their hearts, for they admired the heroism that could do such a thing. The strong and brave men vowed that were they to find the swarthy hero they would crown him with honors, and make him a chief of whom any Indian nation might feel proud.

BUTTON CHIEF.

A grand old man was Button Chief. He was known amongst the white settlers by this name, but amongst his own people—the Blood Indians—he was called Medicine Calf.

He possessed a powerful frame, that must have made him in his youthful days a formidable antagonist. When upwards of three score and ten he could mount his horse and ride long distances. The stalwart warrior strode through the camps in dignified silence, looking with pleasure on the innocent sports of childhood, and giving advice to those who sought his counsel, and relied much upon his wisdom and grace. Feeling keenly the intrigues of many despotic white men when living with his people in Montana, he led the last attack made upon the whites by the Blood Indians.

In his subsequent travels he made many friends among the white people, and the longer he lived his influence amongst them was becoming very much greater. He was ever ready when any of the young men committed depredations to reprimand them severely, and to secure justice and compensation for his white friends. His word was law amongst those who were more closely related to him as members of his band. When he learned that there was stolen property in his camp, he has gone, and, without any solicitation or promise of reward, has recovered it and given it to the owners. Often has he been heard, as he rode through the camp, shouting his orders to the people, and never have I known these to be disregarded. The women have gone out to perform some duty under his instructions; the men have refrained from engaging in petty annoyances or more serious strife; and the children have laid aside their wheels and arrows, and hurried off to school when kindly urged by their worthy chief. He was keenly observant of the ways of the white man, and predicted the downfall of his people by extinction or absorption, and the final supremacy of the pale-face.

In his warrior days he exercised great influence amongst the chiefs and over the young men. A council of chiefs had been held where it was decided to attack the Sioux camp a few miles distant. He was not present, and war could not be declared without his consent. At a subsequent meeting, after the proceedings of the former council had been rehearsed, he was asked for his decision, when, with a deep sense of justice and true dignity, he answered their demands as follows:

"What have the Sioux done?" he asked.

"They are coming too close to our camps," was the reply.

"Have they done you any harm, that you wish to fight with them?"

"No."

After a significant pause he uttered this sententious sentence, which closed the council and decided the whole, "I fight with my enemies."

There are some who could not penetrate the Indian

skin, and see underneath the emotions of a hero. Greed and glory were the impelling powers of the minds of many of the frontiersmen, and to them affection and heroism in an Indian were things unknown. Viewing this man's character after the lapse of years, I am compelled to say that he was a noble man. He had a keen intellect, which could be discerned when dealing with questions relating to his people. He desired that young and old should enjoy the benefits flowing from education and religion. He had a vast fund of traditionary lore relating to his tribe, most of which has died with him. He was supposed to have been one of the few who knew anything concerning the Blackfeet historical song or poem. He was one of the first orators of his tribe. In simple and dignified language he could urge the claims of his people. When Lord Lorne travelled through the North-West, he expressed his loyalty to the Government by taking off his handsome deerskin shirt and presenting it to the Governor-General.

He felt the cravings of a higher manhood within him, and therefore listened attentively to the story of the Cross. Gathering his children around him he would teach them to pray to God. When the missionary knelt by his side to pray, he would join in the prayer and then utter his thanks. One Sunday morning early, as I was visiting the people in their lodges a few miles distant, a messenger rode toward me and said: "Your friend, Medicine Calf, is dead; come quickly to the lodge." When he had delivered this message, he uttered a plaintive wail and left me. With

Captain Joseph Brant.

(THAYENDANEGEA.)

a sad heart I rode off. I knelt beside the women, weeping bitterly, and prayed for grace to the bereaved. Only two days previous we talked about "the home over there," and just before he died he called me by name, and wished to see me once more. My dear, tried, and faithful Indian friend was no more, and deeply I mourned his loss. We raised a lodge on the prairie, and laid him in all his martial glory to rest. The last sad rites performed, we turned away, with heavy hearts. Over on the other side we shall meet again, when the red man shall no longer be doomed by his color, but all shall be as the children of God.

CAPTAIN JOSEPH BRANT.

(THAYENDANEGEA.)

Thayendanegea was a famous Mohawk chief, born in Ohio, about 1742. His family held an important position amongst the Indians, and the influences arising from this became serviceable to him in his military career. Whilst still a lad, he was engaged in several bloody battles. About 1760 he was sent to President Wheelock's school for Indians, at Lebanon, Connecticut. He became friendly with the Johnson family, and the education he had received enabled him, with his natural ability, to accept the position of Secretary to Col. Guy Johnson, who was Superintendent-General of Indian Affairs. Gradually he rose in the estimation of his friends and allies, until, through his connection with the Johnsons, his increased military prestige, and the course of events, he was made the Principal War-Chief of the Confederacy.

In 1775 he visited England for the first time, accompanied by Captain Tice. During this visit a masquerade ball was held, when Brant arrayed himself in the brilliant costume of the Indian chiefs, and as the ladies were closely scrutinizing his dress, he suddenly brandished his tomahawk and shouted the war-whoop. They fled in consternation at the strange demeanor of the Indian chief, but peace was soon restored when they learned that he had played a practical joke upon them. What he saw and learned during this visit caused him to determine firmly to adhere to the British standard, and though many attempts were made to induce him to change his opinion, or to secure his neutrality, he remained true to his purpose. His old teacher and friend, President Wheelock, exerted his influence in favor of the colonists, but his efforts were fruitless. Brant's reply to President Wheelock at once settled the question, and removed all doubts as to his allegiance, as follows: "I recall to mind, with pleasure, the happy hours I spent under your roof, and especially the prayers and family devotions to which I listened. One passage in particular was so often repeated it could never be effaced from my memory, namely, "That they might be able to live as good subjects, to fear God, and *honor the king.*" Efforts were still used by Colonel Herkimer and others to restrain Brant from adhering to the royal cause, but he expressed himself as well satisfied with his treatment at the hands of the king.

An attempt was made at one of these conferences to assassinate Brant, but he was suspicious of treacherous intentions, and had secretly hidden five hundred painted warriors, armed for battle. Freely he expressed his mind, and then shouted the war-whoop, when the whole band rushed around him, brandishing their tomahawks and yelling their war-whoops. Brant incited his Indians against the colonists, while he sought to restrain them from needless cruelty. The Indians formed an alliance with Britain, and then began in earnest the cruel times of warfare between the colonists and the Indians. At the battle of Oriskany the Indians were defeated, but still remained true to Britain, except the Tuscaroras and Oneidas.

Brant was induced, much against his will, by a man in whom he had no confidence, named Walter Butler, to make a raid upon the peaceful inhabitants of Cherry Valley. The wholesale slaughter that ensued has left a stain upon the character of the Mohawk leader, but he was not in command, and was consequently helpless in the hands of the Indians. Several of his own friends amongst the white people were slain; the children were protected by him, and he used his influence, slight though it was, to guard the feeble ones. The Senecas were savagely incensed, and the deeds of cruelty were hideous and terrible. With his faithful band of Mohawks he sought to stay the hand of the bloodthirsty Senecas, but he failed to accomplish his purpose, although he was able to lessen the number of murders that would have been committed. The Revolutionary War still continued, and the Indians under Brant remained loyal to the British Crown. The Indians descended the Mohawk Valley, and by stratagem secured a large quantity of supplies. Then came the last engagement of the war, in which Walter Butler was slain and scalped by an Oneida Indian.

When the hatchet was buried, the Mohawks sold their possessions in the United States, and asked the Mississaugas of the River Credit, in Ontario, to allow them to settle beside them by granting them a piece of land. The request was granted, and though compensation was offered, it was steadily refused.

The Senecas offered them a tract of land to induce them not to go to Canada, but they were determined in their loyalty to the British.

In 1785 Brant went to England, for the second time, to lay the claims of the Indians before the Crown, and to secure some compensation for all they had lost during the war. He was successful in his mission, in securing what he was seeking, and during this visit he was honored with the presence of the clergy, military officers, political leaders and eminent men in literary circles. They courted his company, and rejoiced in his friendship. He exerted himself earnestly, on behalf of his Indians, in raising funds for the erection of a church for the Mohawks of Canada, and the settlement of the land question.

Through his noble efforts there was published, under the patronage of the king, the Gospel of Mark and the Book of Common Prayer, in the Mohawk tongue, and sufficient funds were obtained for the building of the first Episcopal church in Canada, on the banks of the Grand River, a short distance from Brantford.

Kecheahgahmequa, in an interesting sketch of Brant, mentions his untiring devotion to the Indians in striving to secure their rights, and the obstructions placed in his way by interested persons, as referred to in his last speech on the Indian land question, as follows: "I cannot help remarking that it appears to me that certain characters here who stood behind the counter during the late war, and whom we know nothing about, are now dictating to your great men concerning our lands. I should wish to know what property these officious persons left behind them in their own country, or whether, through their loyalty, they ever lost any. I doubt it much. But 'tis well known that scarcely a man amongst us but what sacrificed more or less by leaving their homes. It is well known that personal interest and not public good prompts them." After his return from England, he was attached to the military service of Sir Guy Carleton, in Canada. He was opposed to the confederation of the Indians, and sought to preserve peace between the red men and the United States. He labored earnestly for the welfare of the Six Nations, and sought to prevent the introduction of intoxicating liquors amongst them. The education of his own family and the Indians, the directing of his people toward a life of industry and self-support, and the supply of religious influences, employed the last days of the noble chief of the Mohawks. He died November 24, 1807. Some relics of the revolutionary period belonging to Brant and the Indians are still in existence. Some of these are: the ring which he procured in England and wore, that he might be identified if slain upon the battle-field; the communion service given to the Indians by Queen Anne, when they resided at Fort Hunter; and the watch which was given to Brant by Sir Wm. Johnson, before the Mohawk started on his Cherry Valley expedition. This watch was made by Thomas Linhard, who was a watchmaker in Fleet Street, London, from 1638 to 1658. It was presented by King George Third to Sir Wm. Johnson, and by the latter to Brant. It weighs five and a half ounces, is an inch and a half thick, made in the "British bull's-eye" pattern, and has two rows of figures in the Arabic and Roman characters on the face. It has not been repaired since 1847, and keeps as good time as when made. It fell into the hands of an officer in the Revolutionary army named Evart Van Epps, and by marriage was brought into the Minthorn family, where it is still retained.

In 1876, a proposition was made to the council of the Six Nation Indians to erect a monument to the memory of Brant. After ten years of untiring devotion to his cause by the members of the Brant Memorial Association, the corner-stone of the monument was laid by Chief Henry Clench, an Oneida of the Brantford Reserve.

On the silver trowel used on the occasion was engraved: "Presented to the chiefs of the Six Nation Indians on the occasion of the laying of the corner-stone of the Brant Monument, Brantford, August 11th, 1886."

There was an interested spectator present in the person of Chief Smoke Johnson, aged ninety-four years, who had seen, and conversed with Brant. After the ceremony the aged chief spoke to the large assemblage of two thousand persons. He said "He had known Brant, and had heard much of his exploits and valiancy, and adherence to the British crown. At the time of the Revolutionary War, when the Mohawks were in New York State, they were enjoying many privileges, but the war broke out, and Brant with his Indians fought the rebels. After a long and continuous war the British surrendered America.

"Brant's conduct in carefully guarding the wives and children of British soldiers, and conducting them to Niagara in safety had been universally rejoiced at. Brant was famous as a warrior and faithful ally, and the whole country felt that such a memorial should be erected.

"Brant's faithfulness to the terms of the treaty with the British was marked, and his example was a fit one to follow."

Under the corner-stone, among other things, were placed a copy of the grants of land made by Governor Haldimand, dated October 25, 1784; a copy of deed confirming the grant signed by Governor Simcoe, dated January 14, 1793; a report of the visit of Lord Dufferin to the Six Nation Indian Reserve, August 25, 1874, and a copy of the report of Superintendent General of Indians for 1885. There were also four strings of wampum, the interpretation of which was enclosed in the jar containing them. An abridged interpretation of these has been furnished by Dr. Peter

Jones in a paper entitled by him, *The Indian*, and is as follows:

"*First string.*—Black and white, represents death with grief and mourning; the white indicating removal of sorrow, restoring the light of day with joy.

"*Second string.*—Addressed to the Mohawks, and being white, is in continuation of the white in the first string, removing all sorrow.

"*Third string.*—White. Addressed to the chiefs who, having been in darkness, in consequence of their great loss, are now restored to a sense of duty, while having been to the grave of the departed, where all is, and will be, well.

"*Fourth string.*—White. Addressed to the chiefs, conveying to man a son, new light and sunshine, that they may 'forget sorrow, and do their duty.'"

On October 13, of the same year, the monument was unveiled by twelve Indian chiefs in the presence of the Lieutenant-Governor, Mayor of the City of Brantford, and a vast concourse of Indians and white people. The centre of the monument is a handsome figure of Brant, nine feet high. The pedestal is of Cornish gray granite, and on either side of it are groups of three chiefs of the Mohawk, Tuscarora, Oneida, Seneca, Onondaga and Cayuga tribes. Indian scenes of the camp and battle-field, and a beautiful trophy of war and the chase are accurately depicted on the front and lower base of the pedestal.

The British Government gave the cannon used in casting the bronzes, and the cost of the work was sixteen thousand dollars. This is the first monument erected to perpetuate the memory of an Indian in the Dominion.

We cannot but admire the loyalty and heroism of Thayendanagea, though many of the bloody contests in which he was engaged send a pang to our hearts. Those terrible years of colonial warfare were marked by cruel custom, when red and white alike scalped each other, and sold the scalps to their respective governments.

The noble Mohawk was a sagacious leader, heroic in the hour of danger, kind to his friends, considerate to his enemies, but swift and terrible to avenge when thoroughly aroused. His name shall live as the Indian Loyalist of Canada, hated by his foes, and admired and loved by his friends.

Indian Warriors.

CHAPTER IV.

INDIAN TRADITIONS.

LEGENDS OF THE RED MEN.

THE camp fires are burning brightly, and the aged men are sitting in the lodges smoking, peacefully, long pipes, as one of their number is discoursing pleasantly about the strange things that happened in the distant past. The stories are fascinating, and though in many instances crude, they reveal a wealth of imagination, and strength of intellect that point to a period of culture, and years of education.

The tales told in the lodges of the Canadian North-West are similar in many things to the stories of Hindu mythology related by Max Müller. Amongst the tribes there are local legends which are associated with rocks, trees, landslides, peculiarly looking stones or mounds, and rivers. The North-West teems with wonderful legends of spirits that have performed some mighty deeds, and although many of these are being lost, or are rapidly changing their form, there are very many worthy of preservation. There are myths of creation, the flood, and many other Biblical stories told from day to day in the lodges of the west. There is the story of Napioa—the Old Man—and the creation of the world, the origin of rivers and mountains, the solar myth of Kûtoyis amongst the Blackfeet. The Cree Indians, in their pagan state, pray to the great Evil Spirit. They say that the Good and Great Spirit is kind, and will not hurt them, they do not need to pray to Him; but the great Evil Spirit will seek to inflict injuries upon them, therefore they pray to him and make their sacrifices to cause him to look kindly upon them, and to restrain his wrath. The creation story is the same amongst the Crees, Blackfeet and Ojibways. The differences are slight indeed, the story is substantially the same. The Pottowattamies relate this story in the same way.

There was a secondary creator, under the Great Spirit, called Michabo amongst the Algonquins, Napioa amongst the Blackfeet, Nanaboozho amongst the Pottowattamies, and Glooskap amongst the Micmacs. This personage was good and bad, full of virtue and all kinds of trickery. On the vast expanse of waters which had been formed by the chief Creator, this secondary creator was sitting on a log or canoe accompanied by a woman. The two persons were surrounded by all kinds of animals, and a discussion was held as to the matter that must underlie the water. Four animals were sent down to find out this substance, three of whom failed; the last, the muskrat, returned with some mud in his forepaw. This the woman scraped off, and began to work around in her hands. It rapidly grew, and then was placed in the water, where it continued to increase in size. The wolf began to be troublesome, and the woman becoming angry with him, scolded him, and finally threw him upon the island. He ran around the outside, making in the plastic soil indentations with his paws, and causing the shores of the rivers to be harder than any other soil. Herbs and trees began to grow, and a small shrub planted by the woman grew until it reached the sky. Overhead there was seen a beautiful object which fascinated the dwellers on the island. The woman sent the man up the tree to find out what it was. It looked like an old woman, and he caught it with a snare. The woman was angry, and several animals were asked to go up. The racoon went up, but the heat was so great that he was scorched and fell down. The mole ascended, and when the heat increased burrowed and cut the snare, allowing the sun to go on his course, but in doing so, had his nose scorched.

There are legends directing the mind to the origin of the Indian, the fall of man, the Garden of Eden, the flood, a confusion of tongues, the rainbow, the coming of a culture-hero, or Saviour, and the advent of a white race. Amongst the Ojibways, there is the symbol of the Cross in some of the flint arrow-heads; and the Crees and Blackfeet have the same symbol on the medicine pole at the Sun-dance. Having seen it asserted that this symbol, amongst the Indians, was post-Christian, I made special inquiries, and found that these symbols were in use amongst the red men of our Canadian North-West before the advent of the white man amongst them.

There is amongst the tribes of the Blackfoot confederacy a beautiful solar myth, similar to the Iroquois myth of Ioskeha and Tawiscara, and the Athabascan myth of the Two Brothers. This is the fascinating story of

KUTOYIS.

There was an old man who had three daughters and one son-in-law. This young man had not any distinguishing name, but, for the sake of convenience, we will call him the Bad Brother. This Bad Brother compelled the old man to hunt the buffalo, and keep the family well supplied with meat, wood and water. He would not work himself, but kept the old man toiling hard, and yet he was always poor, and his heart was filled with sorrow.

When meat was brought to the lodge by the old man, the Bad Brother took it all away, and grumbled because there was not more, not allowing enough for his aged parent to eat.

As the old man's wife was cooking meat one day, she picked up off the floor of the lodge a clot of blood, and threw it into the pot. When it began to boil Kutoyis was formed from the clot of blood. He sprang out of the pot a full-grown young man. Kutoyis came one day to the door of the lodge where his father was, and heard him groaning bitterly.

Inquiring the cause of his grief, he told Kutoyis the sorrowful tale of the harsh treatment he was receiving at the hands of his son-in-law. He told his father to grieve no longer, that he would procure for him abundance of game, and all things necessary for his sustenance and happiness. The father and son then went out together to hunt. They saw a fine, fat buffalo cow, and were going to kill it, when Kutoyis said, that now he would find abundance of food. As they were proceeding in company, they heard the Bad Brother scolding, and Kutoyis told his father that if his brother-in-law said he would kill him, to answer him in the same manner. Kutoyis hid himself as the Bad Brother came up, threatening the old man. The father said to him, that he had better not talk in that way, or he would kill him. The Bad Brother ran after the old man and tried to kill him, but he kept out of his way. Whilst thus engaged, Kutoyis sprang up, drew his bow, and shot his brother-in-law, killing him. Peace and plenty then flowed into the old man's lodge, and Kutoyis employed all his time in driving the evil out of the world, and in striving to unite the people and make them happy. The fathers and mothers in the Blackfoot, Blood and Piegan camps told this story to their children to hush them to sleep. Here is a nature-myth found amongst the Indian tribes of America.

Dr. Brinton, in his *Myths of the New World,* has fully illustrated and interpreted these myths. The son-in-law, the Bad Brother, represents the darkness, storm or night, which brings sorrow to men's hearts, and deprives them of good crops, bringing poverty in his train, and threatening to kill them. Kutoyis represents the dawn, morning or sunshine. When the dawn or sunshine comes, there is a contention between the darkness and the dawn, between the sunshine and the storm, and the dawn or sunshine defeats, slays the darkness or storm, and peace comes to men. Then are there abundant crops, joy in men's hearts, and gladness reigns over all the earth. Beautiful, indeed, was this method of teaching by the Indian mothers, and happy were the hearts that fully grasped the full import of these tales.

TRADITIONS OF THE WHITE MAN'S SUPERIORITY.

The Seminole Indians say that when the Great Spirit made the earth, he created three men of fair complexion, whom he took to a small lake and bade them jump in. One immediately obeyed the command, and came forth from the water fairer than before. The second hesitated, and did not jump in until the water became muddled, by which he became copper-colored; and the third, having waited until the water was black, had his complexion changed to a deep black color. The Great Spirit then placed three sealed packages before them, and desiring to make compensation to each, gave the black man first choice. He took up each package separately and tested their weight, judging that the heaviest package was the most valuable, he chose that; the copper-colored man chose the next, and the lightest fell to the lot of the white man. Upon being opened, the first contained spades, hoes and other implements of manual toil; the second had fishing tackle and weapons for hunting and war; the third revealed pens, ink and paper.

Thus the white man had the means of mental improvement, which gave him the superiority over the ancestors of the other races of men.

The Ottawas relate a tradition of the unity of the red race and the final dispersion into tribes. In the beginning the tribes were the same people. There arose a dispute among their ancestors about the foot of a bear, which it was found impossible for them to settle. They finally agreed to separate, and they went their different ways, until in the course of time different tribes were found, speaking other languages and being named after the children of the ancestors of the red race.

The powerful Dakotas relate a wonderful tradition of the white man's influence over their confederacy. Many years ago the Dakotas were a rich and powerful people. They had abundance of horses, their lodges were numerous, their hunting ground very extensive, their women beautiful and accomplished, the warriors were honest and brave, and the people lived to a good old age. They were feared and respected by all the other tribes. Their counsels were sought on all important matters, and when the decision was given none dared to disregard it. As the people were strong, there was seldom any war, and they rapidly increased in numbers. One day there was found on the prairie a stranger, whose body was white, his hair and eyes of a brown color. He was brought to the village of the Dakotas, but they found that he spoke a strange language, and they could not understand each other.

He carried an iron bow without any string, and his

arrows were small, heavy and round. When he fired it off the people became frightened at the noise and fell to the ground. He could shoot very straight and at a long distance, and easily pierced the strongest buffalo shields of the warriors. Many of the people reverenced the white man, and thought he had been sent to aid the Dakotas against their enemies and to make them invincible, but others thought that he stole the thunder of the Great Spirit, and if he was allowed to remain, great calamities would fall upon them. A consultation was, therefore, decided upon, to know what to do with the white man and his iron bow. The council remained in consultation a day and a night. The white man was invited, his weapon was examined by the boldest warriors, he was ordered to prepare it ready to fire, but not to fire it, and then the chiefs closely watched the operation. They saw that the iron was a hollow tube, in which he placed some shining black sand and a small round arrow, which he pressed hard with a long rod; that he put some of this black sand on the top of the tube, near a piece of black stone, and when he touched a small piece of iron under the tube, fire and smoke came out of it. No one could see the little arrow come out of the tube, but they said that it struck a tree before they saw the smoke and fire. It was decided that he should be allowed to remain. A lodge was given to him. He married one of the women, and soon learned to speak the language.

The time came for the Indians to go out and hunt the buffalo, and then the white man went with the tribe to help get in the winter's meat. The buffalo roamed the prairie in large herds. When the white man fired his iron bow he killed the buffalo with one shot, and at twice the distance that the best warrior could shoot. Sometimes it took a dozen arrows to kill one buffalo, but the white man was strong, and in two days sufficient meat had been obtained for the whole winter's supply. Then many of those who hated the white man believed that the Great Spirit had sent him to help the Dakotas. The following hunting season advance parties were sent out to learn where the buffalo were, but they soon returned with the sad intelligence that none were to be found. They were scoffed at for their laziness, and others were dispatched to search, but they also brought back the same news. Consternation now filled the hearts of the people, and they concluded that the white man's iron bow had driven the buffalo away.

The council was called, the warriors and women outside uttered great lamentations, and it was decided that the Great Spirit was angry because his thunder had been stolen. Nothing but the blood of the white man could atone for the crime which the tribe had committed in eating the meat killed by the white man. The white man sat in his lodge, from which he was speedily summoned by the cries of the warriors. As he went to the door, several arrows were fired at him; his Indian wife ran between him and the warriors, and fell dead at his feet, pierced with many arrows. The white man grasped his iron bow and killed one of the medicine men, then picking up his wife went toward the river. The Indians following him were urged by the chief to kill him, but none obeyed. The white man cursed the people for killing his wife, and told them that the Great Spirit would destroy the tribe, that disease would come upon them and cause them rapidly to decrease, that their glory would decline, that white men would come in large numbers, driving away their game and devastating their hunting grounds, and that, from being a great people, they would lose their courage and become very few. The chief becoming angry, bent his bow to shoot, but the iron bow killed him, without uttering a single groan. As the white man ran toward the river, bearing the body of his wife, several arrows pierced his flesh, but he heeded them not. Down the river bank he sped, out into the water, jumping from stone to stone, until he stood at a wide gorge over the falls of the river. Turning round upon the angry crowd of Dakotas he repeated his prediction of their coming fate, and told them that he and his wife should return to them again when the spirits of the people were broken, and disease and death dwelt in their camps. Then, he said, he should know them when the curse had bitterly fallen upon the tribe. Raising the body of his wife he threw it over the falls and cast himself after it. A few struggles in the boiling waters, and he was seen no more. Search was made for the bodies, but they were never found.

Some time after this a party was sent out to search for game, but found none. An old chief assembled his band and went forth to obtain food, promising to send word back if successful, but he never returned. A second party went forth to learn tidings of the first, and no tidings were received from this. A third party were sent to inquire concerning the two bands. but it returned without any intelligence of them. The tribe lived along the rivers hunting and fishing and contending with their enemies. The small-pox came and many of the people died. The white men came with their iron bows and killed many of the warriors. Hunger and disease settled in the camps, and the white man's curse had come. After a time the tribe divided through quarrels, one part remaining and the other going to the mountains. The two lost bands were afterwards heard from. The first had gone toward the mountains, and learned from a trbe of Indians that game was abundant across the mountains. The journey was long, the snow deep, the women, children and aged people tired and hungry. The small band became a large tribe, speaking a different dialect from that of their ancestors. The second party went toward the mountains, but did not cross them. They made their home on the Platte river, and as the years sped on increased in numbers, and rapidly changed their language. The four great bands of the Dakotas felt the influence of the curse that had fallen upon them, although they never beheld the white man and his Dakota wife. The old men told their sons that the white men were avenging the death of the thunder-stealer, and hated the Sioux, but that they should be friendly with them as they were powerful, and could do much harm. The first band is now known as the Brule Sioux, the second as the Ogallalla Sioux, the third as the Santee Sioux, and the last as the Yankton Sioux.

MYTH OF THE PACIFIC AND LEGEND OF QU'APPELLE.

There is a distinction to be made between the myths and traditions of the Indians. The former are stories representing natural phenomena, and were the means employed by the parents for teaching their children lessons relating to natural history. These do not, therefore, represent the actual deeds that have been performed.

The latter are stories representing actual historical facts, and relate to deeds of warfare and adventure that have been done by members of the tribe. Many things are added to these in the course of time, as they are continually repeated in the lodges, and it is oftentimes impossible for the true story to be obtained; besides, many of the people have lost all traces of their meaning, and know them only as stories related to them by their ancestors. Many of these myths and traditions are associated with peculiar things in nature, as trees, flowers, land-slides, canyons, rapids, strange formations of rocks, and mounds.

Upon the shores of the Pacific stands a solitary rock, rising about seven feet out of the water, and being little more than four feet in circumference. The Indians told Paul Kane that this was all that was left of a woman who had been thus transformed into this shape by a whale. A long time ago a Nasquawaley family lived near this spot; the mother was a widow, and had four sons, one by her first husband and three by her second. The eldest son was a great medicine man, yet the brothers treated him very harshly, never giving him any share of their spoils in hunting and fishing, although he was always very generous in sharing his with them. At length he became tired of their unkindness, and resolved to punish them; so one day he entered the lodge and told them that there was a large seal at hand, but he did not inform them that he had created it, and was therefore his favorite and friend. They started with their spears to take it, and having plunged these into its body, they found it impossible for them to draw them out, or to disengage their hands. The seal swam off to sea, taking the three brothers with them, and after having gone a long distance they reached an island, and were then able to free their hands from the spears. They hid themselves amongst the bushes on the island, as they thought they were in an enemy's country, and they dreaded the anger of their foes. In a short time they saw a small canoe, paddled by a diminutive man, come near the island, who, after casting out a stone to anchor his canoe, began to fish. He dived under the water, and after remaining there a long time, came to the surface with a very large fish, which he cast into the canoe. He repeated this operation several times, always counting the fish before he went under the water. As the brothers were hungry, one of them proposed to swim out and steal a fish, when the little man was under the water, and quickly acting upon this, he accomplished the feat. The little man, upon discovering the theft, immediately drew in his anchor, paddled to the island, and discovered the three brothers in their place of concealment. Being very strong, he soon bound them, cast them into his canoe, and started home. Upon reaching his village, the brothers saw that the people were very small, and everything they owned was in like proportion. They were thrown bound into a lodge, and the council was called to consult as to their fate. While the council was in session, a large flock of birds resembling geese flew over the camp and began attacking the people. These birds had the power of throwing quills, like porcupines, and although the people fought bravely, they were completely overpowered, and sank insensible to the ground. When the birds had gained their victory, they flew away, and the brothers, having witnessed the conflict, ran toward the people and began pulling out the quills. No sooner was this done, than they became strong again, and were as well as if nothing had happened. They were very grateful to the brothers, and desired to know what they desired in compensation for the help given. They asked to be allowed to return to their own country, and the council was called to decide upon the best mode of performing this project. They concluded to employ the whale for this purpose, and the three brothers were accordingly placed on the back of the monster, who proceeded toward Nasquawley. They had gone about half the journey, when the whale repented of his task, and thought that, as he was a great animal spirit, he would change them into porpoises, and let them swim home alone. He transformed the three brothers into porpoises, and that is the manner in which porpoises came into existence. As the brothers had attacked the seal, the porpoises and seals are continually at war with each other.

The mother was greatly distressed at the sudden disappearance of her sons, and stood for days weeping on the beach, waiting for their return. The whale happened to pass by, and taking pity upon her distress, changed her into the stone that now stands upon the Pacific coast.

The tribes of the North-West have many beautiful legends, and one of them is the "Legend of Qu'Appelle." An Indian brave was on his way to claim a dusky maiden for his bride. While on his journey in his canoe, as he passed a small wood in the darkness of the night, he heard a voice repeat his name; a strange fear came over his spirit, and he cried out in answer to the voice, "Who calls?" Again he heard the voice repeat his name, and he recognized the sound as that of her who was soon to be his bride. He asked again, "Who calls?" but no sound came to drive away his fears. Sad and lonely he pursued his journey toward the home of his love. At early sunrise he drew up his canoe, and went toward the lodges of his friends. As he neared the camp, he saw a number of people around the door of the lodge where dwelt the dusky maiden. The death-songs fell upon his ear, and then he knew that she had gone to the Island of the Blest. He asked the time and circumstances of her death, and they told him that on the preceding evening she twice repeated her lover's name, and then her spirit fled. His mind went back to the voice in the woods; silently he departed, re-entered his canoe, and was seen no more.

THE WHITE STONE CANOE.

Amongst all the legends of the Indians there is not one that surpasses in sympathetic beauty the legend of the Ottawas, called the White Stone Canoe. This legend has been made the subject of a beautiful poem by James D. Edgar, M.P., and is well worth the study of all interested in the sons of the forest. Abeka, an Indian chief, loses his wife by death, and, consequently, becomes very dejected in spirit. His Wabose has gone "To the Island of the Blessed, to the land of Ghosts and Shadows," and he, weary and disconsolate, wanders through the forests until the powers of the spiritual world throw their influence around him, and he is impelled to go southward in search of his lost Wabose. Fastening his snowshoes upon his feet, he starts upon his journey, travelling swiftly over the snowdrifts that lie in his path, until the sunshine melts the snows, the birds sing cheerily among the branches, and the blossoms burst forth in the south wind. Abeka reaches the home of Pawgok, the dreadful, who is kind to him as a traveller to the land beyond. At last he reaches the lake dividing the Northland from the land of Souls and Shadows. By the side of this charming lake he finds

> "A canoe of dazzling whiteness
> Fashioned out of purest white stone,"

into which he enters, and sets forth to seek his lost Wabose. Soon beside him he sees another white stone canoe, in which is his lost wife. Together they row toward the Islands of the Blest, and though the billows rise high, they never reach the two stone canoes. Upon the same lake are other rowers seeking the Blessed Land, but they sink in its waters, and their corpses strew the shore. Groups of little children paddle gently across the lake, and reach the shore in safety. After passing through many dangers, and witnessing many strange scenes, Abeka, who has filled the wigwams of the aged with venison and corn, and been a true friend to all his tribe, reached the shore in peace. The lovers are reunited for a short time in heavenly blessedness, until a voice comes to him telling him that he must return to his people, that his work is not yet accomplished, and that when his work is done he shall return to find his lost Wabose, as

> "Young and fair as when I called her
> From the land of Snows and Forests."

When Abeka returns, his people doubt the truthfulness of his story, and think that his mind has been agitated by his fastings and vigils, yet they are deeply impressed with his earnestness and noble life. He lives a righteous life, and teaches his tribe to act nobly and live justly, that they may finally reach the Island of the Blest in one of the white stone canoes.

INDIAN TRADITIONS.

The mythological and traditional lore of the native races is of sufficient interest to attract the attention of readers in general, and no traditions possess greater attraction than those of the red race on the American continent.

The Pottowattamies speak of one of the highest mountain peaks at Thunder Bay as the dwelling-place of the thunder, and that at one time there was seen the thunder's nest containing the young thunders. They said that a party of Indians found a nest of young thunders in the vicinity of the Rocky Mountains, in which were two young thunders. Some of the Indians touched their eyes with the point of their arrows, and these were shivered in their hands as if they had been struck with lightning.

The beautiful flower known in the Southern States as the Cherokee Rose, is said to have received its name from the fact that a Seminole Indian chief having been taken prisoner by the Cherokees, was condemned to be tortured, but having fallen seriously ill, the operation had to be put off until he was restored to health. As he lay in the cabin of the Cherokee warrior, the daughter of the latter, acting as his nurse, fell in love with him, and desired to save his life. She urged him to flee from the scene of danger, but he refused unless she accompanied him on his journey. Together they fled, but she had not gone far when her heart went back toward her old home. She asked to be allowed to return, that she might take with her some memento of her home and friends. She retraced her footsteps, and from the blooming roses which clustered around her father's house she plucked a sprig which she carried through her wilderness journey, and finally planted beside her home in the land of the Seminoles.

The loneliness of Saratoga Lake impressed deeply

the hearts of the brave Mohawks. They believed that its stillness was sacred to the Great Spirit, and should a sound be uttered by a human voice in crossing its waters the canoe would instantly sink. It is said that the wife of one of the early settlers was crossing the lake in a canoe manned by several Indians, who warned her before embarking of the dangers of the journey, and earnestly they sought to impress her with the importance of sacredly holding her peace. As they neared the centre of the lake she became anxious to convince the Indians of the falsity of their superstition, and uttered a loud shriek. The countenance of the red men fell, and a deep gloom settled upon them, but after a short pause they redoubled their efforts, and soon reached the shore in safety. As the woman stepped ashore she rallied the chief for his superstitious fears, but the noble Mohawk scornfully replied, "The Great Spirit is merciful, He knows that a white woman cannot hold her tongue!"

LEGENDS OF THE HYDAHS AND OTTAWAS.

There is a beautiful spring that flows continually from the face of a dry, burning rock, near Skidegate, Queen Charlotte Island, concerning which the Hydah Indians say, that many years ago an infant chief, bound to a slightly hollow cedar board, was carried by his mother some distance from their home, and laid down on the beach while she went to gather berries. Although she was absent but a short time, the tide rose and carried the board and its burden out into the

Shooting the Rapids.

channel. His parents went in a boat to search for him, but were unsuccessful. The little bark was carried close to the shore, near this rock, and when the tide receded was left on the dry beach. The infant chief soon became thirsty, and began to cry for water. A raven flying past was attracted by his peculiar cries, and understanding his wants, it flew to the rock, struck it with its beak, from which flowed into the child's mouth a stream of pure water. As the tide rose it floated the cedar board, which was carried by a gentle breeze to the home of the child's parents. In the course of years he lived to become a great and powerful chief.

The Ottawas have a strange legend concerning the flood. A celebrated demigod named Nanaboozho, who possessed miraculous powers, dwelt for a time among men. During his residence among men, he at one time fixed his winter quarters near a lake, in which dwelt malignant monsters. He told his favorite son Wolf, not to go upon the ice when out on hunting expeditions, but always to return by land, lest these monsters should attack him. For some time Wolf followed the instruction of his parent, but one evening as he was returning home very late, being tired and hungry, he came to the margin of the lake, opposite his father's camp, and ventured to cross upon the ice. He had gone about half-way across the lake, when strange, rumbling noises were heard from the depths, the ice began to rise and Wolf became terribly afraid. He made for the shore with all possible speed, but the ice broke and he was precipitated into the waters, where he soon perished. The father was deeply enraged at the loss of his favorite son, and vowed vengence upon the monsters of the deep. He determined to watch for a favorable opportunity in the summer, when the monsters would leave the waters and seek repose upon the sandy beach. When the snow and ice had disappeared, he took his bow and arrows and went to the lake to execute his project. Lest he should be detected, he transformed himself into an old scorched pine tree, and selected a convenient spot upon the sandy beach. About noon the monsters issued forth, and laid themselves down gently on the shore where, not being accustomed to the sun's rays they were soon overcome by a deep sleep. The father now took deliberate aim with his bow and flint-pointed arrows, and severely wounded one of the water deities. Aroused suddenly from their sleep, they were terribly enraged, and immediately plunged into the water, which they agitated until it arose, overflowed the banks, carrying destruction everywhere in its course. Nanaboozho took refuge on one of the highest mountain peaks, but that was soon submerged, and he was compelled to betake himself to a pine log, which he caught as it was floating past, and there he remained, tossed to and fro by the angry elements, until the rage of the water deities was spent. After the storm had subsided, he revolved several schemes in his mind as to the recovery of the lost world. While deeply meditating upon these plans he saw a muskrat sitting upon his log canoe, and he commanded the animal to dive down and bring up a piece of mud from the bottom. In obedience to this command the muskrat plunged to the bottom, where it remained a long time, and then arose to the surface apparently dead. The demigod took it up, examined it, and found a lump of clay under one of the shoulders. This he pressed between his hands until it became thin, and then laid it gently on the surface of the water. In a few days it became a large island, which grew until the earth assumed its present dimensions. Large numbers of men and animals soon peopled the new world, the vegetation was luxuriant, and there was abundance of all things necessary for man and beast. At first the earth was flat, but there came out of the waters a very large animal that began to paw the plastic soil, making deep indentations, which produced the mountains, valleys and river courses. The demigod was of gigantic stature, and had a very gentle disposition. For some time after the flood he dwelt among the people who inhabited the new world, instructing them in all things relating to their welfare, and then finally told them that he was going to leave them, and would make his abode in the north. He said that he felt a deep interest in the new world and its people, and though absent from them, would watch constantly over them. He told them he would kindle large fires at times to remind them of his watchful care, and these would be seen by them. The northern lights are the reflection of the great fires kindled by Nanaboozho, according to the promise he left to his people.

Crossing the Rockies.

CHAPTER V.

THE LAND OF THE RED MEN.

THE CANADIAN WONDERLAND.

THE National Park! The Fairyland of the Rockies! The Wonderland of the West! Bright with anticipation, we boarded the train at Calgary, at one o'clock in the morning, and onward sped toward the grim sentinels of the continent. A run of eighty miles brought us under the shadow of Cascade Mountain, rearing its head amid the clouds, four thousand five hundred feet high.

The wind whistled in our ears as we entered the "bus" for the Sanatorium. But though shivering from the cold of a raw October morning, our hearts were light, for we were nigh to the beauties of nature so vividly pictured in our imaginations.

Strengthened by a few hours of "Tired nature's sweet restorer, balmy sleep," we hastened to gaze upon the strange freaks of that wonderland, something we so ignorantly, yet aptly, term nature.

Where shall we go first? We must see the falls! the beautiful Spray river! the fairy cave! Which shall it be: A swim in the fantastic basin? A bath in the hot springs? So many things to see and yet so difficult to make up our minds. To end our controversy, we began our sight-seeing with a visit to the magnificent hotel in course of erection by the authorities of the Canadian Pacific Railway.

Along a good road, cut out of the heart of the forest, we travelled until there rose in front of us, half a mile distant from the Sanatorium, the object of our search. A beautiful, cone-shaped hill has been selected as the site for the structure, and with indomitable perseverance and energy the top has been literally sliced off, to secure a level and solid foundation. Perched on this lofty eminence, amid the avenue of the mountain pines, the grand array of snow-capped peaks, and within sight and sound of the rushing waters of the Bow and Spray rivers, is this beautiful building. The exterior is very picturesque. It is a three-storied edifice of Swiss design, having basement and towers. The precipitous sides of the hill are covered with lattice work, which adds to the attractions of the whole. The windows are decorated with cedar shingles, shining in their coat of oil. Standing on the balconies of each story, we looked with admiration upon the vast sea of giant trees, the mountains, valleys and rivers. It was a scene imprinted upon the mind, with an indelible impressiveness that generated an enthusiastic rapture, akin to the inspiration of the artist and poet, begotten in the home of genius. Ascending from story to story, until you reach the top, you can look down over the balustrades upon the audience chamber, and there, in imagination, the pleasure-seekers of the Old and New Worlds flit before you, and the merry sounds of sweet converse fall upon your ears. Flitting to and fro, along the corridors, in and out of two hundred and thirty rooms, gazing upon the ornamented walls, where the artist has displayed his skill, we were again in the home of our childhood, where wealth and beauty were in abundance, but a passing glance through one of the windows revealed the grandeur and glory of the mountain-land, and our vision of the anxiety and haste of commercial life was at an end. It is needless to say more. Would you enjoy a feast for the intellect, and carry with you an influence for good as an attendant angel through life, then "Go West."

It is getting late, and we must return to stop the cravings of this weak mortality of ours. A short rest, and we are on our way toward the basin. Three-quarters of a mile over a beautiful road, resembling the avenue of an old English park, and we stand at the Basin Lodge, where, on presenting our ticket, we are admitted to all "the rights and privileges" of this bath-tub of nature. It is a circular basin of warm water, about forty feet in diameter, and from five to ten feet in depth. The spring of warm water rises in the centre, and is sufficiently strong to eject a thick pole thrust into the cavity. Search your vocabulary for words appropriate to express your appreciation of a swim in the basin, and you will utterly fail. "Delicious" is a faint term to use after having spent from twenty minutes to an hour in these waters. I am afraid we should be strongly tempted to follow the effeminate Romans, who spent their days in the enervating baths of the Imperial City. There came to us an infusion of new life, buoyancy of spirit, strength and clearness of intellect, and an excessively rapid growth of physical appetite that was humiliating to us when boarding at a hotel.

"Onward and upward" was our motto. So, after hastily dressing ourselves, we scrambled over the rocks above the basin, and observing an opening in the mountain-side we thrust in our heads, when an exclamation of wonder fell from our lips, for here, out of the bowels of the earth, hot air was issuing, that by the wonderful association of ideas reminded us of certain theological speculations of former days.

Only a few yards distant and we stood over the opening of the Fairy Cave. This hole in the mountain is about three feet in diameter, has a fence around it, is from twenty to thirty feet in depth, and is strikingly suggestive, from its peculiar shape, of an extinct volcano. The terrible illustrations in Dante's Inferno were vividly present to our imaginations as we stood and looked into this eerie home of the Indian gods. For some time after the discovery of this cave a ladder was used to gain an entrance to bathe in its waters, and one lady was courageous enough to descend with her babe in her arms. A tunnel has been made through the mountain into the bathing-place, and at the entrance stands the rustic Cave Lodge. The tunnel is lighted by means of a lamp, and the passage ensures safety and comfort, as it is floored with boards and guarded by a railing on either side. A flight of steps leads up to the cave, which is about twenty feet in diameter, from four to five feet in depth, and has a planked walk around it. The warm water rises from the spring in the middle of the cave basin, and issuing from the rock is a small stream of cold water, which graduates the temperature and keeps the water cooler than that in the basin. Sitting in the cave, weird fancies take possession of the brain, and the fairy tales of childhood seem to become a living reality. The interior is circular-shaped, with stalactitical formations.

Our time is short, and we must see the Hot Springs before we bid adieu to the mountain scenes of the west. Two miles up the mountain side, nestling among the tall trees, are the Hot Springs and the hotels, where reside the invalids who seek health from the mineral waters of the springs. Vehicles leave the Sanatorium daily for the springs, but we wish to enjoy the walk and see the wayside treasures, so we set our faces toward the higher lands and begin to climb. An excellent road, hewn out of the rocks, and winding around the forest-clad hills, leads to the heights of the wonderland. The view at our feet is magnificent. The large hotel, the immense forests, the reservoir, the Spray and Bow rivers, the iron bridge, the beautiful drives, the mountains and valleys, present a panoramic scene never to be forgotten. Here and there along the road, rippling streams of hot water flow from crevices in the rocks. Over two of the springs log buildings have been erected, which are no longer in use by the owners, and are free to the public. Caves and springs are numerous in this region, and pleasing sensations await the traveller, who leaves the road to seek for nature's revelations in the haunts of the children of the wood. The mineral waters of the Hot Springs flow out of the heart of the mountain, and are conducted from a large iron cistern by mean of pipes to the hotels, where bath-tubs and rooms are fitted up to suit the convenience of the visitor. We looked into the cistern, and the sides were thickly coated with sulphur.

Entering the bath-house, we placed ourselves in the hands of the kind attendant, who instructed us to leave our jewelry in the outer room, as the steam from the waters would discolor it. Ten minutes was allowed for the first bath, and we prepared to enjoy it. Dipping the hand into the water, we shrank from plunging in; but slowly, inch by inch, we slid gently, until the delicious consolations of a hot bath were ours. There we lay until, all too soon, the attendant returned, enshrouded us with blankets and left us, for ten minutes, to melt away with profuse perspiration. We arose as men filled with new wine, and ere we left for the haunts of civilization, visited the shower bath and plunge bath rooms.

Many wonderful cures have been effected through the curative properties of these waters. Several persons we have known who, crippled with rheumatism, have bathed at the springs, and in three weeks have returned completely cured.

Our hasty visit is at an end. The return journey is

taken by a "trail" through the forest, along new roads, down by the falls and the iron bridge over the rapidly flowing Spray, and we reach the hotel, tired in body, but delighted with the additions made to our knowledge of the wonderful possibilities of our National Park.

A quiet chat with old friends, a hasty adieu, and we leave for the realms of a lower civilization; but the new life, thoughts and impressions are ours, and often in the future shall we live over again the experiences of "One day at the National Park."

LANDMARKS.

In the eastern ranges of the Rocky Mountains rise, in majestic grandeur, silent and sombre peaks, looking down on their insignificant companions in disdain. Yonder stands the Devil's Head, without a head any longer, for the angry spirits in the mountains warring with each other, threw the heavy mass down the mountain side a few years ago. Southward rises the square-topped peak of Chief Mountain, where the Indians say the winds and thunder come from, and the foolhardy Indian who dares to sleep there will never wake again. One of the Blood Indian chiefs having learned many of the white man's ways, spent a night on the top of the mountain; but the Indians, instead of feeling afraid, only laughed at his folly, and said that he was already part of an Indian and part of a white man, and, therefore, the mountain gods would not condescend to punish him.

The pictured rocks on the Missouri river, the Indians say, were made by the spirits, as they are too high for any mortal to reach.

Southward from Macleod and Lethbridge lies the wonderful writing stone, of which the Indians stand in fear. Some of them have told me that were they to gaze upon this writing made by the gods, they would in the near future surely die. They have related to me instances of Indians who have been slain in battle, through looking upon the writing of the gods.

In the early spring the prairies and foothills in the vicinity of the Rocky Mountains are covered with flowers of every hue. I have known, within one hundred yards, as many varieties of flowers. Two years ago a Western botanist collected in one summer, within four miles of Macleod, about a hundred kinds of grasses and flowers, which included some new varieties.

Some years ago, when travelling from Ghost river to the Red Deer river by way of the Lone Pine, with some friends, we came to a dead forest. A few dead trees were standing in the valley, strange relics of the past, while all over lay huge trees that formerly lived there, but had fallen to decay. Was this a key to the solution of the problem as to the destitute condition of the prairies. Old residents in the North-West have told me that they remembered the time when, in many places, the timber grew plentifully, but ultimately disappeared. In this fallen prairie forest, we had to pass in and out among the huge trees with our horses, and strange thoughts of departed glory passed through my mind.

A few miles from New Oxley stands a natural fort

on the prairie. Not having any means of measuring it I could not give the exact dimensions, but should judge it to be about twenty feet in diameter. It is of sandstone, rising up on the open prairie, has a footpath and narrow, open doorway. It is of circular formation, and has walls three or four feet in height. There, alone, it stands, an empty fortress, half-filled with sand and shrubs, a silent emblem of war amid the peace and desolation that reigns in all the region around.

In that Western country lie cairns of stones marking the sites of famous Indian battles, where Cree and Blackfoot and Sioux fought with pagan cruelty, and carried away with savage delight the scalps of their foes. Strangely shaped stones daubed with clay, or painted in gaudy colors, now streaked with rains and winds, tell of heathen sacrifices and prayers made to the prairie gods. Around them lie articles of various kinds from the lodges of the red men. Circles of stones on the prairie mark the places where the Indians pitched their lodges, but soon the landmarks will have passed from us, or the meaning of these things will be lost. Shadows, all of them, of the races that dwelt on the great plains of our Dominion, whose glory has faded, and day of conquest is gone.

WESTERN AMERICANISMS.

In a new country, which possesses peculiar physical features and local occupations, and where the inhabitants of different countries are congregated, there arises a definite and particular phraseology, instead of the peculiarity of dialect noticed in the counties and shires of the Old World. The stranger is impressed with the new modes of expression which, at first, sound harsh to the ear, but many of them being very appropriate, are soon accepted and used. Many of these Western Americanisms are becoming slowly incorporated into the English language, and tend to express clearly physical features and modes of life that belong essentially to the west. Amongst these expressions we have—coulee, a small valley; canon or canyon, and gulch, a deep ravine; the forks of a road or river, the junction; corral, an enclosure for horses or cattle; shack or shanty, a temporary residence; and lodge or tepee, a tent of circular shape used by the Indians.

The Indian ponies are cayuses; the stockmen and cow-boys' leather overall-pants are chapps, his whip, a quirt; the braided rope, made of cow-hide, cariboo skin or horse-hair, is a *lariat*, which, when he uses, is said to be *lariatting* or *roping*, and if good at his business he is called a good *roper*. A man who breaks in or trains horses is a *buccaro* or *broncho-buster*, and the untrained horse is a *broncho*. There are four different occupations in the country the men engage in, which are called bull-whackers and mule-skinners, applied to freighters who drive oxen or mules, broncho-busters and cow-punchers. A collection of freight waggons travelling under the guidance of a leader, is a waggon-train, and is driven by the bull-whackers or mule-skinners, who are superintended by the waggon-boss. The work-oxen are bulls or stags.

The cow-boy's hat is a sombrero, which is a felt hat of very fine texture, with a very broad brim. When a calf has lost its mother, the orphan is called a mavrock, and becomes the property of the Stock Association, when it is sold to defray the expenses of the annual round-up.

There are old trading-posts with significant terms, Whoop-Up, Stand-Off, Slide-Out, and the Robbers' Roost. Personal names mean something in the west, when you hear Gum-Shoe Jack, Handsome Harry, Tangle-Foot Ben, Rutabaga Bill, and Waggon-Box Julia.

Some of the old timers feast occasionally on hard-tack covered with dope—butter—and in their tea or strong coffee they use the tin-cow—condensed milk.

Seldom do they sleep on goose-hair—feathers—preferring the waggon-box or prairie to the luxuries of civilized life.

The language of every-day life is seasoned with western phrases, sounding strangely to the pilgrim or tenderfoot who wanders into the land of the Chinook winds.

The westerner clinches an argument with "You bet," or "You bet your life," when he has defeated his opponent, he has corraled him, or should he desire him to depart, it is in the expressive phrases, "You git," and "I'll go for you." When the sombre shades of poverty have entered his old shack, he has, in the miner's phraseology, got down to *bed-rock* or *hard-pan*, and then he secures an "outfit" to go elsewhere, but fortune smiles not upon him, as his new found occupation does not "pan out." The western sign-board of a hotel had the device "No jawbone here," *i.e.*, no credit given, and "Jawbone played out."

Hunting in the West.

Going to see a dying man, his friends said to me, "He will have to hand in his checks, and don't you forget it," and after his death they said, "Didn't he die game?" The loafer in the towns or villages is a "bummer" or a "rounder," who "bilks" his friends and foes every chance he gets.

When anything is hidden it is "cached;" money is "Otter skins," "velvet," and "dust," and when the gambler is fortunate, he is "away up in the red." The grumbler is "belly aching," when half drunk he is "feeling lucky," if he is anxious to get some liquor, he asks his "pardner," "Can't you dig up?" and then with his comrades they start out "painting the town red." In the early days women were few, and the dances in which men only engaged were called "stag-dances."

Religion has not escaped the influence of western life, for the "Sky-pilot" and "Gospel-grinder" dispense "soul-grub" to the cow-boys and adventurous settlers among the foot-hills of the Rocky Mountains, where the buffalo roamed in thousands feeding upon the "bunch grass," and have left the impress of their presence in the trails and "buffalo-wallows" that the traveller still may see on the prairies of the west.

THE IRON STONE.

In the museum of Victoria University there is deposited a large meteoric stone, weighing nearly four hundred pounds. Oftentimes have I gazed upon it with that feeling of awe that takes possession of the soul when brought into contact with the wondrous revelations of nature.

The strange stories that I have listened to from the lips of Indians in the land of the lodges, concerning this stone have deepened my interest in its history. It was found on a hill near Iron Creek, Alberta, and from its existence there the stream derives its name. It was claimed as belonging more especially to the Crees, Blackfeet, and Sarcees, the Bloods and the Piegans having only a slight interest in its ownership. The natives say that for long ages it had lain there, and the Iron stone, as they called it, possessed mysterious powers. Reverently the tribes repaired to it, offering sacrifices and praying to it.

The supernatural power that dwelt in the stone, they believed, was the cause of their inability to lift it. Many of them had tried to raise it from its resting place, but all had failed. When told that the white man had lifted it and taken it out of the country, they held their hands to their mouths in astonishment, and said, "The white men are strong." When the Rev. George M. McDougall was living at Victoria, Saskatchewan, he had the stone brought to the mission house there, and afterwards sent it to Winnipeg, and requested the Rev. Dr. George Young to ship it to the Methodist Mission Rooms, Toronto.

Eventually, in accordance with the desire of Mr. McDougall, it was sent to Victoria University and placed in the museum, where it now lies. When the Indians learned that their prairie idol had been removed, they were filled with surprise and fear, and the prophets and conjurers predicted the departure of the buffalo, and serious calamities of various kinds to fall upon the tribes. The prediction failed entirely, as the buffalo returned and the people had abundance.

Dr. Coleman, in the transactions of the Royal Society of Canada, says: "In outline, this meteorite is irregulary triangular and much broader than it is thick. Its surface shows the usual rounded and pitted appearance. It consists of solid metal, with scarcely a trace of stony matter, and only a slight oxidation of the surface.

The specific gravity of the metal is 7,784. An analysis gives the following results:—

Iron......................	91.33	per cent.
Nickel....................	8.83	"
Cobalt....................	0.49	"
Total............	100.65	"

The Indians in their lodges still speak of the sacrilegious doings of the white men, in depriving them of one of the haunts of the spirits, whose help they sought in times of danger and to whom they prayed for success in contending with their enemies. Science and superstition wage war against each other, and the evident conclusion in this matter is, that the red man's idol must pass through the crucible, in order that they may minister to the advancement of the nobler civilization of the white race.

THE CHINOOK WINDS.

The Chinook winds are warm winds from the Pacific, and have, doubtless, received their name from the

Chinook Indians, a tribe on the western coast, where, also, there is in extensive use an intertribal form of speech, called the Chinook jargon. The cause of this singular phenomenon lies in the warm currents of air flowing northward along the coast from the Gulf of Mexico, passing at irregular intervals in large quantities through the mountain passes, and in lesser quantities over the crests of the mountains. In their course eastward they lose their moisture in the form of rain and snow, and as dry warm winds reach the plains on the eastern slopes of the Rocky Mountains. They blow throughout all the seasons of the year, but are most susceptible in the winter, owing to the sudden change in the temperature. Sometimes in force they resemble a gale, driving the snow from the prairies into the coulees, and again they come as a gentle zephyr, causing such a sudden transition in temperature, as to melt the snow in two or three hours. The Chinook Belt of the Alberta District is in width about one hundred and twenty-five miles, extending from Calgary to the International boundary line, not including the stretch of country in Montana affected by it. The influence of the rise in the temperature is felt as far eastward as Swift Current.

During a spell of cold weather the experienced observer will notice a heavy mist gathering around the base of Chief Mountain, and in a short time the change will come. Oftentimes have I gone out when the thermometer registered twenty and thirty degrees below zero, not a breath of wind was stirring, and no sign of a change was apparent, but suddenly I have heard the sound of the wind in the Kootenay Pass resembling the rumbling noise made by a railroad train at a distance, and in half-an-hour the snow began to disappear rapidly, the ice in the river became rotten, and in three or four days, although it had been two feet thick, it was carried away, leaving the river clear. There are striking differences of temperature in these winds; from the cold blizzard driving the snow, and becoming dangerous for man or beast to travel, to the almost imperceptible wind that causes the water to flow down the creek for several days. The first Chinook I experienced was in the winter of 1880, when the thermometer registered a change of eighteen degrees in as many minutes, and the domestic cattle that had remained in town during the short period of cold weather went off alone to the prairie for pasturage. Having spent a few days in Calgary nearly every winter since coming to the country, I was peculiarly impressed, after the railroad had reached there, when a telegram arrived from Winnipeg stating that the thermometer registered forty degrees below zero, and there we were feeling quite comfortable in summer clothing, and the fires in the houses all out, save those used for cooking purposes. I have seen men playing cricket and engaged in out-door occupations on Christmas and New Year's Days. Ploughing has been done in January and potatoes planted in March. Still, we cannot rely upon these precedents, as the winds are irregular. One winter we had a period of cold weather that lasted seven weeks, with not more than four warm days during that time. Were it not for these winds, the prospect of our country being suitable for grazing purposes would be very serious. I have been asked if these sudden changes in temperature were not very injurious to the health of the settlers, and invariably I have answered, "Not to my knowledge." I have had one singular experience on this matter, which may be worth recording. From the time when I buried the first person in the Macleod new cemetery, every funeral at which I have officiated or attended there has been when the cold was over twenty degrees below zero.

Meteorological records kept by the settlers in different sections of the country would prove a great help to our interests, and be an important addition to science. The data thus collected would assist scientific students in solving the difficulties in connection with this important subject.

FRONTIER RELIGION.

The doleful shade of the departing frontiersman recall reminiscences of grief and joy. Miniature cities are springing up on the open prairies, and these are the signal for the spoken farewells of the pioneers of our western land. Seven years ago I received a letter from a Canadian banker, offering me a subscription toward my mission premises, if I would invest in land for him the sum of ten thousand dollars. I replied by stating that he might purchase ten thousand acres of land, and retain it for ten or twenty years before any one would seek to occupy it.

Despite our magnificent distances I am agreeably

surprised to see the women of our country coming among us, to purify by their presence the moral atmosphere, which becomes tainted when woman's influence is not near.

A parting word with our prairie heroes will not be amiss.

The author of "A Summer in Prairie Land," had gone north with his companions. Many days of sweet communion had we spent with these partners in our hopes and joys; and now, lest despondency should dwell in our hearts from isolation, we set to work with a will to benefit the physical, mental and spiritual natures of those among whom our lot was cast. A frontiersman's reception was mine when on visiting the gambling and billiard saloons in quest of hearers, I was accosted by a Roman Catholic who, on holding out his hand, said: "Give us your hand, parson! You are the preacher for me." Desirous of gaining an influence over the stalwart prairie-rangers, I discarded my broadcloth, as unsuitable to their tastes and also to my rough work, and donning my riding-suit of buckskin, determined to overcome all difficulties in the way of hardship and toil. The mud floor of the log cabin was always a welcome spot whereon to lay myself down to rest, after a long ride over the prairie. The stories rehearsed on the long winter nights, descriptive of adventures on the prairie, hunting the buffalo and fighting the Indians, were oftentimes thrilling, although not always agreeing with the narrator in his slang comments and conclusions.

Oftentimes I found it beneficial to listen to the

ideas entertained concerning religion. The religious opinions expressed were suggestive and stimulating to the mind, and enabled me to labor among this class of men more intelligently, and, I trust, with a measure of success.

A Red River Cart.

Away from the civilizing influences of noble womanhood, it is not to be wondered at that many temptations and difficulties beset my prairie friends. I found them very liberal in supporting any good cause. The last cent was often given to help the sick and suffering. Conversing with an occasional hearer as we rode over the prairie, I listened for some time to a perfect harangue against inconsistent Christians, which ended in a declaration that religion was unreal. "Your mother is not a hypocrite, is she?" I asked, in reply. "No, sir," said my friend; "if ever a good woman lives, she is one, and one of the very best Methodists you ever saw, you bet." Muscular Christianity is the delight of these men. Your dyspeptic Christian will not gain much favor or success on a frontier mission.

One evening I was accosted by a friend thus: "Mr. McLean, if you will preach a sermon against our vices, I will get you a congregation that will fill your church." "Agreed. I shall do so on Sunday evening." On Saturday evening, my friend came to me, and said: "Preach us a sermon on our vices, but don't hit us too hard." "A bargain is a bargain, my friend. Get me the congregation, and you shall have the sermon." True to his word, the church was packed full of all classes, and I sought to declare the whole counsel of God.

I stood by the bedside of a man very ill with cancer, and spake unto him of Christ and salvation. "Wait till I'm better, and I'll argue with you," was the only answer I got to my entreaties to seek salvation. A Roman Catholic said: "I'm a Roman Catholic, but I like to go to your church, and I'm willing to help you when you need money." "Ise a Catholic," said another, "but I likes all 'nominations. All 'nominations the same to me." Conversing in the evening, some friend desirous of going to rest, would express his wish by saying, "Give us a prayer, parson." An Indian woman, going to live on the Missouri with her husband, came to bid us good-bye. Putting a five dollar bill in my wife's hand, she kissed her and departed with sorrow in her heart. An old prairie friend lay on his death-bed. Looking up at his comrades who surrounded his bed, he spake of his departure, but immortal hope there was none. The following Sunday I preached to the friends. One of the frontiersmen came to me, and said: "He was an old soldier. Didn't he die brave?" But a few days ago I sat conversing with a sick friend on religion. In answer to my inquiries, he said: "I have not religion now, but I can't seek it when I'm sick. I won't give the remnant of my life to God, when He might have had the best of it. I have lived a hard life. When I get better I will think of religion, and talk with you about it." Alas! I was sent for next day to go and bury him.

Commercial enterprise, mental culture, and moral influence are drawing near, but as they advance, the warm heart, clad in a very rough garb, is departing. I am glad that it is so. Earnest toil has been mine among these men during past years, and many of them I learned to respect. Sin existed, but it was not polished immorality. Rough was their life and manners, but they had affection. Though I cannot point to many trophies won in this field for Christ, I can bow at the throne of the Eternal One, and say, "My heart, O Lord, Thou knowest." It may be that in the great future, when the straggling thousands who now dwell in other lands are gathered home, some weather-beaten traveller shall reach the haven of rest through the tiny beacon-light held up here at the foot of God's majestic hills. Our work is changing, but our hearts remain the same. Patience, enthusiasm and purity we are ever aspiring after. Pray for us and our work. Sympathize with us in our toils. As you pray and sympathize, let us feel it out here by tangible proofs, according as God hath shown you His love.

THE OLD-TIMER.

The civilizing influences of eastern life are driving from us the adventurous and honest-hearted frontiersman. The "old-timer" is not as he was in the past. In the days when the pale-faces were few, and the Indian hunted in all the glory of savage life, the stalwart gold-seeker went out prospecting in the mountains, or traded among the Indians. The gloom and glory of civilized life had no charms for him. A red-skinned Pocahontas presided in his buffalo-skin lodge, and a Winchester rifle was his truest friend. Treachery and theft were unknown to him, and he prided himself on his sturdy independence. The peculiar words embodied in western phraseology were his delight, and were exceedingly appropriate to the man and his mode of life. No weary traveller was ever turned away from his door. Nobly he entertained all, without fee or reward. Winter's weary hours found kindred spirits gathered together around the fire, who,

> "Skilled in legendary lore,
> The lingering hours beguiled."

A love of daring was his leading characteristic. A few of these prairie heroes are still among us, reminding us of the joys and sorrows of mountain solitude. The abrupt speech is but the expression of an honest heart, and the rough exterior enshrouds a true and noble child of nature. We honor the men who were the pioneers of the energy that now is manifested in our western land. I have lived with the cow-boys and the old-timers in lodges, shacks, and old log houses, and always there was given the best they had, and the greatest respect was shown. Sitting around the camp-fires on the prairies, during my early years in that country, oftentimes was I amused and enlightened with their peculiar ideas on religious matters. Life on the frontier in those days was careless, rough and daring. The men were uncouth in manner, and though many enjoyed an excellent education and home-training of a superior kind, these were thrown aside for the free and easy style of western life. There was a large-heartedness and genuine liberality lying underneath the rough exterior, and it mattered little what denomination was represented, it was made welcome, if its advocate was a man of the proper kind. Hypocrisy was not tolerated, and a feminine manner especially was disgusting. Their delight was in deeds of physical strength and acts of bravery. They were strong believers in muscular Christianity. The missionary who could ride fearlessly, handle an axe, sleep on the prairie, and undergo hardship and toil as they were accustomed to, was admired by them. A straightforwardness characterized their religious tendencies. There was no beating about the bush. The missionary was told that all was in readiness for the party to roll themselves up in their blankets, and go to bed on the floor, by one of their number saying, "Give us a few lines, parson," and then, on bended knee beside the rough wooden benches, the evening prayer ascended to the Father of all.

Oftentimes in the same halls Roman Catholics and Protestants held services, and some of the people comprised the same congregations.

Money was freely given to help on the spread of both religious systems, and it was only when disagreement came that sides were taken. Men of every creed were found, and it needed religious teachers of broad sympathies and a genuine love for men to toil in such a field. There was needed a freedom in conversation, a feeling of equality in men, pleasure in partaking a rough meal, and the way was thus opened up for doing good for their bodies and souls.

Dressed in my suit of buckskin, I have travelled on horseback fifty miles to preach once a month, carrying the mail for my worthy hearers. My congregation consisted of four persons, two of whom were Roman Catholics. The mail delivered on Sunday morning, the letters were read and then service held, after which they read the papers, which had been a long time on the way. The Gospel songs we sang together, and, with a hearty good-bye, away I sped, preaching three times, and travelling on horseback on the Sunday thirty-one miles.

It was Sunday evening in the old town of Macleod, and I had a bill to pay on Monday morning. The billiard-rooms were open—for at that time we had no Sunday-law—and as the mail had reached the town before time for holding the service, my congregation had departed to get the mail. "*Nil desperandum*" was my motto, so at once proceeding to the billiard room, I went to the head of one of the tables, and took off my hat. The hats of the entire company were doffed, the cues dropped on the floor, and then I delivered my message:

"Gentlemen, I am here on important business, and as you all know me, there is no use beating about the bush. I am here to-night to get some money. When your comrades were sick, I have visited them, without first inquiring whether they were Catholic or Protestants."

"That's so, parson!"

"When you have called for me, at all hours of the night, winter and summer alike, I have gone to see your friends when they needed help."

"That's true!"

"When they were sick and poor, I have gone around and collected money to help them."

"That's true, parson!"

"Now, I have a church bill to pay to-morrow morning, amounting to fifty dollars, and I want some money to pay it. My friend here, Mr. V., will take a hat and go around to get your contributions."

They gave me thirteen dollars. I went to other billiard rooms, and the following morning visited the fort of the North-West Mounted Police when all the men were assembled in the mess-room, and then I finished up with the full amount to pay my bill.

There lay a sick man in the Police Hospital who

had no relations in the country. He was anxious to go to the Hot Springs at Banff. In two hours I had about seventy-five dollars subscribed and paid, by going around the town.

The old type of the honest trapper and pioneer is fast passing away, and the new type has sprung from other circumstances that lack in opportunity and fail in results.

A Pawnee Chief.

CHAPTER VI.

FRONTIER TALES.

THE THREE CAPTIVES.

THE half-breed lodge and the old-timer's shanty have oftentimes been refuges for me during storms, and welcome resting-places at night, and there have I listened to the tales of adventure, some of which were true and others were creations of the imagination employed to drive dull care away. After a hard day's work we sat one evening around the camp-fire, and one of our party related the following story as part of his own experience:

An emigrant party, journeying toward California in the early days, was escorted by five soldiers of the United States army to protect the men, women and children from the sudden attacks of hostile Indians. Despite their watchful care, they were surrounded by a band of Sioux Indians, who seized all the men and children, fastened the waggons belonging to them together and tied them to this portable corral. Heaping the provisions and travelling outfit of the company around the waggons, they set fire to the whole, burning up the human sacrifices with fiendish glee. Having retained the women as prisoners, they abused them in a terrible manner, as they travelled toward the lodges of the west.

A party of Comanches on the warpath came sweeping down upon the Sioux camp in great numbers, and would have killed and scalped their hereditary enemies had not the chiefs pleaded for their lives and offered the lady prisoners as compensation. The Sioux were left unmolested, and the white women being accepted, they were delivered in care of a chief called Left-Hand. This chief was a Spaniard, well educated in Spanish and English, and fluent in the use of the Indian tongue. When a boy, he had run away from home, entered the Indian lodges, gained an influence among the people by adopting their mode of life, until they showed their high appreciation of his shrewdness and valor by electing him as one of their chiefs.

Left-Hand told the prisoners that as soon as they approached one of the forts of the United States army they should be set at liberty. A military scout, having learned from the Indians of the presence of ladies in the Comanche camp, sought an audience with some of the chiefs, and bargained for the purchase of the freedom of the captives. Returning to the fort, he informed the Commandant, and persuaded him to use his influence on behalf of the prisoners. A subscription among the soldiers resulted in procuring a handsome sum, and two men were sent out to buy them, which they did, at the rate of seven horses per head.

A party of soldiers well-armed and under the guidance of their Commandant departed, and after three days' travel reached a camping place on the edge of a ravine, which the leader determined to enter, despite the protests of an outrider, well trained in Indian customs and law. Heedless of the opposition of the hardy Indian fighter, he entered the ravine and camped there, when scarcely half-an-hour had elapsed before a whoop and yell announced the approach of a large party of Indian warriors. The soldiers being surrounded, were filled with fear, but Left-Hand, followed by several chiefs, rode to the spot where the Commandant and his officers were assembled, and inquired the cause of the great military display. He was told that they had not come to fight, but had brought with them cannon, as they were liable to meet with different bands of hostile Indians, and it was a legitimate necessity to protect themselves in time of danger.

Being satisfied of their peaceable intentions, Left-Hand mounted a cannon and delivered a very conciliatory speech, in which two of the chiefs joined him. The head chief and a minor chief were angry and sullen, refusing to converse with white dogs, and Left-Hand perceiving this gave a shrill whistle, when, like the lightning's flash, several hundred naked warriors, on splendid horses, rushed down the embankment and stood around their chief. Addressing the two hostile chiefs, the Spaniard told them to get ready to fight, as they had not only to contend with the soldiers, but the members of their own tribe. Brave and daring words like these compelled those antagonistic to the sentiments of the majority of the Indians to slip away quickly and quietly, lest their lives might be taken. Left-Hand told the soldiers that he would go to the camp and return with all the prisoners next night. The Commandant said he would wait for them, but, fearing treachery, he left on the following afternoon. The outrider, understanding Indian customs, and relying firmly upon the integrity of the Comanches, said that he would wait the appointed time, and, having fastened the horses to some trees, bided their time. Five chiefs, with their warriors, returned, having the ladies with them, who rejoiced in seeing once more the face of a white man. The chiefs, having exacted a promise of safety from the scout, marched toward the fort, where they arrived in due time, amid the rejoicing of all. The ladies were detained there for some time, when a large subscription was raised among the soldiers, to help them on their way home. The stage proprietors gave them free transit over their lines of road, and in a few days they were landed safe and well among rejoicing friends, who had given them up for dead.

Honesty of purpose, and strict adherence to promises, characterize many Indian tribes, until the influence of the fluctuating and immoral pale-face injects evil thoughts and tendencies into the minds of the untutored red man.

THE DOCTOR'S RIDE.

Several years ago, I formed the friendship of a devoted worker in the mission field, for whom, as the years sped on, I entertained the deepest respect for her piety and zeal in labors abundant among the Indians. For years Mrs. S. had toiled with a purpose true, to better the condition of the Indian youth among whom her lot was cast. It was a beautiful evening in the fall of the year, when we camped on the spot where the enterprising city of Calgary now stands. We talked long over past events, and the hopes of the different members of the party were bright for the civilizing of the red men. Early next morning we cooked our breakfast by the camp fire, and hastily partaking of it, a kind adieu was bidden, and I turned my horses' heads toward the south. Seven or eight days passed away, and I was preaching in the little log church in the old town of Macleod. I had just concluded the service, and was attending to my duties as caretaker, when a young man entered, and holding out his hand, said excitedly, "Mrs. S. is dying. You are to come with me, and bring the doctor with you." "When are you going?" "To-night!" One hundred and fifty miles distant lay the dying woman, and no medical help nearer than Macleod. For years we had been in the same position, but fortunately we had now a doctor at the Mounted Police Fort. The young man had ridden over one hundred and sixty miles in two days, having had to make a detour on account of a large prairie fire which was raging. Sending my friend to the mission-house, I repaired to the fort, and requested the doctor to accompany us on our journey. He informed me that it was impossible for him to go, but that there was another doctor there who in a few days was going to Calgary, and I might arrange to have him proceed at once. Fearing that I might meet with an excuse or refusal, I went to the commandant of the fort, and related to him all the facts of the case, urging him to do all in his power to save the woman's life. He manifested deep sympathy, and quickly gave me an order to present to the doctor, for him to hasten at once. Not being able to induce the doctor to go that night, it was arranged that we should depart at six o'clock next morning. Getting the loan of horses and taking my buckboard, the young man and the doctor started at seven o'clock, while I accompanied them on my little black horse. Over the Old Man's river and out on the prairie we sped at full galop. We travelled at such a rate that, when we had gone but ten miles, I was fast losing ground, as the others were urging their horses and keeping far ahead. It was a race for life; we were striving to defeat the king of terrors if we could. I saw that it was impossible to keep up with my friends, so unsaddling the horse, I turned him loose on the prairie, hoping to find him on my return. Jumping on the back of the rig, we sped onward, and the faster we travelled the more excited we became. Continually there rose before us the vision of the stricken household, and help drawing near. At ten o'clock we had gone twenty-eight miles, but our horses were exhausted, and as we had lost some time with the saddle-horse, we had to make it up. Two hours were spent at a ranch getting fresh horses, and again we pursued our course. Thirty miles more, and then a detour of five miles to a horse ranch, where we had to wait for the return of the manager, who kindly allowed us to leave our horses and furnished us with a pair of wild bronches. At seven o'clock at night the cow-boys gathered around us, to help us to start. Two men held each horse while being hitched up, and with a shout from the men the frantic animals bounded into the darkness. Without a trail we flew over the prairie, heedless of the danger, for we carried succor for the helpless, and hope urged us on. Over the hills, down through the coulees, dashing into the creeks and rivers, we wildly pushed on, until midnight found us at the Mounted Police Fort at Calgary. Sergeant-Major Lake was in charge, and to him I hastened for the loan of a team of horses. Kindly and quickly he came to the rescue, taking our wearied bronches, and giving us a splendid team of police horses. At one o'clock in the morning we bade adieu to Calgary, and on toward the mountains we drove. The road was rough and mountainous, the morning raw, with heavy dew falling that soaked our clothes through, and we felt tired with our long journey, but we could not sleep for the excitement, and we slackened not our pace. At six o'clock we dashed into the clear, cold waters of the Bow river, and a few minutes sufficed to bring us to the house where our friend lay. We had been twenty-three hours on the road, five of which had been spent in getting fresh horses and refreshments, and during that time we had travelled over one hundred and sixty miles. It was no wonder that when the friends came out to welcome us they expressed their astonishment, as they had not expected us for two days more. Sad were our hearts as we gazed upon the wasted form, which but ten days before we had seen in all the strength, beauty and freshness of womanhood. Alas! all our efforts were in vain. Medical aid had arrived too late to save the patient toiler, yet such hopes were given as to shorten my stay, because of the necessities of the work at home.

After making arrangements for the sad event, should it come, and spending two days amid the solitude of the sick room, I turned southward, taking with me two half-breed boys who had been residing there.

At the different places where horses had been obtained we returned them, and not one of the owners would take any fee. Upon reaching High river, we were left with one saddle-horse and one horse for the buckboard. Not having any shafts or wood to make any, we placed the two horses in the rig and proceeded on our journey, accompanied by the stage which was carrying the mail between Calgary and Macleod. It had snowed heavily all night and was still snowing when we left, but as we had only thirty-five miles to travel that day, we concluded that we could easily reach the stopping-place, so took with us only a few crackers for lunch. The storm kept raging, and, although we had started early, we had travelled but sixteen miles by the middle of the afternoon.

Resting for an hour to partake of our luncheon, which had become well soaked with snow, we prepared to go on, but the saddle-horse objected strongly to draw the rig any further. Gentle persuasion with alternate whipping availed nothing, so we had to give up the contest, and leave the buckboard, harness and camping outfit on the prairie, hoping to get them at some other time.

I was now forty-five miles from home, and had nothing left me but a borrowed horse without any saddle. The delay caused by the balky horse had turned us completely around, so that we had some difficulty in finding our way. At last we found the ruts in the road, and I had to go ahead of the stage, dragging one foot in the rut, lest we should lose our way, and shouting when no longer I could find it. Darkness overtook us, and the snow became so deep that I lost the road, and then the stage-driver undertook to travel, guided by the wind. We pursued our course until pitch darkness settled upon us, and then we camped, picketing the horses near the waggon, lest they should stray during the storm. We were cold and hungry, but food and bedding we had none. My buckskin riding suit, which I had on, was wet through with the snow, but we had to make the best of our disadvantages. The stage waggon had a cover over it, and into this we all crept, four of us sitting up all night with our clothes and boots on, for we dared not take them off else they would have been frozen stiff in the morning, and we had no wood to make a fire. The night was bitterly cold, and the wind howled around us in our fragile home, yet grateful were we for the shelter.

Before day-break next morning we hastened on, hoping in a few hours to reach a ranch, where we might thaw out our garments and obtain food and rest. The snow was deep, and my horse exhausted, plunging in the snow belly deep, stumbling every few paces, the poor little animal was compelled to walk.

As I rode bare-back with my wet clothes, and my feet touching the snow, the skin peeled off my legs, and I suffered great pain. The stage went on ahead, and soon I was left alone on the prairie, three miles behind. For years, when travelling, I had slept on the prairie, with nothing to cover me but my saddle-blanket, and invariably without a single companion. I had gone out in all kinds of weather, with the mercury sometimes frozen, yet I had never endured such agony as on that last three miles ride alone, toward the ranch. Alternately walking and riding, I reached the place early in the afternoon, and the log shanty, with a blanket for a door, became a palace in my eyes. We remained there all that day, resting and drying our clothes. On the following morning a small Indian saddle was lent me, that I might comfortably reach my home. We got along well for sixteen miles, where we intended to camp for an hour. The spot we had chosen was destitute of snow, and toward that we rode. The stage was ahead, and I was following close behind, when the horse which I rode stepped into a badger-hole, fell and rolled completely over, with its rider under him. As he got up, he placed his hoof on my left cheek, close to the eye, and made a deep cut, but I was aroused from the awkwardness of my position by the stage-driver swearing at his horses, and letting my horse go, I went to see what was wrong. He had driven into a heavy snow-drift, and the horses were unable to extricate themselves, so we set to work to clear away the snow as rapidly as possible. Whilst doing so, the blood was dropping freely on the snow, from the wound on my face, but that was of little consequence, when all were in trouble. The rest of the journey was made in a few hours, through the deep snow and heavy snow-drifts, and the people gladly hailed the stage, with letters from the north. The doctor sewed up the wound which, under his skilful care, healed rapidly. The little black horse was caught on the prairie and given to me, a few weeks afterward; and the buckboard, harness, and camping outfit were found and brought in by a stockman, the coyotes having had a meal or two off the harness. The sad news reached us that the weary sufferer had ceased to live, and amid the grandeur and awe of God's majestic hills, they laid her to rest, awaiting the meeting again in the land beyond.

THE LONG HAIR.

In former years numerous were the engagements between the Blackfeet and the whites in the country, and these were at times of a sufficient nature to make a lasting impression upon the minds of the traders and Indians. A few years ago there lived in Choteau county, Montana, a white man known amongst the Blackfeet as The Long Hair. In 1871, about four hundred lodges of Blackfeet, Bloods and Piegans were camped on the St. Mary and Belly rivers. A trading post had been built, and whisky was freely traded to the Indians for robes and horses; many deeds of theft

Indian Woman Carrying Wood.

and murder were, therefor committed as the result this traffic, and much su fering consequently ensued. The buffalo were abundant in the country, and the trade in robes was good. Teams were getting ready to transport the robes to Benton, when a Blood Indian, named Strange Dog, shot Joe Spearson, one of the principal traders, in the knee, shattering the limb in a terrible manner. It was proposed to amputate the leg, but the wounded man was anxious to go to Fort Shaw to obtain efficient surgical aid. Tenderly he was cared for by the traders; a team was sent with him to take him with all possible speed to his destination, but he died at the Marias river on his way there. After his death the traders loaded up their teams and burned their buildings, preparatory to leaving the country. A Blood Indian, becoming angry at his wife, took his pistol and shot her in the leg. As she was supposed to be dying, no one took any particular notice of her, but as she lay near the burning buildings, and dreading being roasted alive, she began to cry out. Her husband came up with his pistol, intending to kill her outright, when Long Hair stepped forward, and standing over her with his Winchester rifle pointed at the cruel husband, dared him to molest her. The coward gazed in astonishment at the heroic Long Hair, who ordered the white men to remove her to a place of safety. She was gently nursed until restored to health, and then she returned to her people. The Bloods ever afterward feared the man who would fight for a woman, and they learned to respect him for his kindness, courage and power.

THE WHITE CHIEF.

Amid the mountain scenery of Montana, where streams and rivulets expose to view the mines of precious gold, the Crees, Crows and Blackfeet raised their lodges long before the pale-faces erected buildings and made homes for themselves among the lovely valleys. The prairies were their chief locations for toil and recreation, and there joy and sorrow filled their hearts as they hunted from necessity or for sport, and engaged in bloody warfare with their foes. Sadness must have fallen at times on the hearts of the old men in the camps, as they remembered and recited to their children and followers the legends which continued a prophecy of the white man's supremacy and power. The aged Indian warriors were accustomed to relate that—

> "In the fulness of time with wings shall come
> An angel race from the rising sun;
> Myriad in number, like light in their thought,
> Time shall not end till their destiny's wrought,
> And peace and prosperity with them shall reign."

Just as this prophecy was beginning to receive fulfilment, a young Frenchman, prepossessing in appearance and of good intelligence, was sent by his employers to trade at an Indian post. One year was spent with much success. For, practising the politeness for which the French nation is noted, he had traded extensively and made many friends among the noble red men. He had labored hard for his employers, and expected a handsome remuneration for his year's toil, but imagine his consternation when, instead of his salary, he received a pair of corduroy pants and a horse. Disgusted with such inhuman treatment, and bitterly enraged, he left his situation, rode to a hill a short distance from the trading post, drew his revolver and shot his horse dead. At once he became completely enamored with the Indian's customs and modes of living, and with characteristic alacrity cut his pants into Indian leggings, threw his saddle-blanket over his shoulders, and started off in search of a camp, dressed in the garb of an Indian. Entering the camp, he was received with all due respect, and, as the Great Spirit had taught his red children, they gathered together and smoked their pipes as a pledge that no animosity lay between them. In a short time he became fully confirmed in his opinion that color amongst the Indians was hereditary, and he concluded though

> "The floods may pour from morn till night,
> Nor wash the pretty Indian white,"

he would take unto himself a daughter of the heritage of Japheth. There was brought unto him one of the fair Winonas of the tribe for his acceptance. The result was better than that recorded in the legend of Winona, who, when espoused to an Indian brave whom she hated, went to the edge of a cliff, now known as "Maiden Rock," and there, on the day appointed for her marriage, sang her death song and then threw herself into "the jaws of death." He was soon made a chief in the tribe, and all the honors of the position were duly accorded him, so that he became influential through his position, which was still more increased through his superior knowledge and strength. In the fiercest contests he led his warriors to victory, and in the sports of the chase he excelled. His superior skill gave him a position among the mystery or medicine-men of the tribe. Among all the Indian tribes the medicine-man is an important personage. The Mandans, or "people of the pheasants," had their rain-makers, who were promoted to the rank of medicine-men. The rain-maker, by showing his ability to make rain descend, demonstrated that he was possessed of power given him, either by the Good or Evil Spirit, to make strong medicine by his system of conjuration. The Cree and Blackfoot medicine-men are conjurors who depend chiefly for their success upon their charms and incantations. They possess a peculiar sanctity, especially during the performance of any religious ceremony, and they are not slow to add to their influence by appropriating the skins of rare or poisonous animals to the paraphernalia of their office. The white chief was held in high esteem as a mystery man, and thus was enabled to enjoy peculiar privileges, which made Indian life more pleasant to him.

For thirty years he enjoyed all the festivities of the Indian camp, helped the needy in their hour of distress, gave advice on all important matters relating to the Indians and whites, and honorably filled the position which his abilities and devotion had obtained for him. When the ever-adventurous pale-face made his appearance, and the tidal wave of emigration advanced westward to the Rocky Mountains, the white chief adopted the dress of his forefathers, but still retained his love and allegiance to the people of his choice. Old age found him surrounded by many of his Indian followers, who loved him for his heroism, and trusted him as their most worthy friend. As he lay in his lodge in the Indian camp, the shadows of death gathered fast around him, and the light of his life was fast ebbing away. The gray-haired sires waited to receive his dying counsel, the medicine men performed their incantations, and the women and children sobbed aloud in the intensity of their grief. With bitter lamentations they made for him a warrior's grave, and the remains of the noble white chief found a resting-place in the home of the braves who loved him with the unfailing love of the faithful red man, and honored him with an endearing monument in their hearts and lives.

Making a Portage.

CHAPTER VII.

INDIAN LANGUAGES AND LITERATURE.

AMERICAN INDIAN LITERATURE.

CARLYLE expressed a truth deeper than is understood by the majority when he wrote: "There is not a Red Indian hunting by Lake Winnipeg can quarrel with his squaw, but the whole world must smart for it."

A knowledge of American Indian literature, to a slight degree at least, is a necessity for men of culture. The American Indian problem is employing some of the most eloquent of men, and some of the most efficient literary talent. Because of the relation of the Indians to our country, it is incumbent on us to seek to know something concerning them.

Their traditionary lore, consisting of fables and fireside tales and facts regarding the early history of the tribes, has constituted their unwritten literature. It is estimated that the number of American Indian languages and dialects is nearly thirteen hundred. Before these languages had reached that stage in their development when they were made intelligible to the people by means of symbolic signs, they were represented through a system of picture-writing which gained its highest point of perfection among the Mayas and Aztecs. In the first period of picture writing, the full picture is drawn, and thus represents all the ideas intended to be conveyed; the second period is symbolic, wherein the leading characteristic of the individual or circumstance is expressed by means of its representative symbol; and the third stage is phonetic, when a symbol is made to represent a sound. Specimens of picture writing or hieroglyphics may be seen on the rocks of Lake Superior and the Upper Missouri, and on the lodges and buffalo robes of the Sioux, Blackfeet, Bloods, and other Indian tribes. From these ideographic symbols were evolved by continual abbreviation phonetic signs, which were ultimately classified in the form of an alphabet. Hence we have the Aztec and Maya hieroglyphic alphabets. The Spanish priests who succeeded Las Casas destroyed many of the manuscripts belonging to these nations, but Bishop Landa, though engaging in the same disreputable work, preserved for the student of American antiquities the Maya hieroglyphic alphabet with some notes thereon. In the English alphabet the development from pictorial writing to its present form may be seen by studying the letters and tracing their origin. Draw the head of an ox, and notice how easy is the transition from that to the letter A, or describe a *hand*, with the forefinger pointing upward, and see how close is its resemblance to "h."

Turning aside from the purely native literature, there confronts us an extensive field of English literature devoted solely to the Indians. Works in Latin, French, German and Spanish, have been issued, wherein much information is detailed concerning the Indians of the American Continent. Alonso de Ercilla (1533-1594) spent eight years among the Indians in the wilds of Chili, where he witnessed a continual warfare between them and their Spanish conquerors. The exciting scenes of which he was a spectator were recorded every evening, sometimes on scraps of paper, leather or parchment. The result of his labors was a long historical poem of thirty-seven cantos, "Araucana," the fame of which has engraven the name of its author upon the historical records of Spain. The Jesuits gave much valuable information concerning the Huron Indians in the "Relations des Jesuites," written to the Provincial of their Order in Paris between 1611-1672.

The works written concerning the Indians during the last century, and the early part of the present, were confined chiefly to a narration of missionary effort among them, but many books of great value on American antiquities have sprung into existence within the past fifty years. Very important philological works have been lost to the student of Indian literature through the poverty of the authors, preventing them from publishing the result of their labors. A large number of works still remain in manuscript, and can only be found in the libraries of historical societies and private persons.

John Eliot, the apostle to the Indians (1649), published "The Glorious Progress of the Gospel among the Indians," and other works in English. Through his efforts in seeking to enlighten the people of England regarding the state of the Indians amongst whom he was laboring, he incurred the displeasure of the colonists, and his life was thereby placed in great danger. Animated by a heroic spirit, he continued his labors until the success of his work overcame opposition, and he rejoiced in God.

The memoirs of David Brainerd and his brother John (1744), have been the forerunners of a class in this great department of literature that have thrown much light on the character and customs of various tribes of Indians. The memoir of David Brainerd was written by the celebrated New England divine, Jonathan Edwards, and an abridgment of it was prepared by John Wesley. The reading of this book so impressed the mind of Henry Martyn, that he determined to become a missionary, a resolution that was nobly kept.

John Heckewelder, a Moravian missionary (1754), wrote "An account of the History, Manners and Customs of the Indian Nations who inhabited Pennsylvania and the neighboring States." He also published a work on the Mohegan and Delaware Indians.

James Bradley Finley narrated his experience and observations in "Wyandotte Mission" and "Life among the Indians," and Peter Jones (1861), following in the same path, published a "History of the Ojibway Indians."

George Catlin spent eight years as a wandering artist among the Gros Ventres, Crees, Blackfeet and other Indian tribes, and the results of these years were embodied in pen-and-pencil sketches, which were published under the title "North American Indians."

Henry Schoolcraft has been held in high estimation as a laborious collector of legends and facts relating to the history and customs of the Indians. His long residence among the Indians gave him abundant opportunities for gaining this kind of information, and his enthusiasm enabled him to make good use of all that lay within his power.

Very different from these books was the richly illustrated work of John L. Stephens, on the antiquities of Central America, which was exceedingly popular, and has been largely drawn upon for information and illustrations by succeeding authors.

The writers on American antiquities of the present day have succeeded in grasping more clearly and firmly the various sections of the whole subject than those of any other period. A philosophical method has been adopted in discussing the various theories propounded as to the origin of the Indian tribes, and the relations of their mythology and language to that of other tribes or nations of people. Men of extensive scholarship have devoted years of research, and have thus bequeathed to us works of abiding interest and accurate information. Amongst the ablest writers on American Indians are Bancroft, John T. Short, Ellen

Russell, Charles G. Leland, President Wilson, of Toronto University, Dr. D. G. Brinton, and Horatio Hale. Bancroft's "Native Races," and Short's "North American Indians of Antiquity," are books for the student who wishes to study the question in its relation to philology, sculpture, painting, theology and history.

The legends of the Indians have ever been a source of attraction for all kinds of readers. The study of these is fascinating, and they possess points of especial interest to the historian and the theologian. "Indian Myths," by Miss Ellen Russell, and "The Algonquin Legends of New England," by Charles G. Leland, open up a field of study of intense interest. The poetic legends reveal a mythology that is inspiring, and that fills the mind with astonishment. Novelists have found abundant material for entertaining the reading public in writing about the joys and sorrows of the Red Man. Washington Irving, in "Knickerbocker's History of New York," exposed the claims of the Dutch settlers to the Indians' land under pretence of defending them. Fennimore Cooper wedded fact and fiction in a large number of volumes, wherein the virtues of the representative Indian were graphically described. Joaquin Miller, the poet of the Sierras, has espoused the cause of the injured Indian in his "Shadows of Shasta," and Mrs. Helen Jackson has written in "A Century of Dishonor" a tragic account of the organized wrong-doing brought to bear upon the aborigines in the United States. This is a book very highly recommended by Joseph Cook, and teeming with terrible facts which are officially authenticated.

In the realm of poetry, Longfellow added to his fame by studying long and deeply the writings of Heckewelder, Catlin, Schoolcraft and others, and embodying the results of his investigations with his poetical aspirations in that exceedingly popular poem "Hiawatha." Ten thousand copies of this Indian poem sold in America within a few weeks after its publication, and fifty thousand within one year and a half.

In the fifteenth century La Casas went among the Indians in Mexico. There was a tribe that would not be friendly with the Spaniards, and could not be conquered. La Casas translated the doctrines of the Roman Catholic Church into verse in the Quinche language. He introduced the poem set to music by means of four traders, who sang it to the Indians after the day's trading was over. They sang it accompanied with Indian instruments of music, and the effect was grand. The Indians were delighted, and called for it to be sung again and again. They sent for La Casas and his fellow-priests, and the men who could not be subdued by the sword were induced to submit to the gentler influences of religious truth.

Works of special interest to the student of philology may be noted. David Zeisberger (1732), who spent nearly sixty years as missionary among the Indians, especially the Mohegans and Delawares, wrote grammars, dictionaries, phrase-books and several religious works of the Onondaga dialect of the Iroquois language, and also in the Delaware. The manuscripts of his works are deposited in the libraries of the American Philosophical Society and of Harvard University.

In the National Library at Paris there are several manuscript works on Indian languages, among which are an Algonquin grammar and dictionary, a dictionary of the Iroquois language of the Agnier nation, and a pamphlet on the rudiments of the Micmac language. The best Cree grammar in existence is one published in 1815 by Henry Howse, a chief factor in the Hudson's Bay Company. Only a few copies remain of this valuable work. Dr. Friedrich Baraga, a Roman Catholic missionary, spent several years among the Indians around Lake Superior, and was made Bishop of Sault Ste. Marie. He published a grammar and dictionary of the Ojibway language, which are still in use and of much service. James Evans, a Methodist missionary at Norway House, invented the Cree syllabic characters, by means of which an intelligent Cree Indian will learn to read the Bible in his own language in one or two days. He whittled the type out of wood with his penknife, and made ink out of the soot of his chimney. So great have been the influences of this invention that very few Cree Indians are to be found who cannot read in the Cree syllabic. The Rev. Mr. Watkins, an Episcopal missionary, prepared an excellent Wood Cree dictionary, which is the only one published. Pere Lacombe's French-Cree and Cree-French dictionary and grammar is a book of nine hundred pages, and the best book on "Plain Cree." In Wood Cree, the grammars of Archdeacon Hunter and Bishop Horden are worthy of notice. The former consists of a lecture on the Cree language, with the paradigms of the verb. It is a book for the philologist. The latter is a pocket grammar, to be used by those who wish to acquire as much of the language as will enable them speedily to converse with the natives.

Among the Dakotas there are seven tribes having differences of dialect, and in the Dakota language Dr. Riggs has published an excellent grammar, a dictionary of nearly sixteen thousand words, the New Testament, translated into Dakota from the original Greek, and lately the entire Bible.

In the interests of the Indians, the press has been brought into action. Thus we have newspapers bearing the names, *The Indian Missionary*, *The Southern Workman*, and *Our Brother in Red*. Much valuable information may be obtained on this question in the reports of Historical Societies, and especially of the Smithsonian Institution at Washington. *The American Antiquarian* is a monthly magazine published in the interests of this subject, with several branches of study arising out of it.

The literature prepared specially for the Indians themselves, and in their own language, is chiefly of a religious nature. Bibles, hymn-books, and works of devotion comprise nearly the whole range of this branch of literature. John Eliot translated Baxter's "Call to the Unconverted" and a work on logic for the use of the Natick Indians, but the great literary monument of his life was the translation of the Bible into the Natick language. Eight years were spent, with the assistance of an Indian, in the translation of the Old and New Testaments. With the help of an Indian the New Testament was printed.

This was the first Bible printed in America, and was received with admiration and gratitude by the leading divines and also by the Christian people of England and America. Only a few copies are now in existence. In 1868 a single copy sold for $1,150. There lives but one man, the Hon. J. Hammond Trumbull, of Hartford, who is master of the language and can read the Bible. Not a descendant of this New England tribe exists, but the Bible remains a silent token of the industry and enthusiasm of the apostle to the Indians.

In 1813, the Gospels were translated into the language of the Eskimo Indians of Labrador. In 1825, the Wesleyan Methodist Missionary Society of Canada issued its first Missionary Report. Therein we read that Dr. A. Hill, a Mohawk chief, had translated the Gospels of Mark and John, and had nearly completed translations of Matthew and Luke. This chief translated also some most excellent hymns for public worship. A princess of the same nation was engaged in translating the Acts of the Apostles. In 1840, the Rev. H. B. Steinhauer, an Ojibway Indian, recently deceased, went out to the Hudson's Bay Territory with Jas. Evans. After a residence of a few years he and John Sinclair, a half-breed, translated the Bible into Cree. Sinclair translated the Old Testament to the end of Job, and the New Testament to the end of the Acts of the Apostles. Mr. Steinhauer translated the remaining parts of the Old and New Testament. I have in my library a manuscript copy of Genesis written in the Cree syllabic characters by John Sinclair. It is a beautiful specimen of penmanship.

Archdeacon McDonald, of Peel river, a tributary of the Mackenzie, has spent the past twenty years among the Indians. Fort Yukon is situated one mile within the Arctic Circle, and this for eight years was the headquarters of this missionary. The language spoken is the Tukudh, but at Norton's Sound and beyond the Indians speak dialects of the Tinné language, which has a slight resemblance to the Tukudh. In the Cree there are thirty syllabic characters and ten affixes or auxiliaries; but in the Tukudh a syllabary has been made, which contains four hundred syllables. Some Indians have been known to learn these in two weeks, and to read the Gospels in three months. The New Testament, nearly all of the Prayer Book, and a large number of hymns have been translated, and are now being published in this language.

Chief Justice Onasakenrat, of Oka, when in the prison of St. Scholastique, began translating the Scriptures from French into Iroquois. At his death he had translated the Gospels and a large number of hymns, and was engaged in the Epistles.

In 1827, the Indians on Grape Island used a small hymn-book containing twelve hymns translated into Chippewa and printed in New York. Seth Crawford assisted, about the same time, in correcting some Mohawk translations of the Scriptures for the New York Bible Society. Peter Jones translated into Chippewa, Methodist hymns, the Apostles' Creed, the Lord's Prayer, Ten Commandments and a spelling book. In the Lenox Library, New York, there is a copy of the Mohawk Indian Prayer Book printed in New York in 1715.

An Eskimo Traveller.

The very names of translations of religious books for the use of the Indians in Canada and the United States would fill many pages. Many of the tribes for whom these translations were made have been swept away by the hand of cruelty, or have succumbed to the gentler influences of civilized life. The history of Canadian Indian literature would fill the pages of a large volume, and several articles could be written on the translations that have been made for the use of the Indians in the Canadian North-West alone. There are few Indian tribes that have not a literature of their own. Bishop Horden, Archdeacon McKay, Orrin German, and many others are using their linguistic ability toward developing this literature, and the energy just displayed is an important factor in aiding in the solution of one of the problems of to-day. A subject embracing so many languages and dialects, and relating to such a diversity of peoples, past and present, possesses a deep and abiding interest for the student, and to such the field is inviting, and will amply reward for all the labor bestowed.

ESKIMO LITERATURE.

The Eskimo are scattered over a very widely extended territory, embracing the northern portion of the continent from Labrador to Alaska. A large number of dialects are in use among these people, all traceable to the Eskimo family of languages. The Aleuts, Kadiaks, Greenlanders, Atnahs, Koniagas, Malemutes, Kadjacks and Innuits are only a few that belong to this interesting group. In 1656 a vocabulary of the Greenland dialect was published in the voyage of Olearious. The most prolific writers were the Egedes, father and son, Hans and Paul Egedes, who were Moravian missionaries to Greenland. Hans Egedes spent twenty-five years in Greenland, and was made bishop. He wrote a work on Greenland, descriptive of its natural history, the rise and progress of the Norwegian Colonies, the native inhabitants, and gave very many interesting facts relating to the flora and fauna of the country. He published a dictionary of the language in 1750, translated the four Gospels, and began a grammar. His son Paul having learned the language more perfectly, finished the translation of the New Testament and completed the grammar. Other noble workers followed in their footsteps, and treasured up the folk-lore and songs of the people. Many works relating to the mythology and traditions of the Eskimo have been published in French, German, Swedish and Russian. It is surprising to note the large numbers of books treating of the Indians, which have been written by German scholars. As specialists in this department of literature, they have done some noble work.

Our knowledge of the Eskimo and their customs has been derived chiefly from books relating to Arctic exploration. Several notable articles on this subject have been prepared by officers of the Hudson Bay Company, and the governments of the United States and Canada, and read before philological and historical societies. A short time ago, two papers were read before the Canadian Institute, on "The Eskimo of

Stupart's Bay" and "Marble Island," which gave interesting facts about these people. Several important works in the English language have been published, revealing reliable information concerning the vast extent of country inhabited by the Eskimo, and giving facts of ethnological value about them. Among these may be noted, "Dobbs' account of the countries adjoining Hudson's Bay," published in 1744; "McKeevo's Voyage to Hudson's Bay in 1812;" "Franklin's Narrative of a Journey to the shores of the Polar Sea in 1819-1822; Parry and Ross' volumes on the "North-West Passage;" "Stearn's Labrador;" "Hall's Life with the Esquimaux," "Haye's Adventures in Greenland," and "Hooper's Ten Months Among the Tents of the Tuski." Several volumes in later years give the results of modern investigation, as Whymper and Dallis' books on Alaska, Schwatka's important work, and Gilder's volume on Schwatka's search in the Arctic in quest of the Franklin records.

Owing to the energetic labors of the Moravian missionaries in Greenland, the native literature has been well developed. Some of the books were printed in Denmark, and others in Greenland. There are schoolbooks on geography, history and other subjects, and several story books. About two years ago some very entertaining letters, relating to the Eskimo of Labrador, were written by Mr. Tuttle, and published in the Winnipeg papers. The linguistic department of Eskimo literature is extensive. Numerous grammars, vocabularies and dictionaries of the various dialects of Greenland, Labrador, Alaska, and the intervening stretch of country lying between, in the northern part of our Dominion, are in existence. Apart from the very thorough work done in this section, by the missionaries already mentioned, exploring parties and travellers have made full notes on many of the dialects, and these are to be found interspersed throughout their records, in the journals of learned societies, in magazines, and in newspapers. The United States Bureau of Ethnology has several manuscript copies of vocabularies in its library, and a work published under its auspices is very full of interesting matter, viz., "Pilling's Eskimo Bibliography." Dr. Frank Boas has been lately studying, enthusiastically, the folk-lore of the Eskimo of Davis' Strait. He has been toiling in the same field among these people, as has Dr. Rand among the Micmacs, and Charles G. Leland among the Algonquins of New England. The Church of England missionaries are laboring among the Eskimo on the Yukon and surrounding country, and good work has been done by such worthy laborers as Archdeacon Kirby and Bishop Bompas. The bishop has published his western Eskimo primer, while Mr. Peck has translated portions of the New Testament, Book of Common Prayer, and other religious works. The various translations of the Old and New Testaments in Eskimo are very extensive. There are several complete translations of the Bible in the dialects of Greenland and Labrador; and, also, there exist partial translations in many of the other dialects. There are given to these people translations of Luther's Catechism, Krummacher's Parables, Kempis' Imitation of Christ, and other religious works. There is one noticeable feature about the literature of all Indian tribes, the lack of works on social and political science and travel. Without these as aids to the religious literature in existence, it is next to impossible to develop the idea of citizenship which ought to result from a progressive civilization.

INDIAN SYLLABICS.

Several years ago the Venerable Archdeacon McDonald, whose mission is on the Yukon, and who for a term of years dwelt one mile within the Arctic Circle, invented a very elaborate syllabic, which he applied to the Tukudh language, one of the family of the Hyperborean languages. The syllabary consisted of 400 syllables, which, when thoroughly memorized, enabled the Tukudh Indians to read their own language with perfect ease. Having translated the New Testament and Prayer Book, he utilized his syllabic system, and so accurate was its construction that in four months the natives could read the Word of God. Great benefits flowed to the people from this invention, as they speedily learned the truths of morality and religion for themselves.

A young man belonging to the Cherokee nation, named Sequoyah, brooded long over devising a method by which he could teach his people to read as he saw the white men do. He taught himself to read English, but he thought that he could perfect a more complete system by which the Cherokees could read in their own tongue. After much experimenting he prepared a syllabary consisting of eighty characters, which he bequeathed to his people. Eagerly they grasped this linguistic treasure, and they were not long in mastering all its difficulties. They were profited and delighted with the system, and felt proud of its inventor. His fame spread among the Indian tribes, honors were thrust upon him, gifts were bestowed, and for a time he felt glad. Congress voted him a sum of money, and he was on a fair way to affluence and peace. But Sequoyah was unsettled. He believed that a remnant of his people lived unknown on some other part of the American continent, and he determined to discover the lost band of his tribe. Taking with him a young lad as guide and companion, he bade farewell to his people, and set out on his journey. Weary, lonely and sad, he travelled on his errand of peace; but the friends he sought were never found. Halting on his journey, his strength departed, and the inventor of the Cherokee syllabic passed to "that bourne from whence no traveller returns."

In the early history of Methodist Indian Missions in Canada, James Evans spent some time at Alderville, under the Rev. Wm. Case. Subsequently he lived for some years on Indian missions among the Ojibways, and translated hymns into their tongue. He began comparing the construction of Indian languages, and thus laid the foundation for that perfect linguistic work which he was to accomplish in after years around Hudson Bay. About 1840 he was sent out to labor at Norway House. In studying the Cree language he found an efficient helper in Mrs. Ross, the wife of the

Hudson Bay factor. He devised the famous Cree syllabary. It was composed of about forty syllabic characters, the types of which he cut from wood with his knife, and made ink from the soot of his chimney. By the aid of this system a clever Indian could learn to read the Bible in one or two days. Six happy active years of service were spent, and then he went on a visit to England, where he died. This stands today as a memorial of the enthusiasm and ability of one of our pioneers. The Cree confederacy is indebted to him for work. The religious denominations use his invention, and it aids them materially in their work. A few years ago it was adapted to, and utilized for, the Eskimo tongue. These systems are highly beneficial to the people when they are isolated, but when they are in close proximity to the haunts of the white man, they hinder in the progress made toward true civilization, as they prevent the growth of ideas, and lead not to the important duties of citizenship. The syllabic systems have, however, proved to be a most important factor in elevating the people, and leading them to grander conceptions of truth and God.

THE CREE LANGUAGE.

The Cree confederacy is one of the largest branches of the great family of Indians called Algonquin. In books written during the early period of the history of our country, the people were named Knistineaux and Kristineaux, but for several decades they have been known under the simpler term, which is now universally used. They occupy a vast extent of country, embracing at the present time principally Athabasca, Saskatchewan, Alberta, Assiniboia, Manitoba and Keewatin. Among the Indian tribes, there are distinctive names applied to the tribes by the people themselves, and not in use among the white people. The members of the Blackfoot confederacy use as a national appellation—Netsepoye, which means the people that speak the same language, and the Cree national distinction is, Naheyowuk, the exact people.

Judging from the grammatical construction of their language, its harmony and beauty, and the influence it has exerted over the other languages, the Crees have a righteous title to their significant name. Invariably among the tribes inhabiting the North-West some persons will be found who are able to converse in the Cree language. Like all languages during the early stage of their development, it is agglutinative in form, and like Indian languages in general, the entire language becomes a language of verbs. There are two leading dialects of this tongue, the Wood and Plain Cree. Differences of pronunciation are manifest among the tribes using the language, induced no doubt by separation, the influences of religion, population and local surroundings. There are few sounds in use, and consequently few letters are needed to give expression to them. Sexual gender is not denoted, but instead there are two forms employed, namely, animate and inanimate, referring to things with and without life. There are two numbers, singular and plural; and in the latter there is a distinction peculiar to Indian language, namely, two first persons plural, the one including the first and third persons, and the other, first and second persons; as Notawenan, our father, and Kotawenan, our father.

In the formation of nouns, the termination in general reveals the class to which they belong. Thus, abstract nouns end in win, simulative nouns in kan. Nouns referring to water have their termination in kume, and those denoting abundance in skau.

Diminutive nouns are formed by adding is, or sis; as, iskweo, a woman; iskwesis, a girl.

The verb has seven conjugations, with a very elaborate display of moods and tenses, and a large number of different kinds of verbs. Many new words have been adopted from the English language, and after being thoroughly Indianized, have become incorporated in the Cree tongue.

Early in the history of Protestant missions among the natives, the Rev. James Evans, residing at Norway House, invented the Cree syllabic character, and with the aid of Mr. and Mrs. Ross, of the Hudson's Bay Company, made translations and utilized this syllabic system in teaching the Indians. For a long period previous to his residence at Norway House, Mr. Evans had been making a special study of Indian languages, and the result was the invention of this system. It is evident from the formation of the characters that the inventor had acquired some knowledge of phonography, and applied its principles in the construction of his syllabary. There are about fifty characters including the auxiliaries in this syllabic system. It is so simple in construction that an Indian with average intelligence can memorize the whole in a day, and in less than one week read fluently any book written upon this plan. The Indians of this confederacy, with very few exceptions, read and write these characters; and many of them, with no other teachers but the Indians around the camp-fires, have so grasped these principles that they can read with fluency the books printed in the syllabic system. It is a rare thing to meet Wood Indians of the Cree confederacy who cannot read, so great has this educating influence been exerted over the minds of the people. The inventor of this syllabic system having spent his entire residence among the northern Crees, the Indians of that portion of the country learned the characters more rapidly and used it more extensively, but in later years the Plain Crees, with some exceptions, have acquired it, and utilized it in the different relations of life. The Stony Indians read the books printed in this system fluently, and write letters in it; some of which I have in my possession. A short time ago, a band of Indians in the far north sent a letter written in these characters on a piece of birch-bark by one of their number, imparting information concerning their ideas of liberty and government. It is used by the Protestant and Roman Catholic missionaries, and has lately been adapted to the language of the Eskimo. There are several works published of great importance to the student of philology. Joseph Howe, Esq., of the Hudson's Bay Company, published a grammar of the Cree language in 1815, learned and accurate, which is now out of print and difficult to obtain. Bishop Horden, of Moosonee, has a grammar of the language, neat, compact and very suitable for the student. Archdeacon Hunter prepared and published a lecture on the "Grammatical Construction of the Cree Language." It is a very elaborate work on the Cree verb; invaluable to advanced students of the language. The Rev. E. A. Watkins prepared the only Cree-English and English-Cree dictionary ever published. With commendable perseverance he has tabulated nearly fourteen thousand words. The Rev. Albert Lacombe has published a Cree grammar in French and a dictionary in the same language. This is the only grammar and dictionary in the Plain Cree that has been prepared.

The religious development of the people has demanded and supplied a literature of its own. The Rev. H. B. Steinhauer, aided by a half-breed, named John Sinclair, translated the Bible, and this is published in the syllabic character. In the same character, "Cree Family Prayers, Psalms and Hymns," by Archdeacon J. A. McKay. Archdeacon Hunter prepared the English Church Prayer-book, and his wife translated and prepared a Hymn-book, both of which were printed in Roman characters. Besides these works, Evans, Mason and Hunter, translated parts of the New Testament, which were published. The Rev. Father Lacomb has prepared a series of readings from the four Evangelists in the Cree language.

The same author has prepared manuscript copies of a hymn-book, prayer-book, catechism, and book of sermons for the use of the Roman Catholic Cree Indians.

The Rev. Father Vegreville, of St. Albert, has prepared manuscript copies of a grammar and dictionary of the Cree language, and the same of the Chippewayan language, which is the same as the Montagnais.

The Rev. Father Legoff, of Cold Lake, Fort Pitt, has prepared manuscript copies of a dictionary and grammar of the Chippewayan language, also in the same language a history of the Bible and Roman Catholic catechism.

Bishop Faraud, of Lac la Biche, has also written a Bible history and catechism in the same language.

The Rev. Father Petitot has published "Legends of the Tinné Indians" in the French language, and has manuscript works in the Tinné language.

Among the latest publications in the Cree are "The Pilgrim's Progress," by Bishop Horden, and the Methodist Hymn-Book, by Revs. Messrs. McDougall and Glass, in Plain Cree, and by Orrin German, in Wood Cree. The Methodist Catechism has also been translated into the same language.

Camping Out.

CHAPTER VIII.

THE INDIAN PROBLEM.

THE CIVILIZING OF THE INDIAN.

POLITICAL and ecclesiastical leaders earnestly desire the speedy and permanent civilization of the Indian race, but they differ in their conception of what is included in the term "*civilization*," and in their methods of elevating the people. It must be acknowledged that there is such a thing as an Indian problem, which requires years of study and experience to train the mind to grasp fully its difficulties, and even then it is a problem that wears a different aspect for different tribes. It is amusing to listen to the very quaint remarks and sometimes serious discussions relating to the Indian question by persons eminent for their political acumen and religious zeal, but who lack the necessary knowledge and experience to judge wisely on these matters. The very difficulties of the situation seem rather to invite than deter some persons from freely expressing their opinions, and urging speedy and definite action in accordance with their theories—untried, puerile and antagonistic to the customs and training of the Indians.

The work of civilizing the Indian race is surrounded by innumerable, but not insurmountable, hindrances, because therein is implied the full transformation and development of the nature of the individual, the complete overthrow of religious, political and social customs, and very many changes in the domestic relations of the people.

There must of necessity be the training of the Indian toward self-support, salvation from a life of pauperism, and the begetting of a love for honest labor. It is believed by many that the Indian is naturally lazy, but that is a mistaken idea. The change that takes place after the advent of the white man introduces different kinds of work to that to which the red man was accustomed to attend to, and these bring into play other sets of muscles which become quickly tired out, and hence arises distaste to the particular kinds of labor. The young and middle-aged are generally ambitious, and aim at perfection in toil. Not being trained to the new kinds of work, they do not produce first-class specimens of their handicraft, and consequently, their spirits being dampened, they throw the task aside, and long for the good old days when congenial toil was theirs.

Let the commercial and mechanical races follow the hunting tribes of red men, and they will soon be wearied with the labor and long to depart for "pastures green." If the same principle of condemnation as applied to the Indians were brought to bear upon the race of pale-faces, a sweeping verdict of unfitness and laziness would be theirs. As the white man's civilization grows, sympathy and liberality are begotten in the just appreciation of the work that belongs respectively to every individual, tribe or race.

Legitimate training includes the guiding of the native love for freedom and independence out of the nomadic life into the stationary residence attending a life of agriculture. True development never means the suppression of a noble principle or emotion, but there exists the keen discernment that seizes every just desire, energy or affection, and leads them into channels of usefulness among men. The barbarian love of freedom is our heritage. We dare not frown upon the holy aspirations that dwell in other men's souls. Part of the work of the red man's teachers is to mould the nature of the natives until their ideas on freedom and independence will be similar to those of the white men in their relation to each other.

The civilizing of the Indians does not mean the compulsory acceptation of the white man's customs, but it is the transformation of the whole man. It means the physical, mental, moral and spiritual development of the individual and the race. Custom unjustly has compelled us to accept a division of this work, namely, that the temporal welfare of the Indians belongs to the State, that the moral and spiritual training is the duty of the Church, and the education of the young is a scheme of co-partnership. Church and

State are equally interested in the civilizing of the red man, but the division of labor as a permanent separation is one that is injurious to all concerned and detrimental to the interests of the work.

There are times when mutual help is needed in every branch of work, and sometimes it becomes the duty of the one civilizing agent to reprove the other. The Church has seen fit to reprove the State for neglect, inefficient toil and lack of intelligent enthusiasm; and the State, impressed with its sense of duty, has censured the Church for its inferior management of its work, self-lauded yet defective methods of procedure and want of visible success. Impartial oversight on the part of each is beneficial and just, but jealous criticism must be severely condemned. False ideas have arisen regarding the relation of the Government to the churches in the Indian work. Between the two agencies for the red man's culture there exists a difference of opinion as to which is the most important and should precede the other. The Church says, "Christianize first and then civilize;" the State replies, "Teach the Indians first to work and then to pray." True civilization includes the work of both these agencies, and it is not antagonistic, but the one is the complement of the other. It should be unity in labor, not precedence. Pious sentimentality will raise its hands with sanctimonious horror at the very thought of politicians criticising the doings of ecclesiastics, but a just criticism will promote heathfulness, and the work of teacher and taught will rapidly improve.

There is a tendency on the part of departments to intrude, so easy and pleasant it is to find fault. Mistakes are easily made and quickly noticed. The State does wrong when it interferes with that which is the distinctive *right* of the Church, from the expenditure of money, long experience and the employment of specially trained talent; and the Church oversteps its bounds when it begins to dictate to Government employees the course that must be pursued in training the Indians. A case of the former nature took place when the United States Indian Commissioner forbade the use of the native language in the schools of the Dakotas, under the supervision of the Rigg's family, who had spent half a century laboring among these Indians.

It would be well, however, were the Government to promulgate laws regulating the existence and work of the denominations on the Indian reserves; that is, equal rights to all creeds and classes, and only one denomination to be allowed to labor on each reserve.

The work of civilizing the Indians will always suffer so long as men study it in the light of party politics, but progress will be seen when affairs are managed by men whose creed is broader and purer than party. The past few years have seen a change in that direction, and success has followed the labors put forth.

Over and over again have reports been published by careless or ignorant persons of "Indian Scares," disturbances, horse-stealing and wars that never took place.

The Church must recognize the religious element in politics, and assist in training the Indians in manual labor, while the Government must suppress all kinds of immorality and set an example of purity and justice in all things. The machinery employed by the secular power is working well, and the results are satisfactory

An Indian Boy.

to those who understand the difficulties attending the work. Indian mission work in Manitoba and the North-West has been successful, but it is not the kind of success desired by those who know nothing of life and labor among the Indians. The average Christian's idea of success is an impossibility. More is asked from the Indian missionary than any other laborer in the field of religion.

The Christian politician and the political Christian seek to labor so that there shall be the impartation of a new affection in the Indian heart, changed modes of thinking, a new religion of higher and nobler import, training for intellect, surer means of support, and a more useful and happier life. These results will be the reward of enlightened toil on behalf of the red men.

MOVE ON!

The author of "The Making of New England," relates that a government agent was sent to an Indian tribe to inform them that they were again to move from their location. The chief told the agent to sit down on a log, which was done, and then he repeatedly requested him to move on, until he reached the end. Again the chief said, "move on," but the agent replied, "I cannot." "Just so it is with us," said the chief; "you have moved us as far as we can go, and then ask us to move still farther."

Occasionally the cry is raised by a few persons in the country that the Indians should be moved to other locations, as more suitable for the red men. Some of the arguments used appear at first sight as very plausible, and as begotten by genuine sympathy for the Indian race. There may be some individuals sincerely desiring the welfare of the people in this direction, but self-interest is generally the foundation for all these schemes. Some of the reservations are beautifully situated, and the encroachments of civilization arouse the selfish desires of those who are seeking land.

The depredations of renegade Indians cause an aversion toward the whole tribe, and vengeance is vowed upon their guilty heads. The petty annoyances that arise from the proximity of the races, and the antagonism existing between them; the reports, real and false, of uprisings, and the abhorrence shown by the whites toward the blanketed Indian with his barbaric customs, cause the periodical cry to resound in our ears, "Move on!" The independence, generosity and love of justice inherent in the refined intellect, compel men to study the question and test the arguments before agreeing to any measure involving pain to a single community of another race.

A strange argument was used to justify the policy of the people of the United States for the expulsion of the Indians from their lands. This was based upon the theory of the origin of the American Indians elaborated by Dr. Ezra Stiles, President of Yale College, in a sermon preached by him at Hartford, in 1783, before Governor Trumbull and the General Assembly of the State of Connecticut, entitled, "The United States elevated to Glory and Honor."

President Stiles considered the Indians to be the Canaanites expelled by Joshua. One branch coasted along the Mediterranean to its mouth, and was then wafted by the trade winds to the coasts of Mexico and Peru. Another branch travelled north-eastward, and from Asia went from island to island through the northern archipelago until America was reached. In the strange inscriptions on the rocks in Narraganset Bay, which he copied and scientists informed him were Runic characters, he noted the fact that the ancient Carthaginians had at one time visited the shores of the new world. He also believed in the identity of the Siberian Tartars with the American Indians. Naturally those interested seized upon this theory, and felt justified as modern Israelites in expelling the Canaanites from the land. Increased knowledge prevents us from accepting such statements and adopting such a policy. "The Indians must go," becomes a very attractive heading for a sensational article in the columns of the western press, but justice is blindfold, and the reasons urged for and against a change of policy must be placed in the scales before a verdict is given.

The Indians' residence in a district implies benefits past and present to the white settlers located there. Because of the existence of Indians on a reserve in a district where white people have made homes for themselves, there arises the necessity for supplies in the shape of beef, flour, and numerous other articles. Hired labor is employed as freighters, farm laborers and clerks. The money received by these persons, besides the annual payments to the Indians, is spent in the district to a great extent.

Without the Indian in particular sections of the country there would be no need for the Mounted Police, with the attendant outlay of money. The Indian Department and Mounted Police create a demand for labor for farmers and stockmen, and give to the country a large supply of money which would not exist were the Indians driven out. It may be only removal to a remoter district, but is that just? In former years the Indians were almost the sole means for the existence of many people, and now that the demand is not so great, because of other means of securing a living, must they be sent to the north because of our whims? When they have gone there, settlers will follow, and the same expulsion will be demanded. Because they are no longer of as great service to many as formerly is no just reason for removal. Suppose the red men in their years of strength had demanded the expulsion of the white people, the country would have still been a barren waste. Equal rights must be given to all, and justice sacredly meted out. When Indians and white people commit crimes, let them be punished to an equal degree. Petty annoyances arise through contact of the races by not understanding each other's language and customs. There are subtler influences at work that tend oftentimes to engender strife. The reports of the eastern press relating to Indian troubles are, in the majority of instances, exaggerated or totally untrue. The prevailing sentiment of the people of the Dominion is, to treat the Indians firmly and kindly in accordance with the principles of justice, and in the end this will prove most beneficial to all concerned. Red and white are the subjects of one Sovereign and the children of a common Father, and to each belong respective rights that must be sacredly revered and upheld.

BIBLE AND PLOUGH.

The Rev. J. H. Wilbur, who labored very successfully among the Yakima Indians, made the following quaint and suggestive remarks in relation to mission work among the Indians: "The plough and the Bible go together in civilizing Indians."

This idea is practically forgotten by the majority of persons interested in the Indians. The one sole idea presented by our white Christian brethren and sisters is the conversion of the red men, and seldom are the questions asked: "Are the Indians adopting the customs of the white men? Are they learning to toil as we do for their daily bread? Are they imbued with the principles of loyalty and justice? Do they appreciate the educational efforts put forth, and avail themselves of the means used for the civilizing of their race?" Hand, head and heart training must go together in elevating the Indian race. By a just combination of influences relating to these objects, there will result true development.

The progress made, however, will not be proportionate with that of any of the civilized people of the nineteenth century, with whom it is not just to compare them. After centuries of severe training there have been evolved the men and women of the present period, and the difference between these and their ancestors of a few hundred years is as great as between the red and white of to-day. It is very easy to criticise men and methods, and fault-finding has an agreeable and fascinating influence over some minds. There is nothing too sacred that the hands of the unholy iconoclast will not touch, and ignorance oftentimes gives an impetus to the political zeal of the disappointed. Knowledge of Indian customs will invariably increase sympathy, if it does not entirely destroy all tendencies to condemn in the slightest degree the work of the men who live and labor among the Indians.

Missionaries toiling for the welfare of the Indian race are confronted with customs different from their own, and these must be studied, so that wise measures may be adopted for the silent overthrow of all those that are injurious to the advancement of the red man. The sudden change that comes over the mind and heart of the Indians by submission to the Divine, compels a rejection of many customs that are detrimental to their ultimate civilization. Still there are some that remain that must be gradually undermined by the introduction of influences and counter-customs, before the end is reached which we desire. Direct opposition to native customs will stir up strife, and the object sought will be lost; but if the religious, social, political and domestic customs are thoroughly understood, and discretion used in imparting others, there will result abundant success. Few study the native customs, hence mistakes are made, and unjust statements are heard injurious to the natives and the earnest toilers in the field.

The man who would be successful must spend his days and nights in the study of the native language of the people among whom he labors. Without this there can be no intelligent acceptance or appreciation of the truths taught. There are few interpreters qualified to grasp the ideas and accurately translate them in the true spirit with which they should be given.

Financial help is a necessity to carry on labor in any field. It is sad to be compelled to state that it is much easier to raise funds for missionary work in India, China and Japan than for the missions carried on among the aborigines of our Dominion. "The child of sorrow" of missions is the work of Christianizing the red men.

It is true that the results are not so great and as speedily secured as in the lands of the east, but there are hindrances innumerable that retard the progress of the work. Considering well the training of the race, the attendant circumstances of their lives, and the difficulties to be overcome in prosecuting the one great object of consecrated toil, the results, measured by these and other influences, are good and full of hope.

The previous training of many of the men employed in the fields is at variance with the toil now undertaken. The spiritual qualifications are excellent, the enthusiasm and devotion much to be admired, but these end all. Our ideas must be enlarged to embrace the entire nature of the individual. Food for body and soul must be obtained; but, alas! helpless often are we in leading the Indian toward self-support. Divine truth aids in this direction by changing the native idea of independence. The union of the forces emanating from the missionary societies and the Indian Department are directed toward the united lives of body and soul. The inconsistencies of white men, intelligent and honest, destroy in a measure the fair prospects of success. "Be pure, just and peaceable," says the teacher of truth, and the Indian answers, "Your holy book teaches us that, but surely the white men don't believe it, or they would not disobey the lessons that God's Son has taught." Responsible is our position in the land of the red men, and we cannot spurn the teachings of our home and friends.

The antagonism existing between the customs, intellects and lives of the two races, and the despondency consequent upon the changed life of the Indians are important factors in frustrating attempts for their amelioration in the present and the great beyond.

Church and State are related in this important movement. There may arise conflicting influences tending to destroy the work of each, but there are broad principles which are common, and these must be seized upon as a basis of unity whereby success may be insured. "Lend a hand," should be the united cry. Help each other. The great object should be to train the spiritual, intellectual and physical powers. Our motto must be: "Religion, Education, Self-support—*The Bible and the Plough.*"

The wards of the Government are being trained. Noble work is being done. Success has followed the toils and trials of missionary toilers and Indian Department employees in many fields. Enlarged knowledge relating to reserves and missions, with the study of the history of the conquest of countries and the training of races, will dispel despondency and create brighter hopes for the ultimate civilization of the Red Race.

RED AND WHITE.

Modern philanthropists desirous of aiding any legitimate agency for the amelioration of the red race, look for speedy results from energetic and well-directed labor, and become greatly astonished when they behold the red man pursue the even tenor of his way, irrespective of all the combined influences of kingcraft and priestcraft.

Hastily and rashly they judge the means employed for the Indian's enlightenment, while they have forgotten one of life's golden rules, eminently practical in missionary toil, "Learn to labor and to wait." They make a valuation of missionary work on a strictly mercantile basis, and heed not the difficulties peculiar to this branch of missionary toil, and the higher criterion of spiritual labor which recognizes the unity of our race, but a diversity of soul-culture with its consequently different responsibilities and rewards.

The resistless tide of civilization, ever advancing westward, overwhelms the native culture of the red race. There has arisen an antagonism between the frontiersmen and Indians that has destroyed, in some measure, the peaceful relations they formerly held with each other. The Indian is suffered to exist, but he is regarded as an encumbrance to the country and a strong barrier to its speedy development.. The early settlers are greedy in their desires for beautiful locations for their farms, and there are many fine tracts of good farming land in the hands of the red men, who do not make any use of it. They have felt that at times their property was unsafe, and their lands consequently of less value because of the presence of their enemies. But if the pioneers have felt thus, so much the more have the Indians realized the evil consequence of the white man's residence in the country. They blame the white man for driving the buffalo from the country, and as they sit in their lodges, they narrate instances of the white man's avariciousness and strength. The vast tracts of land are gone, game is becoming scarce, diseases of various kinds have been introduced, and the Indian brooding over his loss bewails his departed independence, "and his heart is on the ground." The red men know that the white people do not love them, and there exists a feeling of animosity between them. There is such a striking difference between the civilization of the two races, that unity of sentiment and aims becomes an impossibility. The different tendencies arising from the construction of the languages, development of literature, modes of thinking, systems of education and the labors and pleasures of life lead to a diversity of results, where exists ultimate separation, unless a powerful factor is introduced, to overcome these influences, and utilize them in one common direction. There is a civilization of the red race as well as of the white, and the culture of the one should be studied and admired as honestly as the other. The Picts and Scots, the Celts and Gauls of the early centuries of the Christian era did not exhibit any higher civilization, and in many instances a much lower state of culture was manifested, than is now inherited by the majority of the Indian tribes.

The law of composition was accepted by the Barbarians, with the right of judicial combat. The Arabians, Germans, Hungarians and other nations placed a price on the head of their friends who were slain, besides a fine was imposed, by payment of which, an injury might be forgiven, unless the injured party chose to go to war. The Indians follow the same law. "A scalp for a scalp," or a certain number of horses as a compensation for an injury or the loss of a friend. Two Blood Indian chiefs had relatives killed by some members of a southern tribe, and in conversation with both of them on the matter, one said, "Two of my relations were killed; if I can get two scalps for them by killing two of my enemies, I will be satisfied;" and the other expressed his feelings by saying, "My son was killed by these people; I must have the scalp of one of them for it, and that will satisfy me; but if my enemies wish my people not to go to war against them, they can give us some horses, and that will end the whole matter."

A Piegan chief accidentally killed a child belonging to his own tribe, and the difficulty was set at rest by the payment of several horses. When a case similar to this happens in some tribes the injury is repaired by the guilty person offering himself for adoption into the family to supply the place of the deceased, which offer is generally accepted.

When Indian criminals have died in the penitentiary the Bloods have asked what compensation the Government was going to give them for their loss.

In the mode of life of the Germanic tribes and the

Indians there is a striking similarity, As the Indians are at the present day, the Germans were inveterate gamblers, drank liquor to excess, feasted when they had abundance, and fasted when their food was gone; prized liberty above everything, paid great respect to their war-chiefs, yet recognized no king; punished adultery by cutting off the guilty wife's nose, beating her severely and then driving her away; exercised great hospitality and lived a nomadic life. The Hungarians lived in leathern tents, seldom cultivated the ground, wandered from place to place hunting and fishing, sought out good pasturage for their horses and cattle. In their war customs they pursued the same tactics as the Indians. The Scandinavian youth rejoiced in a life of piracy.

The Germans scalped their enemies and observed marriage customs similar to those of the Indian tribes.

This condition of things was a necessity at the period, as land virtually had no value, there was not among the tribes any landed proprietors, and when the people were not engaged in the labors of the chase they were idle. When they were compelled by a change in their circumstances to adopt a sedentary life, and follow the pursuits of agriculture, there arose an inequality among the people from the fact that the chiefs became landed proprietors and employed those under them as laborers. The former equality, arising from their tribal relationship, gave place to an individuality which paved the way for the evolution of the Germans, Hungarians and other civilized nations of the nineteenth century.

It has taken several centuries to evolve the English-speaking race of to-day, and ignorantly we look for as great a development in the red race from half a century of training. This transformation of civilization includes a great deal. It means the substitution of a foreign language for a large number of dialects, an entire change in their modes of life, the rejection of old ideas and modes of thinking, and the accepting of that which is difficult to comprehend, because foreign to their minds. It is unjust to expect, and impossible for us to conceive, the development of Indian tribes in the space of a single century to the high standing of civilization enjoyed by the white race of the present age.

It is natural that the Indian should remember the teachings of his forefathers, and prize them highly, clinging to them in preference to the new ways of the white man. But the change will come, though it must be slow; and much depends upon the Indians' environment as an aid to the principles of religion, to the time necessary for its accomplishment.

Gradually the old customs will die out, new ideas will be generated, and the tendency will be upward, if the term of existence is sufficiently long for this development.

AMONG THE LODGES.

Wandering through our western towns and villages, the solitary Indian becomes suddenly aware of his obnoxious presence by the barking of dogs, and the screaming of children. Gazing upon the workmanship of his white brethren, he is compelled, by the force of circumstances, to keep a wary eye upon the stealthy cur who frowns upon the red intruder, and warns him with significant growls, that he is treading upon forbidden ground. The gentler portion of society exhibits signs of uneasiness when first ushered into the presence of the people of the plains, and the strange questions sometimes asked, reveal the depth and genuineness of their fears. The pale-faced child trembles and cries in its nurse's arms when the painted visage of the Indian is seen. Change the scene, and these striking peculiarities of the different modes of life of the two races are repeated. Going from lodge to lodge, the low growls of a dozen wolfish, snappish, detestable whelps arouse all our latent energies, and firmly convince us that, in features at least, we belong to another race.

It seems impossible, even after years of toil, to establish any bond of sympathy between these parasites of the lodge and the white man. Travel through the camps accompanied by a dusky friend and protector, and they will speedily recognize you as a stranger. Enter the lodges, and the youthful occupants will flee for safety to their mother's knee, unless oft-repeated visits have made you familiar to young and old. Oftentimes, in stormy weather, have I sought the cheery warmth of the lodges, and sat listening to the wondrous tales of the days of yore, yet never has my confidence been sufficient to trust to the dignity and self-respect of an Indian dog. I have made friends of the children, enjoyed their prattle and childlike stories, but patience has fled when, after bidding adieu to my youthful companions, I have been pursued by a band of despicable, lank and long-haired curs. Despite the poverty of the lodges, there are treasured in the book of memory many pleasant reminiscences of joyous hours, with painted warriors and youthful heroes, who have gone to the red man's elysium. Song and story quaintly sang, and vividly told, fill up the weary round of hours until the absorbing passion for gambling gains the ascendancy, and the evening song gives place to the game of chance. Strange fascinations that will compel a man to stake his entire fortune on the result of a race or a few turns of a small wheel; and yet they but imitate the race noted for its superior intellectuality and physical organization.

Light and shade make up the sum total of man's little life; still the clouds may have a silver lining by the presence of hope, harbinger of abundant peace and joy.

THE LAZY INDIAN.

The brave and faithful Uncas, the last of the Mohicans, as depicted by Fennimore Cooper, is a reality much desired to be seen among the red men of the plains and forests of the North-West. Transatlantic travellers appear crestfallen when they first gaze upon the natives of our land. We are not surprised, therefore, to find expressions of disappointment, and even disgust, from the pens of these travellers in many leading newspapers, relating to the Indians. The day has not yet passed for a faithful representation of a devoted Pocahontas or the loyalty and intelligence of a Tecumseh. Surely there exist principles in the hearts of the noble men of the pale-face race which will compel them to recognize ability and honesty when circumstances arise to call them forth.

Instead of pity and mockery, give to the Indian honesty and firm dealing, and the latent goodness of his nature will be aroused. The Stonies, Sarcees, Blackfeet, Piegans and Bloods have ever been numbered among the bravest and most loyal to the white man on the American continent. Records of Indian

Indians Fishing Through the Ice.

warfare in the North-West reveal the daring spirit exhibited by members of these tribes. The dull and listless manner commented on by travellers is the result of training, whereby they conceal the struggles of their emotions and exhibit the stolidity now characteristic of the Indian nature. Permit that same dull-looking red man to enjoy the exciting influence of camp life with its festivities, or the exhilarating atmosphere of a buffalo hunt, or, in fact, anything necessary to call forth the cunning and daring of his spirit, and you will witness a complete transformation. When the buffalo roamed the prairie in thousands, the skin lodges, nicely tanned and well made, presented a fine appearance. Then the average Indian dress, with its ornaments, of the young men of the Blackfoot nation, was of greater value than that worn by professional men in the cities. Then the Indians were wealthy, and each man owned a fine band of horses. The introduction of whisky and the departure of the buffalo, brought poverty to the brave red men.

These Indians were noted for their hospitality. Never was a white man sent away from an Indian lodge hungry and tired. The choicest pieces of meat were given to the stranger. Now their circumstances are changed, and an expression of sadness sits upon their countenances. Still, they are not hopeless, as may be evidenced by their success in agriculture. Their mode of life is entirely changed, hence their apparent laziness. They see their lands occupied by white men, the buffalo gone, disease undermining their constitutions, and no way of maintaining their independence. They are now in the critical period of the conquered, which, if they pass over, will be of great benefit to them.

There is just cause for complaint on the part of some at the annoyance resulting from the intrusion of Indians. But have the Indians no just reason why they should complain against the doings of the white people? Certainly they have. When the railroad was being built past Blackfoot Crossing, advantage was taken of the Indians' ignorance of money; and some parties bought new moccasins, worth two or three dollars, for a cent, which had been polished till it was bright, and taken by the Indians for gold. White men have, after using tea for themselves, dried it, and then sold it to the Indians as good tea. Promises have been made to them of one or two dollars for sawing a quantity of wood which white men would not do for less than five or six dollars; and when it was finished, the "noble" and honest (?) pale face has grossly cheated, by paying the Indian but twenty-five or fifty cents for the work. These things have happened repeatedly, and certainly they ought to be put a stop to by the law compelling the despicable Christian to pay what was due. There is nothing surprising in the Indian's demeanor. He does not exhibit the spite toward his intelligent brother which the pale-face genius shows toward everything Indian.

In several of our western towns the hatred toward the Indians is great; but when the treaty payments are made, the ambitious trader becomes the servant of the Indian for the sake of his gain. Expressions of hatred will oftentimes be heard. One man was heard to say that he would supply them, free of charge, with all the vermilion they required to paint their faces, if they would only paint their eyes as well, so that the poison contained in the vermilion might destroy their sight; another would give so much money, if all educational and religious influences were taken from them. Ask the medical men who have spent several years in the country why so many Indians are dying, and they will tell you that it is because of the diseases introduced by white men. Point not to the influences of civilization as the cause of the deterioration of the Indian nature, but rather ascribe their degeneracy in morals and their debilitated physical constitution to the evils that follow in its train.

286 An Indian Missionary.

CHAPTER IX.

CHRISTIANITY AND THE RED RACE.

THE GOSPEL IN THE WIGWAMS.

THE Marquis of Lorne, in his observations of Indian life, as narrated in *Canadian Pictures,* writes: "In Canada, as in Africa and the South Seas, the Gospel of Christ has won victories over ignorance and sin. The preaching of redemption through the death of Christ on the cross, has touched and cleansed savage hearts, and the Indian manifests no less than the white man the power of the Spirit of God." There are many doubters as to the success attending the labors of missionaries among the red men. With them it is the practical question of dollars and cents. A definite amount has been expended on an Indian mission, and the exact equivalent in conversions according to some ideal standard must result. Comparisons are made between missionary work in Japan and India with missions to the Indians, and because there are quicker returns, the answer is given to all questions on the matter by a wholesale condemnation of the work.

It is urged that the money should be expended on promising fields, rather than wasted on the Indians. Now, we do not believe that were the missions withdrawn, the money raised for Indian missions would be subscribed for Japan, China or India. There are many persons in the churches strongly impressed with the responsibility of the Church to "preach the Gospel to every creature."

It does not mean that they are to civilize or convert every heathen, but it implies that the duty of preaching the Gospel belongs to man, and the results belong to God.

Carey and Judson were condemned for their long years of waiting, but the harvest followed the seedtime, and ultimately they had cause for rejoicing. Even in laboring in highly civilized communities there are difficult places to toil in, as well as easy churches and homes. In political life and in military affairs, the strongest and best men are placed where the enemy is the boldest, and has the surest foothold, but it is oftentimes the opposite in ecclesiastical matters.

Where ignorance, superstition, custom and religion have full sway over the native mind, the untrained are sent to labor, as if any kind of talent, education and piety were good enough for the Indian.

We train men for the ministry, and send them fully equipped to labor among the white people, but where is the training for the Indian work?

The religion of the Nazarene is antagonistic to the

natural desires of the Indian, hence arises a hatred of it, and oftentimes a secret and determined opposition to it. Despite this native antagonism, the hearts of thousands of the red men have been touched during the period in which Indian missions in the Dominion have existed. When we remember that many of these people are the descendants of the ancient lords of Canada, who owned the land which has become our heritage, and when we see the sad change from progress to poverty that has come over many tribes, does it not become our duty to send them the Gospel, that we may, in part, restore their best fortunes, their peace and joy?

The spiritual insight imparted to the native intellect when entirely submitted to the Christ, flashes anew with strength and directness, but it is a purified and enlightened intelligence that is the result. The shrewd wisdom of a Brant became refined, and increased in vigor under the teaching influences of the Word of God. Polygamy has ceased to be practised among the tribes who have fully embraced the Gospel.

The medicine man's incantations, the death-song, the scalp-dance, the drunken orgies, the native burial customs, and many of the revolting ceremonies consequent upon a degrading and retrograding civilization having taken root among them, have, to a great degree, come to an end. Christianity has destroyed the hideous immorality of the camps, and introduced a noble standard in the life and person of Christ. It has suppressed many of the tribal laws which were injurious to the best interests of the people. Native customs have become subject to the Christ, the social life of the camps have become more uniform and refined, and the domestic relations of the people have been changed to accord with the views of the great teachers of life.

The Indian division of labor has given place to the nineteenth century interpretations of the Bible, and the combined wisdom of the people. The hunter has become a farmer or mechanic, the breechcloth and blanket have been replaced with tweed and broadcloth garments, made by a fashionable tailor; and the wild fruits of the forest no longer exercise exclusive sway over the red man's palate and table. When there has been the impartation of a new affection dislodging the unholy principles of mind and heart, there have followed many changes in the life and labor of the Indians.

Contrast the condition of the wild nomads of the prairies, devoted to their native religion, with that of the Christianized tribes of the old provinces, and the influence of the truth of the religion of Christ will be seen. Civilization without the Gospel changes the position, power and intelligence of Indian manhood, but to a very great degree the division of labor, as it touches womanhood, is slightly affected, and the morality of the camps is very materially injured, indeed, is almost totally destroyed.

We have met members of the Muncey, Ojibway, Shawanese and Pottawatamie tribes, who were prosperous farmers, courteous and refined in manner, eloquent speakers and devoted Christians. Several young men belonging to the Caughnawagas, Ojibways and

Six Nation Indians in Canada have graduated in arts, medicine and law.

The history of Protestant Indian missions, from their inception in New England until the present time, reveals the power of Gospel truth in reclaiming the wanderer from the paths of sin.

The transition of a tribe from Paganism to Christianity, is an interesting study. Sterling examples of piety have dwelt in the lodges, and the camps have forgotten their war-whoops in the sweeter songs of the Prince of Peace.

LANGUAGE-STUDY.

The Master's marching orders are obeyed year after year by hundreds of devoted men and women, who go out into the desert places of the earth to teach the despised races of men the way of life. The one prominent desire of their hearts is for success, and yet many fail in reaching the ideal set before them. There are numerous causes preventing the acceptation of the Gospel by the heathen; but though some are local, there is one that is a barrier to spiritual conquest among all peoples, and that is the lack of knowledge concerning the language of the people to whom the Gospel is to be preached. There have been instances where missionaries have employed interpreters, and they have been eminently successful in the conversion of the heathen, but these are few indeed.

Again, missionaries with a thorough knowledge of the language of their people, have had to pass through the stages of seed-sowing and soil preparation before success was theirs. But let us listen to the voices of the successful missionaries, and follow the lessons they would teach us. The men who have toiled in the fields where we are to labor are the best teachers we can have, therefore let us be content and obey them in all things.

After the devoted Moffat had labored for some time in Africa without any apparent success, he appealed to his wife for sympathy. "Mary, this is hard work; think how long we have been preaching to this people and no fruits yet appear." The noble-hearted wife replied, "The Gospel has not been preached to them in their own tongue wherein they were born." Moffat says, "From that hour I gave myself with untiring diligence to the acquisition of the language." Great was his success in after years through following the advice of his wise helpmate and friend.

The Rev. Edward Webb spent nineteen years as a missionary in India, and at the ordination of his son, Samuel G. Webb, who was going as a missionary to the same country, he made some important statements affecting the success as related to the study of the language of the natives. He said, "When you have sailed over the ocean lying between this land and that, you will find another, broader still, and much harder to cross. Their tongue will separate them from you more effectually than Himalaya ranges or broad Atlantics, and you must scale those heights and cross that ocean. In full view of the labor involved, you must plan to acquire a wide and thorough acquaintance with the Tamil, including minute accuracy of pronunciation, full comprehension of its grammatical structure, some familiarity with its literature, and, above all, an idiomatic and free use of the vernacular. Without this, close contact with the people is impossible. But with it, you will be accorded a high place in their regard. You will be an authority, with position and influence. If your plan includes such thoroughness, there is, be assured, hard work before you. I had such a plan when I landed in Madras. But I had a theory that to study the language by lamplight, after dark, was unnecessary and even harmful in that climate, and so spoke. The remark of a missionary present was, 'Then you will never get it.' No native was ever more accurate in his own tongue, or more fluent, than that brother came to be in Tamil—the Rev. Dr. Scudder, now of Chicago. His power and proficiency came by study and practice, night as well as day. Make no plan to relax your effort after one or two years of missionary life. You cannot graduate from that school till your work among the people closes. The first missionaries from this country to the Tamil people were giants in their language—Spalding, who through fifty years of service, even to the fiftieth, spent many hours daily in the study of it; Poor, a match for any native in rapid, idiomatic, and eloquent speech; Winslow, our Webster in Tamil lexicography."

Who has not read of the linguistic studies and labors of Dr. Carey, of India? At his cobbler's bench he taught himself Latin, Greek and Hebrew; and in India he pursued the study of the languages with the same enthusiasm, until he became eminently successful. He was appointed examiner of candidates for the service of the East India Company. For thirty years he taught Bengalee, Mahratta and Sanscrit in Fort William College. In 1801 he published the New Testament in the Bengalee tongue. He prepared grammars and dictionaries in several Indian tongues. The Bible he translated in whole and in part, assisted by others, into twenty-four different languages. The Bible was thus made accessible to more than three hundred million people.

Dr. Morrison, who rose from the last-maker's bench to become a missionary to China, translated the Bible into the Chinese language, and thus prepared the way for the evangelization of the millions in the Celestial Empire.

John Hunt, of Fiji, mastered the Fijian language, translated the New Testament, besides preparing books for the people, thus making it possible for cannibal Fiji in fifty years to become a civilized country, supporting her own ministry, and sending missionaries to the lands beyond.

Whoever, therefore, would be successful must devote his days and nights to the study of the language of the natives, and the sooner this is done the better. Much depends upon the progress made during the first year. The sounds of the strange words will for some time be confusing, but there will follow gradually and surely, clearness and strength, such as will finally give the mastery. In the study of the languages of the American Indians, the key to success lies in the study of the verb. These languages, especially the Algonquin, are languages of verbs. Study day and night with enthusiasm the verb of the Indian language, and you are on the safe road to victory. Study in the lodges and wigwams, with your note-book in your hand, and the grammatical construction of the language will become clear to you without any teacher. O, how I have longed for some kind friend to tell me how I might master the language, and what course I might pursue, that speedily I might be able to speak fluently the words of life to the people in the native tongue. Little children of five and six years of age are found in the camps speaking English or French and the native language; and yet, though those little ones study neither grammar nor dictionary, they speak the Indian language grammatically.

Dr. Riggs, in his "Forty Years with the Sioux," writes: "Before we left the States, it had been impressed upon us by Secretary David Greene that whether we were successful missionaries or not depended much on our acquiring a free use of the language. And the teaching of my own experience and observation is that if one fails to make a pretty good start the first year in its acquisition, it will be a rare thing if he ever masters the language. And so, obedient to our instructions, we made it our first work to get our ears opened to the strange sounds, and our tongues made cunning for their utterance."

This faithful missionary lived to prepare a grammar and dictionary of the Dakota language, and translate the Bible into the same.

There will be hard work, but the missionary's motto is "*Nil Desperandum.*"

When Howard Vincent, late Director of Criminal Investigations, Scotland Yard, London, was going to spend his furlough, he visited a new country each year and mastered its language. When he went to Russia, he advertised for lodgings with a Russian family, where he could receive help in the study of the language. He employed four tutors, each having a different system, with whom he studied eleven hours a day. In six weeks he was able to converse fluently in the Russian language. There are different methods for studying a language, but none supersedes direct and continual contact with the people, and an intelligent enthusiasm in the study of the language, so as to classify words, and grasp accurately its grammatical construction.

The Rev. Mr. Clough, of the Telegu Mission in India, related his experience in language-study, which may help us in our work. "I learned the native language by committing Bible verses to memory one at a time, and repeating them on the street-corners to little crowds of natives. I had to change my corner very often, as the natives would get tired of hearing a single verse repeated. My stock of verses gradually accumulated, until I had enough to make a respectable sermon, and soon afterward I mastered the language."

By preaching to the natives in their own language, you will reach their hearts and gain their confidence and love. Should you live to translate or prepare works for the use of the natives, there will follow you a teaching benediction that will gladden your heart, and meet you again on the other side of life with ten thousand bounties as your glorious reward.

THE ANTAGONISM OF RACES.

The great war chief of the Dakota nation, Sitting Bull, gave utterance to a sentiment that is peculiarly suggestive to us in studying the Indian question, "There is not one white man who loves an Indian, and not a true Indian but hates a white man." The noble attempts of Hiawatha and Tecumseh to form a grand confederacy of the Indians were expressive of the antagonism existing between the red and white races of men.

Bitter and sad memories are traced by the hand of history relative to the contact of the red and white races with each other. The songs of the pale faces and the stoics of the woods have oftentimes been mingled together, only to be broken by the sound of the white man's rifle, and the hideous war-whoop of the native tribes. When the Pilgrim Fathers landed at Plymouth Rock, in 1620, the brave Indian chief Samoset gave inspiration to the minds of the exiles for conscience' sake by proclaiming, in the name of the natives of the land, "*Welcome, Englishmen.*" The language of their lips was but the expression of the language of their hearts. This first token of friendship was the harbinger of peace that lasted for many years.

The labors of John Eliot, the apostle of the Indians, were confronted by the hostility of the early settlers in the country. The peaceful relations at first established between the early settlers of our own country, and the Indians were ultimately destroyed by the overbearing spirit of the Saxon race. There are other influences, however, not apparent to the casual observer, which are at work continually undermining the foundations of peace and loyalty that are being laid.

The Indian tribes of the West learn, by contact with each other, to speak each other's language sufficient to converse on matters affecting their common welfare, but the Saxon learns not the tongue of the Indians, unless in a few instances where force of circumstances has compelled him to do so. The Indian loves his own language, and shows a strong aversion to the language of his conquerors. Although he may have learned some words and phrases, he prefers his own beautiful language to the foreign tongue introduced by the white men. And he has good reason for loving intensely the native language which he speaks. It is so full of beauty, possessing an unwritten grammar before the genius of the white man had reduced it to writing.

It is accurate in all its grammatical distinctions and full of euphonious arrangements and harmony. When the missionary seeks to engage in labor amongst the Indians there confronts him this conflicting element, the native language. He must master it, if he would reach the hearts of the Indians. This means a vast amount of labor, because it is constructed differently from the English language. In order to remove this antagonistic element there must be a determination to grasp the intricacies of the tongue which belongs to the natives. The more that I have studied the language, the stronger have become my convictions that there is a divinity in language. A little child will enter the Indian camp speaking only the language of the white race, and in one or two years it will speak *grammatically* the language of the Indians. How has the language of an uncivilized people become so civilized? Because God is in it.

There are to be found customs antagonistic to those of the white race; many of these customs point to a period of civilization, antedating the advent of the white man among the tribe. Their domestic, social and political customs are different from ours, and in order to help the Indian to a nobler life we must undermine them with our own, or bring them into harmony. Our Blood Indians in former years buried their dead in the crotches of trees, the bodies being wrapped in buffalo robes or blankets. They also placed them on raised scaffolds, on the prairies where no wood was to be found. Beside the bodies were laid boxes containing the relics of the deceased, and with them whatever treasures they possessed. Now we are bringing them into harmony with ourselves. The people are burying their dead in coffins and placing them in the ground. This may not seem much, and yet it is one of the influences at work as the result of missionary labor. They are laying aside the domestic duties of the camps, and adopting the domestic life of the white people.

There are differences of opinion between the red and white races as to what constitute their respective rights. These can only be brought into harmony by acting according to the principles of justice.

The native religion of the Indians is at variance, in many things, with the Christian religion.

True, there is the belief in a God—a Great Spirit or a Great Sun—but there are also inferior deities. There are prayers and sacrifices, traditions of the fall of man, the flood, the coming of a great Teacher, and many others closely related to those of the Christian religion, and yet there are many others that are of a conflicting nature. There is the opposition of the medicine men, and the intense devotion of the people to their own religion. Here is but one instance of many that I could mention, illustrating this fact. Several years ago there went a priest to Blackfoot Crossing to teach the Blackfeet the way of life. As he was doing so, there appeared upon the scene a Blackfoot Indian, who told the Indians that the aged priest was speaking falsely. He said that some time ago a Kooteenay chief had died, and his spirit went to heaven. He had accepted the Christian religion, and accordingly he went to the white man's heaven. When he had knocked at the door, seeking admission, a messenger inquired his name, and then informed him that he was not a white man, and could not, therefore, be admitted. He retraced his steps, proceeded to the heaven of the Indians, and besought the door-keeper to grant him an entrance. On learning his name the person informed him that he was not an Indian, but had an Indian skin, with the religion of the white man. As he had departed from the faith of his father, he could not be allowed to enter.

There were two religions given by the Great Spirit, one in a book for the guidance of the white men, who, by following its teachings, will reach the white man's heaven; the other is in the heads of the Indians, in the sky, rocks, rivers and mountains. And the red men who listen to God in nature will hear his voice, and find at last the heaven beyond.

When the Kooteenay chief found that he could not get a resting-place, but must be left out in the cold, he was puzzled to know what to do. The attendant, taking compassion upon him, said, that one more chance would be given him, and that he would be permitted to return to earth on condition that he told all the Indians to retain their own religion, and not listen to the instructions of the white men.

"Now," said the Blackfoot prophet, "the old Kooteenay chief has returned from the dead, and he is living at the Kooteenay village, and he says that all the Indians are to keep their own religion, or they will not reach the Indian's heaven."

The aged priest was baffled, but soon recovering himself, he said, that as it was getting late he would postpone his answer for a few days, when he would call the people together for his answer.

That evening he sent out from the camp two young Blackfoot Indians, who were instructed to proceed at once, and as stealthily as possible, to the camp where the old Kooteenay chief lived, and learn all the facts, returning as quickly as possible.

A long journey of over two hundred miles lay before them, but they were not long in going and returning. In a few days they entered the Blackfoot camp at night unseen, and reported themselves to the priest. Early next morning a crier went around the camp, calling the people together to listen to the answer of the priest.

The people were assembled, the Blackfoot prophet being among the number. He felt proud of the position he occupied among his people, and felt confident that no answer could be given to his statement.

The aged priest emerged from a lodge, approached the people, and began to address them. He told them how he had sent the young men to the camp of the Kooteenay chief, and found the old man enjoying good health. The chief said that what the Blackfoot prophet had said was not true. He had not died, and had never seen a vision of heaven. "And," said the priest, "here are two of the sons of the old chief who have come to our camp to corroborate the testimony of the two young men whom I sent."

When the people saw the sons of the Kooteenay chief assenting to the speech of the priest, they looked at the prophet, and beheld his crestfallen appearance. He had lost the day, and the white man's religion was allowed to be taught in the lodges to young and old.

The Indians love intensely their own religion, which in many things is akin to the Christian religion, yet there are antagonisms. It is not by determined opposition that we must win our way, but by continued labor, undermining the customs of the Indians by giving them a superior religion, grander and purer customs, and a nobler civilization than they enjoy. The Gospel of Christ is winning its way gradually, by spreading its influences among the people. It is affecting their religion, mythology, traditions and customs. We are preserving the past in written form, and supplanting it with a nobler present. In former years, when the Indians were asked to tell the story of the Creation, they related their native tradition; now they relate the Bible account of it. Whilst we mourn, in the interests of science, that much is being lost of great interest relating to history, we rejoice in the progress of the race. The differences existing between the red and white race will not be removed by a sickly sentimentality, but by according justice, and in seeking to use all legitimate means for the elevation of the red race. By earnest missionary effort, there will be for the Indian the impartation of a new affection, and the suppression of evil.

ENVIRONMENT AND RELIGION.

The rapid extension of the kingdom of the Nazarene, its acceptance by some tribes of men and rejection by others, has caused students of missions to inquire concerning the causes of the different attitudes of races and communities toward the superior religion of life. At first sight it seems strange that one tribe should eagerly embrace the teachings of the Divine Book, and another, removed two hundred miles distant, should persistently refuse to accept the same truths. Yet there are causes which time, patience and devotion can overcome. It is a well recognized fact, that the physical features of a country wherein a race of people is located, have much to do in developing the individual members, and the race as a whole. The people who dwell in a thickly wooded country differ from those who live on inland rivers. The stunted Eskimo and Lapp are not to be compared to the stalwart Indians of the plains. Geographical position and climate exert powerful influences in producing a progressive or retrogressive civilization. Tribes, physically and intellectually well developed, are not found in the remote places of the earth. War, famine, or crime has driven the cowardly, weak, or immoral to seek a shelter out of the reach of their enemies.

When comparing races and their characteristics, we are unable to push our study to its utmost conclusions, from lack of data, as their history is unwritten, save in their languages and arts. Yet we can gather sufficient, from their languages, mythology, traditions, native religions and arts, to gives us true ideas as to the influence which geographical position and climate exert upon the minds of peoples in their relation to Christian missions. In the study of the Indian races of the American continent, a striking difference in development, physical, mental and moral, and in their attitude toward Christianity in any form, when first presented to them, will be found between the Indians of the forest, the coast, the mountains, the prairie and the inland rivers.

The *Blackfeet* of the plains are tall, with well proportioned bodies, but the arms and limbs lack muscular strength, elasticity and form; the *Mountain Stony* is short of stature, lithe in form, and active in his movements, and the *Chinook* Indians, on the rivers, are short, stout and heavy. The place of residence begets its own peculiar kind of labor, which acts upon the mental power of the individual, and upon his morality.

The study of a single nation will reveal the influence of environment upon labor, and the civilization resulting therefrom. The grandeur of the sea produced the adventurous Norse rovers, and the daring Venetians. The mountainous scenery of Switzerland, Wales and Scotland begat a race of heroes and bards, and subsequently eloquent preachers and people famed for their intelligence and thrift. The language and literature of a mountainous people is grand and rugged, presenting a striking contrast to the mellow tones and gentle strains of the famous Troubadours of the sunny plains of Provence. Some countries are better adapted than others for developing a high state of mental activity. The resources of land and sea which bound the residence of a tribe, determine the kinds of labor in which they shall engage. These necessarily act upon their intellectual development and morals. Labor requiring energy and daring will create corresponding mental excitement and moral courage; while idleness, or a desultory kind of toil, will beget debasing appetites, bestial thoughts, and a listlessness toward a spiritual life.

The Chinook Indians lived for a time in a wild section of country where their food was berries and grasshoppers pounded together, and their abject condition made them cowardly and sensual in the extreme. That kind of labour which necessitates the constant use of the reasoning faculties will prepare a tribe for thinking upon matters of religion. This may result in its acceptance or rejection, according to the ability of the religious messenger, or the motives which prompt the tribal leaders to admit the approach of the missionary.

Country and climate exert their influences upon the literature, morals and religion of communities. Were Canada possessed of a warmer temperature, a greater coast line, and a larger number of mountains scattered throughout the various provinces, she would probably have a more extensive literature than she has to-day. Dr. Oswald, in an article in the *Popular Science Monthly*, on the moral influence of residence and climate, puts it thus:

"Modern French scientists are nothing, if not methodical, and have repeatedly called attention to the curious regularity in the geographical distribution of certain vices and virtues; intemperance, for instance, north of the forth-eighth parallel; sexual aberrations south of the forty-fifth; financial extravagance in large seaport towns; thrift in pastoral highland regions. It is, indeed, a remarkable circumstance that in the home of the best wine grapes, in Greece and Southern Spain, drunkenness is far less prevalent than in Scotland, or in Russian Poland, where Bacchus can tempt his votaries only with nauseous vodka. The idea that a low temperature begets an instinctive craving for alcoholic tonics seems disproved by the teetotalism of the Patagonian savages, who horsewhip every Spanish stimulant-monger without benefit of clergy. The Lesghian mountaineers, too, observe the interdict of the Koran in the icy summit regions of the Caucasus; but there is no doubt that the bracing influence of a cold climate affords a certain degree of immunity from the debilitating effect of the alcoholic vice, and that a Scandinavian peasant can for years survive the effects of a daily dose of alcohol that would kill an Egyptian fellah in a single month."

The reception of Christianity by different Indian tribes will be seen, when compared, to depend somewhat upon the influence of country and climate, as related to labor, mental activity, morals and native religion, making all due allowance for the hindrances, arising from inefficient religious teachers, and the advantages resulting from isolation and excellent food.

The Indian tribes of the Dominion may be conveniently divided into five classes, namely: Forest, Coast and Island, Mountain, Prairie, and Inland River Indians.

The Hurons and Iroquois, when first met by Jacques Cartier, dwelt in the beautiful valley of the St. Lawrence. Subsequently they went westward to the region of the lakes, and lived within the area embraced by Ontario and the western part of the State of New York. Though at that time separate tribes and allied races, they were bitter enemies, and for a long term of years waged deadly war against each other. Dwelling in palisaded towns, they still belonged to the class which I have named—Forest Indians. The Iroquois were tall, proud and energetic, fitly called by Parkman, "the Indian of Indians." Morgan, in his "League of the Iroquois," says of them: "They achieved for themselves a more remarkable civil organization, and acquired a higher degree of influence than any other race of Indian lineage, except those of Mexico and Peru. In the drama of European colonization, they stood for nearly two centuries with an unshaken front against the devastations of war, the blighting influence of foreign intercourse, and the still more fatal encroachments of a restless and advancing border population. Under their federal system the Iroquois flourished in independence, and were capable of self-protection long after the New England and Virginian races had surrendered their jurisdictions and fallen into the condition of dependent nations; and they now stand forth upon the canvas of Indian history, prominent alike for the wisdom of their civil institutions, their sagacity in the administration of the league and their courage in its defence."

The Hurons were a "patrician order of savages," fitful in temper, superstitious in religion and terrible in war. The attitude of this "typical race of American aborigines" toward Christianity, will present one phase of the subject under consideration. The Hurons were taught Roman Catholic Christianity by the Jesuit missionaries, under the guidance of Brebeuf and Lalemant, and the spiritual teachers labored for a long time before there were any permanent results.

The influence of the French under Champlain, the missionary-soldier, on the side of the Hurons against the Iroquois, prepared the way for religious instruction. Success in war was of greater consequence to them than the religion of the pale-face, but if they could gain the former, they were willing to adopt the latter. The sensuousness of the native religion appealed to their minds with stronger force than the truths taught by the priests. They found nothing in the new religion to replace the "*medicine*" of the old. The wretchedness and poverty, induced by frequent wars, broke the power of the Hurons; and the missionaries, by nursing the sick, feeding the hungry, teaching incessantly by precept and example, at length won the affections of the people and gained adherents to the cross.

Isaac Jogues, the founder of the "Martyr's Mission" among the Iroquois, after many months of intense suffering, trod the way of the cross, and went home to God. As he entered the wigwam of an Iroquois chief, in obedience to a summons, the swift stroke of a tomahawk dashed him to the ground, and his red-handed parishioners rejoiced in his death. The story of this pious Jesuit and his mission, as told in Withrow's "Adventures of Isaac Jogues," reads like a thrilling romance whilst having the charm of reality, and enforcing the truth, "The blood of the martyrs is the seed of the Church."

Not till war had weakened the Iroquois, and laid their hearts on the ground, did they accept the teachings of their spiritual advisers. The strength of intellect that devised the wonderful political organization of this race, should have caused them to examine the new religion for themselves, but there were reasons for postponing its acceptance. They were a race of warriors, who devoted all their energy in gaining a superiority over other tribes. They loved intensely their native religion, and the medical priesthood opposed the new religion, as they foresaw the loss of prestige and power. Bloody warfare does not prepare the hearts of men for spiritual meditation; and the history of the introduction of Christianity among the Huron-Iroquois by the Jesuits, strongly enforces this truth.

The Coast and Island Indians, although addicted to many barbarous customs, are possessed of considerable power of intellect. Living near the sea, and constant adventurous toil to gain a livelihood, increases and sustains this mental power. Sir George Simpson wrote concerning the Indians of British Columbia, residing near Fort Simpson, that they were very clever and ingenious. They carved steamers, animals and many other objects very neatly in stone, wood and ivory, imitating, in short, everything that they saw, either in reality or in drawings. He saw at Fort Simpson the head of a small vessel that the Indians were building, so well executed as to be taken for the work of a white mechanic. One man had prepared very accurate charts of most parts of the adjacent shores. Henry S. Welcome, in "The Story of Metlakahtla," says of the Tsimsheans: "Despite their atrocious barbarity, these people showed evidence of superior intellectual capacity. Their language, abounding in metaphor, is copious and expressive, and, with few exceptions, the sounds are soft, sweet and flowing. In front of every hut was erected a totem-pole, elaborately carved with the figures of birds or animals, or other objects designating the crest of the clan to which the occupant belonged. Sometimes the entire front of the hut was carved and stained to represent the head and face of an animal or bird, the mouth or beak of which served as a door-way. Every article, whether canoe, fish-spear, war-club or spoon, serves as examples of their skill in carving. Among their various occupations they wrought and exquisitely engraved bracelets and other ornaments of gold, silver, and copper, and made baskets and pouches of a peculiar grass so closely woven as to hold water, all embellished with unique heraldic designs."

Large quantities of salmon are caught by the coast tribes, and were they to engage in this kind of work in order to get sufficient for food only, there would follow periods of idleness, and consequently mental inertia. They have, however, sought other kinds of labor, making oil from the oolachan and dogfish, and toiling in saw-mills and canneries. When the natives first came in contact with the teachers of Christianity, their wars, prevailing superstitious practices, and opposition from the "medicine men," presented a strong front to the new doctrines. The missionaries employed the Chinook jargon for a time, only to discard it as useless for the purpose of teaching religious truth. Assiduously studying the native languages, they preached, worked and lived heroically, and the artistic natives gradually pondered over, and finally accepted the Gospel. The different denominations engaged in Christianizing the natives of British Columbia have been eminently successful in their labors. Whilst not detracting in the least from the honors due these earnest and worthy teachers of the faith, their success, in part, follows from the influence of country and climate.

The mountain tribes introduce to us a people with country and labor entirely different from those that have been mentioned. Feelings of reverence and awe take possession of the soul when contemplating the eternal hills of God. Is there not good reason for the mountain Indian associating the mountain peaks with many of his traditions, and for many of the Indian tribes believing that the ancestors of the Indian and some of the native deities sprang out of the mountain tops? The grandeur of the hills, however, implies hard toil for the Indian. Hunting on foot, climbing the slippery slopes, is excellent exercise, inducing good digestion, sound health, clear intellect, strength of limb, cheerfulness of spirit and courage. Surely there should follow religious thoughts—reverence for the Supreme, dread of evil, and a prayerful disposition. The Mountain Stonies are a hardy race. They listened reverently to the story of the Cross as told them by Rundle, Woolsey and the McDougalls. The truth has found good soil, and the harvest is abundant.

The prairie tribes are the Goths and Huns of the

New World. The introduction of the horse to the new continent by the Spanish conquerors, and the later reception of firearms by the Indians, have changed the life and labor of the natives of the plains. Expansion of intellect and sterling independence, closely allied to a lordly haughtiness, are begotten by a life on the broad prairies of the south and west. The excitement of the chase, and the fear and glory of continual warfare nourished the pride of these people, and made them feel that in everything, even in religion, they were superior to all other peoples. With the simplicity of children, curiosity and a love of novelty, caused them to listen attentively to the teachings of the Bible. When they heard of salvation they were eager to embrace everything included in the new religion; but they would not give up their practice of polygamy, their sun-dances, religious and social festivals, and their martial raids upon their foes. They expected that by submitting to the rites of religion, some mysterious influence would be imparted to them whereby they would become superior to all the other tribes. But the tree of knowledge yielded evil only. There came not the fulfilment of their expectations, and they were disappointed. The advent of the white man brought disease and death. The native prophets of the plains said the Great Spirit was angry, and was punishing them for allowing the white men to enter their country, and for listening to the white praying men. There were minor influences at work which induced sentiments like these. As late as 1846, the Snake Indians were found without horses and firearms. When the emigrants were travelling to California, some of the Snake Indians followed on foot, keeping close to the horses, which were going at a gentle pace, and for fifteen or twenty miles they jogged along, chattering to the people, returning homeward as easily as they came. The peaceful Indians were changed in a few years to revengeful red men, because many of their people had been wantonly shot down by selfish and angry white men.

Drs. Riggs and Williamson, of the Dakota mission, with the brothers Pond, toiled earnestly for years, seeing little fruit and enduring many hardships at the hands of the Sioux. After twenty-five years of labor, there came the Minnesota massacre, when the mission was destroyed. But in the prison the Sioux began to see that their medicine-men and their religion had failed, and they sought help in Christianity. Three hundred were baptized in one day. Dr. Riggs tells the story:

"In a few weeks a deep and abiding concern for themselves was manifest. Here were hundreds of men who had all their life refused to listen to the Gospel. They now wanted to hear it. There was a like number of men who had refused to learn to read. Now almost all were eager to learn. And along with this wonderful awakening on the subject of education sprang up the more marvellous one of their seeking after God—after some god. Their own gods had failed them signally, as was manifest by their present condition. Their conjurers, their medicine-men, their makers of *wakan*, were nonplussed. Even the women taunted them by saying, 'You boasted great power as *wakan* men; where is it now?' These barriers, which had been impregnable and impenetrable in the past, were suddenly broken down. Their ancestral religion had departed. Their hearts were aching after some spiritual revelation. They felt that there was such a thing as sin, and there was such a person as Christ, God's Son, who is a Saviour from sin. These impressions were made by the preaching of the Word."

The prairie tribes lived by hunting the buffalo, and so great were the numbers that in a few days enough meat could be procured for making pemmican that would last for months.

After the excitement of the chase, there was feasting, revelry and idleness, with wars with the neighboring tribes. Camp-life was then debasing to the intellect and morals. What has been the attitude of the other Plain Indians besides the Sioux? The Plain Crees have been harder to reach in religious matters than the same people included in forest tribes, these are the Swampy Crees. The Blackfeet, Bloods and Piegans have had Roman Catholic and Protestant missionaries for nearly a decade, and still there is not a single conversion. What are the causes of this? Country, climate, modes of life and labor, proximity of white population, missionary sectarianism, and tribal relationship. The Indians expected physical benefits from religion, and their expectations were not met. The whisky trader preceded the missionary, and the people were debased in mind and morals, while they were fast going to destruction physically. Disease, immorality, the departure of the buffalo, and consequent change of labor from hunters to agriculturists; the opposition of the medicine-men, the influence of tribal relationship, by means of which a leading chief can control the confederacy in favor of the native religion; depression of spirit arising from decrease of population, difficulty in procuring persons capable of interpreting religious ideas, or acting as efficient helpers in studying the language; proximity of the tribes to the International Boundary Line, having the same people residing in Montana, hence arising a strong temptation to the young men of the camps to horse-stealing; the immorality of the border population, and the presence of representatives of different churches on the same reserves, are some of the influences that have thus far hindered the progress of Christianity among the people. But the day is coming when they shall follow the other tribes in accepting the truth, and become disciples of the Master of Life.

The Inland River Indians are the lowest in the scale of civilization, that is, in comparing the tribes in their native state, before the influences of the white population have reached them. The Chinook Indians, a tribe of the Flathead confederacy, may be regarded as representative of this class. A distinction must be made in this classification on the scale of civilization between the Chinooks, which I include under coast tribes, and those of the inland rivers. It is not an ethnological division, but nevertheless, in the study of the Indians, is an important one. The Chinook Indians on the Columbia may be regarded as the most uncouth and lazy, in their native state, of all the Indian tribes, if we except the Digger Indians, of California. Washington Irving, in contrasting them with the prairie tribes, says: "The effect of different modes of life upon the human frame and human character is strikingly instanced in the contrast between the hunting Indians of the prairies and the fishing Indians of the sea-coast. The former, continually on horseback, scouring the plains, gaining their food by hardy exercise, and subsisting chiefly on flesh, are generally tall, sinewy, meagre, but well formed and of bold and fierce deportment; the latter, lounging about the river banks, or squatting and curved up in their canoes, are generally low in stature, ill-shaped, with crooked legs, thick ankles, and broad, flat feet. They are inferior also in muscular power and activity, and in game qualities and appearance, to their hard-riding brethren of the prairies."

The country in which these people lived, when Paul Kane visited them, was almost destitute of furs. Fish were easily caught; and although they were expert in the management of their boats, and could ride safely over the boisterous waves, their mode of labor induced laziness, and exerted a stunting influence upon their intellects. They were deficient in decorative ability, and showed little taste in the arrangement of their dress, or in ornamenting the implements of peace and war. The tribes of the interior of British Columbia and Washington Territory were in a similar state. Missions were established among the inland river tribes, and success has followed the labor of faithful men. When they receive the Gospel there is imparted an incentive to labor, desire after improvement, domestic and social, and a love for justice and truth. There being little or no change in labor succeeding missionary influence, such as in the case of the prairie tribes, the resources of the country are laid hold of and developed, and the people become self-sustaining. The advent of the white people introduces whisky and work. Christianity teaches the Indians to reject the former and accept the latter, and that is what is being done.

The Gospel was preached to the Indians on the Fraser river, and in a short time many were converted. The Indians have become missionaries to other tribes. In the vast territory of Alaska, converted Indians were the pioneers of Christianity; and now many Alaskans are rejoicing in the presence of churches, schools, missionaries and teachers. About 1850 the Roman Catholics began work among the Twana Indians, at Skokomish river, Washington Territory, but were compelled to leave, and shortly after were succeeded by Protestant teachers. Missionary work was carried on, with some interruptions, until 1874, when it was renewed with energy and enthusiasm. The additions to the Church from that time among the Clallam and Twana Indians, until 1883, were chiefly from the ranks of the Sunday-school children, after that the people sought the way of life, and now industry and religion go together.

Studying the tribes as a whole, making all due allowances for exceptions as to persons and individual tribes, and for all the influences which affect them before and during the time Christian agencies are brought to bear upon them, the following, according to my judgment, as affected by the study of the history of American Indian missions, is the order in which they will receive the Gospel:

1. The artistic tribes residing on the coasts.
2. The mountain tribes.
3. The inland river tribes.
4. The forest tribes.
5. The prairie tribes.

The Divine Spirit does not, however, act according to any set rules, and there are individuals and tribes that have been reached despite the influences of country and climate.

LIGHT ON THE PRAIRIES.

Westward advances the tide of immigration, carrying the flowers and the filth of our eastern provinces and the Old World. Over the fertile fields of Manitoba, the boundless prairies of agricultural and mineral wealth, the massive ranges of mountains, to the shores of the mighty Pacific, friends and foreigners are speeding their way, and we are destined to follow them with churches and schools, to make them a united people in our glorious Dominion. Who shall guide us but the great Master of Life, in whose hands are the destinies of nations and men? God has given to us a blessed heritage in that western country, with its vast areas of excellent land. There is Manitoba, with one hundred and twenty-five thousand square miles; Assiniboia, with ninety-five thousand square miles; Saskatchewan, with one hundred and fourteen thousand square miles; Alberta, with one hundred thousand square miles, and away in the north, Keewatin and Athabasca, with their vast areas of land, well adapted to supply the wants of tens of thousands of people. Thriving agricultural settlements and prosperous villages are scattered over the provisional districts of Assiniboia, Saskatchewan and Alberta, and Manitoba is already teeming with many thousands of wealthy settlers. Nearly the whole of Alberta is underlaid with a thick bed of coal of excellent quality. It crops out of the banks of several rivers, five and six feet in thickness. Over nearly all of this provisional district the soil is rich; the crops for the past three years have been wonderfully abundant, and the people are contented and happy, save in their desire for increased railroad facilities. In the Macleod district of Alberta, the cattle roam in thousands, summer and winter alike, for they dwell in the land of the Chinook winds, and need not the shelter of colder climes. This is God's heritage for our children, and we must go up and possess the land for our Lord and Christ.

Within these vast areas of land, included under the names of Manitoba and the North-West, there dwell twenty-five thousand red men, who need our help, as they have given us their land. There are located on reservations under the authority and guidance of the Government in the North-West Territories, Wood Crees, Plain Crees, Blackfeet, Bloods, Piegans, Sioux, Stonies, Sarcees, Swampies or Saultcaux, and Chippewayan or Montagnais. Away far in the north are a large number of tribes belonging to the Tinné family of Indians.

The Indian tribes of our western country are the possessors of a civilization that is fast decaying, and the followers of the mountain, prairie and forest gods, who no longer sway the minds and hearts of these red men, as in the days of yore.

The Indian conjurer performs his incantations, and the people repair to him in times of trouble. The sick children writhe in agony as the medicine-men bleed them with a piece of glass for a lancet, or scarify them with a burnt stick or piece of heated iron. The prairie lodges are still filled with painted men and women, rejoicing in the fact that they do not belong to the race of white people.

These native customs seem strange to us, because they are so near, and point to a period and a people of whom history has told us very little. The history of these people reveals to us many tribes great in numbers, rich in lands, buffalo and other kinds of large and small game, independent in spirit, full of superstition, yet thoroughly imbued with religious zeal in all their ceremonies connected with hunting, war, medicine and social life. The change that must inevitably come to all inferior races has at last fallen upon them. The advent of the white men, and the introduction of Christianity and civilization amongst them, has affected their whole life. The religious words and phrases existing in the native languages are losing their former meaning, and many new terms belonging to Christianity have found their way into these languages, and are exerting a powerful influence upon their minds and hearts. Many of the Indians do not take kindly to the new life at first, being rather suspicious of the benefits to be conferred by accepting it, and being also somewhat at variance with their own. In their transition state, between losing faith in their native religion and accepting Christianity and civilization, they rapidly decrease. Despondency takes possession of their hearts, the oppressive feeling that they are a conquered race presses heavily upon them, and, like the wild caged birds, they sicken and die. When, however, they have fully learned the lessons of man's equality, the brotherhood of man and the fatherhood of God, as revealed to them by Christian teaching, they become strong and independent.

Christian teachers have rapidly followed the adventurous settler, supplying him with religious teaching for himself and family. Representatives of all the religious denominations have followed the trails into Manitoba and the North-West, pushing each other too closely in their zeal to carry the Gospel, thus retarding each other's progress and spending money in a needless way. In every little village there are ministers of the Episcopal, Presbyterian and Methodist Churches. Along with these, the Congregationalists, Baptists and Salvation Army are numerous, and doing good work in Manitoba. But in the North-West, the three largest denominations are working hard to win the country for Christ.

Missionaries have gone into the camps and among

the lodges of the red men, and oftentimes have they followed them in their hunting expeditions, urging them to lay aside the war-paint and cease going on the war-path, for the Prince of Peace has come to unite the Red and White Races with bonds of Christian love. The English Church has the greatest number of missionaries amongst the Indians. These teachers are laboring amongst the Cree, Blood, Blackfeet, Sarcee and Piegan Indians; and in the northern country, amongst the Linné and Eskimo families. The Presbyterians have workers among the Cree, Sioux and Stony tribes. The Methodists are toiling among the Cree, Saulteaux, Sioux, Stony and Blood Indians. Heavy manual labor, isolation, poverty and sickness is the lot of the majority of these workers, but the tales of suffering they do not tell, for they are toiling for God, and He will reward them. The greatest burden is that of the slow growth of success, when compared with that of Japan and other countries. The modern student of missions, and the general Christian public, have raised a wrong standard of success, and by this they judge all missions. Missions cannot all be measured by one standard; and the Indian missionaries who toil for many years and report few conversions, are doing God's work as effectually as those whose lot is cast among a people who are born again in a single day. There may be an apology made for the people, but none is needed for the earnest, faithful toiler in the mission field, and yet his work is sometimes severely criticised by men much inferior to him in learning, ability, self-sacrifice and devotion.

Seldom do we hear or read of those who bear the heaviest burdens in the missionary work, namely, the women who toil silently and unseen. The religious newspapers and missionary magazines seldom mention their names or their labors, and yet they nurse the sick, teach the Indian women and girls by precept and example, cheer the missionary in his lonely toil, and keep starvation from the door by dint of economy and love. When the missionary returns from his field on furlough, the hardships and suffering are never told at missionary meetings, but the thrilling accounts of victories won are the burden of his song. We have lives of missionaries in abundance, but few of missionaries' wives. Oh! cruel custom, that shuts our mouths and straitens our pens, in giving the women their meed of praise. God shall reward them, if men fail to grant them their due.

Mission work has been successful amongst the Indian tribes. The Gospel has reached the hearts of the dwellers in the lodges, and their lives have been changed. The songs of the medicine-men and the beating of the *tom-tom* of the Indian gambler have ceased when Christ has won the heart. The mother's wail for her lost children has given place to the joyous hope of immortal life. Pagan burial rites have been forsaken, and Christian ceremonial has been accepted as a token of peace. Christian civilization has transformed the Six Nation Indians from savage warriors to peaceful and industrious citizens of our Dominion. The wild, roving Sioux of the Minnesota massacre forsook their gods, and became farmers and mechanics, with schools, churches, native teachers and ministers, through the power of Gospel truth. The Sioux Indians of Manitoba received a native missionary through the intercession of the Rev. Dr. Black, of Kildonan, with the veteran Siouan missionary, the Rev. Dr. Riggs; and to-day there is a thriving community near Birtle, rejoicing in the purity and power of the religion of Christ. The Wood Crees, Stonies and Saulteaux have learned to reverence the Sabbath, rejected their heathen practices, adopted many of the nobler customs of the white race, and are advancing toward a life of civilization and truth. The power of Christ saves the aged women from a cruel death, the virgins from a life of shame, the children from neglect, and gives education, cleanliness, respect for others' rights, and love in the home. The words of the Great Teacher have been heralded within the Arctic Circle and along the Great Yukon river, and the hearts of the hardy natives have been made glad with the joyful sound.

The wealth and piety of our churches must be utilized to send the Gospel to the white settlers and the red men. Christians dare not shirk their responsibility in this matter. An hundred-fold will the outlay return to us, in maintaining the peace of our nation, and preparing a people to serve the Lord.

Indian Brush Lodges.

CHAPTER X.

DO INDIAN MISSIONS PAY?

DAVID ZEISBERGER, the famous Moravian Indian missionary, labored for nearly sixty years among the Indians, and rejoiced in many trophies won for Christ in the camps of the red men. Sixty-four years after his death, four Indians from Canada visited the spot where the aged missionary was buried, and together sang the same hymn that was sung at his funeral, which was one of Zeisberger's own translations. What impelled these red men to make this pilgrimage? The power of the Gospel of the Nazarene.

The Indian, in his native state, is ambitious to be a warrior. He boasts of his prowess in slaying his enemies, taking their guns, and carrying off their scalps. In our western country, there came from the north, a noble Cree Indian, determined to avenge the death of his son at the hands of a Blackfoot Indian. On his way south, he visited a camp where a missionary was preaching, and there, for the first time, heard the story of God's love to man through the gift of His Son. His heart was touched, and he became obedient unto the truth. Southward he travelled, until he reached the Blackfoot camp, and there beheld the murderer of his son. Looking upon him, he told him of the story he had heard, and the absence of a desire for revenge, but he said he wished not to look again upon his face. The Cree Indian became a true Christian, and adorned the truth. He used his influence to avert a war between the Crees and Blackfeet, and was successful. In subsequent years, the Blackfeet slew him while he peacably sought to teach them the truths of the Christian Master of life. Woman was a mere chattel in the Indian camp, but Christianity taught a true regard for Indian womanhood. The heathen customs of mutilating the body were discarded, and men and women were taught to regard their bodies as temples of the Holy Ghost. The aged people were left to perish upon the prairie by their children in the days of heathen warfare, lest the lives of the whole tribe would be taken by their enemies; but the religion of the Christ taught them a true regard for the helpless, and the tottering parents were protected in the camps on the plains.

Heathenism taught revenge in death, and compensation when any kind of injury was inflicted. "A scalp for a scalp" was the principle acted upon; but the Christian teachers recognized the principle of forgiveness. War was thus averted, and the lives of many saved.

Heathenism buried its dead in the crotches of trees, on scaffolds raised on the prairie, or in lodges; but the influence of Christian teaching changed the modes of burial, and directed the minds of the people to an immortality, spiritual in its nature, freed from the sensual pleasures of pagan hearts.

A nobler individualism, superior religion and grander civilization, was given to the red men, by the followers of the Christ, than that promised by the priests and doctors of the lodges and wigwams of the forests and plains. Loyalty to the Queen and country was the burden of the message given by the Protestant teachers of religion, and the Indians of the west listened and obeyed, thus securing peace in troublous times.

The missionaries are a part of the standing army of our Dominion, who, by the principles they instil into the minds of men, and the enthusiasm they arouse in a noble cause, save to the country every year thousands of dollars, and help to maintain the peace and prosperity of our land. The work of educated and pious men prepare the new districts for the advent of the settler, and the grand heritage that God has given us, is made accessible for the enterprising poor who seek their fortunes in the west. It pays to send the Gospel to the Indians, and to maintain our work among the aborigines of our own land.

THE CHURCH AND THE INDIANS.

Missionary work among the Indians of Canada began in 1614, when four priests arrived from France. They conceived the project of founding a colony and fortifying a village to ensure safety in the event of an attack from hostile Indians, and to gather the friendly tribes to be instructed in matters pertaining to their temporal, intellectual and spiritual welfare. Seven or eight years afterward five others joined the priests already mentioned, and began their work of converting the natives. These were sustained by the leading French statesmen in the country, one of whom took holy orders that he might win the Indians for the Church, and another was heard to say repeatedly, with intense earnestness, "The salvation of one soul is of more value than the conquest of an empire."

The Jesuits at once established an institution near Quebec for instructing the Indians. The missionaries combined with their spiritual labors political objects, and for a time gained immense power. They used their influence, and succeeded in prohibiting the sale of intoxicating liquors to the Indians. These early missionaries were enthusiastic in their labors.

The story of the sufferings of such men as Brebeuf and La Jeune is of thrilling interest. They labored among the Iroquois, but had little success. In the midst of their toil the missions were attacked and the people slain. They found the Hurons tractable, and were rewarded by baptizing, in a short period, 3,000 of them. All over the Dominion these men have labored amid privations of the severest kind. When persecuted by the Indians, they have held up their fingerless hands to God and implored His protection and grace, and so great was the impression made that the haughty Iroquois agreed to make overtures for peace, and asked for missionaries to teach them the way of life.

The Roman Catholic Church has been successful in making converts, but not in civilizing and elevating the Indian. Their ritual is attractive to the Indian mind, and the ceremony of baptism admits them to the Church, but they lack the inspiring influences that flow from the faith in Christ, and the indwelling of the Divine Spirit in their hearts.

The Episcopal Church began her labors among the Indians with prospects of good being accomplished, but the early years were not blessed with abundant success. The work was new, and there were many difficulties in the way. From the days when Archdeacon Nelles began his labors on the Tuscarora mission, many good men and true have toiled in this noble work, and the Master has blessed them abundantly. For more than fifty years this good man labored amongst the Six Nation Indians, and their present state of civilization is but one proof of his zeal and intelligence in missionary toil.

In 1820, the Rev. John West began his labors in the Red River Settlement.

In 1840, Bishop Anderson entered upon his missionary labors in this country. His diocese extended from Labrador to the Rocky Mountains, and from the International Boundary to the North Pole. With the care of the churches of the white settlers resting upon him, and the many inconveniences of travelling in those years, he forgot not the red men of Manitoba and the North-West. He was the great praying-father of the Indians. Laborer after laborer he brought into the field, until his missions were extended to the Arctic Circle. These worthy men sought out intelligent natures, placed them under missionary teachers, and trained them to labor among their fellow-men. All over the land they have travelled, visiting the missions, opening up new fields, preparing a religious literature for the tribes, and then filled with the holy enthusiasm which they caught in the home of the northern lights, they have gone east to the haunts of civilization to arouse the sympathies of Christian people, returning with the missonary coffers well replenished to carry on their works.

At Metlakahtla, near Fort Simpson, the Rev. Mr. Duncan has done noble work in Christianizing and civilizing the Indians, and is now toiling earnestly in Alaska with his people.

Archdeacon Vincent, resident for thirty-one years in the Diocese of Moosonee, has labored with enthusiasm among the Esquimaux and Indians. The New Testament and Prayer-Book have been translated, and the books printed and bound by the missionary. Very many of the Indians have been converted, and abundant success has attended the labors of this noble man.

Away in the frozen north, and within the Arctic Circle, Archdeacon McDonald has toiled, and God has blessed him. He invented a syllabary, consisting of about four hundred syllables, and in these characters he has himself printed and bound the New Testament and Prayer-Book in the Tukudh language. In a few weeks the people are able to read for themselves, in their own language, the Word of God. Tribes hitherto unvisited he has gone amongst and taught them the way of life.

Bishop McLean for a long period toiled among the Cree Indians, in the Saskatchewan country, some of whom were educated under his supervision in Emmanuel College. Descended from Scottish Presbyterian stock, he inherited an excellent physical constitution, to which was added sterling piety, and a freedom from theological bigotry. Never can I forget my last interview with him, when, on parting, he prayed for me personally, and for the success of my work. Then, grasping my hand, he said, "God bless you, I shall rejoice as much at your success as if you were one of my own clergy." He has gone to his reward, followed by the blessings of many half-breeds and Indians in the northern land.

The Presbyterian Church has been engaged chiefly in teaching the Indians, preferring to spend her labors upon the young. Work among the white settlers of Manitoba and the North-West has exacted the talent and funds of the work, and great success has followed this wise expenditure in the new country. The labors of McKay, Flett and Solomon among the Crees and Sioux have been blessed in the conversion of the Indians, and a few noble men and women are teaching scattered bands of Sioux and Crees in the land of the west.

The aged and devoted David Zeisberger, who spent over sixty years as a Moravian missionary among the Indians in the United States, was compelled at one time to seek refuge with his people in Canada from the persecution of the settlers, and the attacks of the American soldiers. He labored among the Delaware Indians, a tribe of the celebrated *Lenni Lenape.* It was among this same tribe that David Brainerd spent four very successful years, and then went home to God. In 1792, some of these Delawares belonging to the Moravian Church settled on the Thames river, at a place now called Moraviantown, where they have received the ministrations of their own missionaries. This pioneer missionary church has spent much of her energy in hard and lonely fields among the Indians. They are engaged successfully among the Indians and Esquimaux of Labrador. There is no church that can surpass this for the enthusiasm and self-sacrificing spirit of the men and women who have bled and died for the sons of the Red Race.

Indian missionary work in Canada by Protestants began in earnest with the labors of the Rev. Wm. Case, of the Methodist Church. So deeply was this man of God impressed with his responsibility in carrying to the Indian tribes the word of God, that he travelled almost incessantly, visiting the Indians, urged the missionaries under his care to study the languages, sought out true and well-qualified men to labor, and devised new methods for winning the tribes to Christ. He took several Indian boys, and had them sing at missionary meetings in the United States, much to the joy of the people there, and with great profit to the funds of the Church. He organized the Manual Labor

School at Alderville, as a training institution for Indian youth. This school became the Indian college, where several of our most successful Indian missionaries were trained. The men directed by Elder Case became the most successful missionaries among the Indians of the Church. His heart was in this work, and, like the sainted John Elliott, the Apostle of the Indians, he only ceased to labor for them when his breath ceased.

As he attended a camp-meeting, he beheld the face of a youth among the converts, who was destined to become one of the most successful Indian missionaries that ever lived. That lad was Kahkewayquonaby—Peter Jones.

The father of this youth was a white man, who, having loved a modern Pocahontas, married her. Although the lad had spent his childhood in the Indian camps, his father, being a man of education, sent him to school, where he received a fair education. After his conversion, he held prayer-meetings among the Indians, taught an Indian school, pursued a course of self-education, and travelled with the missionaries as assistant preacher and interpreter. After his ordination, he became an Indian missionary, with a roving commission. Tribe after tribe, and band after band, he visited; and, as he preached, the power of God fell upon the people, and many were led to rejoice in salvation. On his own mission he went with his Indians into the fields, and taught them how to plough and sow. He encouraged the women to persevere in the study of domestic economy. All day long he would labor in the fields with his people, and, in the evenings, they gathered together in their prayer-meetings. A week or two at home, spent in this manner, and then away he would go on a missionary visit to the tribes scattered throughout the Province of Ontario. He was intensely energetic in his labors for the salvation of men. Such was his influence among the Indians that, when they heard that he was passing through a section of country to attend a meeting at a distant point, the Indians and whites would come for miles to see him, prevail on him to speak a few words to them on religious matters, and, of their own accord, would take up a collection, and, with tears in their eyes, give it to him, as expressive of their love for the Gospel, wishing that they could make it more.

He married a white lady from England, who still lives.

Twice he appeared before royalty in England. Everywhere he was preaching to the Indians, or preaching and lecturing in the interests of his work. He did a noble work. Thousands of Indians heard from him the way of life. Many, very many, were led to Christ through his instrumentality.

Though he is dead, he is still preaching to the Indians by his Ojibway Hymn Book and New Testament.

John Sunday—*Shawundais*—was a Mississauga Indian. Dark and lonely were the early days of his life; but the Gospel reached his heart, and, impelled with love for his fellow-men, he began to tell the story of God's love to fallen man. A roving commission was his; for in our forests, and along the rivers and lakes of Ontario, and farther west, on the shores of Lake Superior, he sped to declare, in the lonely wigwam and among the scattered bands of red men, the everlasting truth of God. From that day till the present, the songs of Zion have been sung, and souls won for Christ by Evans, Rundle, Woolsey, McDougall, and a host of other honest toilers, in the mission fields.

God has blessed with His presence the ministrations of His servants of all the churches in the camps of the Indians of our land.

THE RED ALIENS.

When first the white men came in contact with the Indians of Canada, they were treated with the greatest kindness and respect. The Indians entertained them in a hospitable manner, and, in return for their generosity, the white men gave them wine. Thus came the *first curse* upon the native tribes of our Dominion. When Donnacona, the Lord of Canada, visited Jacques Cartier, he was compelled, with two of his chiefs and eight of the natives, to accompany an expedition to France, where they pined away and died, thus alienating the good will and love of the Indians from the white man.

When Martin Frobisher discovered the Frobisher Straits, he took with him to England a man, woman and child belonging to the Indian race.

Compulsory banishment was *the second curse* that fell upon the native tribes.

Champlain was solicited by a band of Indians belonging to the Algonquin nation to aid them against the powerful Iroquois, and consented; and then began a series of Indian wars that lasted in Canada for over a hundred years. The records of this period teem with accounts of treachery and cruelty of the most hideous kind. The white men and Indians joined hands against their fellows. Then, sections of the red and white races slaughtered other sections of the same races, and the war-whoop of savage and the battle-cry of the civilized resounded through the forests of our beautiful land.

Thus came the *third curse* upon the Stoics of the woods. Friendship fled, and bitter animosity sprang up in the hearts of the Indians toward the pale-faces, which increased as the years rolled on. Aliens to society, they have been hated by many, because of their customs, and especially because they stand in the way of advancing civilization.

Mission work has been opposed by the greed of the land speculator, and hindered through the lack of sympathy and financial help from the Christian public of the land. We have not been guilty of gross injustice toward the red man, but we have failed in not answering fully the demands of the aborigines for education and Christian teaching.

President Cleveland fairly represents the duty of the nation in treating the Indians, as he says: "The conscience of the people demands that the Indians shall be fairly and honestly treated as wards of the Government, and their education and civilization promoted with a view to their ultimate citizenship."

The Sword and the Bible will not Christianize them;

harsh treatment will develop a spirit of animosity, and nobler methods must, therefore, be employed to elevate and direct them in the way of peace.

On the seal of the charter of the colony of Massachusetts is represented an Indian standing, calling to the white men, "Come over and help us!" One hundred and twenty-five thousand red men in the Dominion look up to us for spiritual help.

The educational facilities must be increased with more fully qualified teachers to instruct the Indian youth.

The Indian tribes are passing away, and what is done must be done quickly. We dare not linger in the face of such grave responsibilities. On the western plains, native songs, wafted on the evening breezes, are the dying requiem of the departing savage.

Enthusiastic missionary labor will arouse the despondent occupant of the lodge and make of him a man of pure and earnest life.

SUCCESS OF INDIAN MISSIONS.

The successful labors of eminent missionaries among the Indians attest the value of intelligent enthusiasm and consecrated effort in this distinct field of toil.

Roger Williams, John Eliot, and Mayhew were the pioneers in Protestant mission work among the red men of the American continent. The peaceful policy of William Penn disposed the minds of the Indians to listen attentively to the teaching of the Holy Book.

David Ziesberger, amid toils and difficulties, many and varied, sought to lead the red men from the paths of savage warfare in the way of peace and truth.

David and John Brainerd labored with success among the Indians, the former laying down his life after a short but brilliant career, the latter, taking up the fallen mantle of his brother, went on to win fresh conquests for Christ.

Finlay, among the Wyandots, and Williamson and Riggs, among the Dakotas, saw the fruit of their labors in the conversion of many souls, the reformation of the lives of the red men, and changes in the native customs of these people.

In our own Dominion, the ministers of righteousness have won many trophies among the Micmacs of Nova Scotia, the Iroquois, of Quebec, the Ojibways and Mohawks, of Ontario, and the numerous tribes in Manitoba, the North-West Territories and British Columbia.

The Rev. Silas Rand began his work in 1846 among the Indians of Nova Scotia. He found the Micmacs and Maliseets in a state of primitive barbarism, but, having strong faith in the possibility of the Indian being made a useful and pious man, he labored assiduously for the temporal and spiritual well-being of these tribes. Amid many difficulties he has toiled, but he has lived to see great advancement in their temporal and social condition. Whilst seeking to elevate the people, he has studied earnestly their history, customs, mythology, traditions and language, and is now the recognized authority on these matters.

The whole of the New Testament has been translated and printed in Micmac, with several of the books of the Old Testament. The Gospel of John and some religious tracts have been published in the Maliseet language; tracts, catechisms and hymns have also been prepared in the Micmac language, and a dictionary of Micmac and English, containing nearly thirty thousand words, is about completed.

Dr. Rand says concerning his work: "Mark, also, the change that has taken place in the condition of the tribe as respects *civilization* since we commenced our labors, despite all kinds and sorts of obstacles that have been placed in their way and in ours. Mark, for instance, the change in their *dress* and their domestic habits—in their culture generally. Forty years ago, you could not tell Indian men and women, as far as you could see them, by their dress. A few old women still wear the old-fashioned head and *shoulder* gear: but these cases, so far as my own observations go, are few and far between.

"And at the present you will meet with no intelligent man who will contend stoutly that an Indian 'can never be persuaded to live in a house,' or that 'Indians are like partridges, that no skill can tame,' all which nonsense, and much more of the same stamp, I used to have to meet. The rare thing *now* is to see a wigwam.

. . . .

"More than this, I have found everywhere a determination to obtain learning, to learn the English language, to send the children to the English schools and to adopt all the habits of civilization. To be able to read and write, well and fluently, is what but few comparatively of their white neighbors have attained to, if the truth should be told, and I will not pretend that cases are very often to be met with of such an attainment among the Indians.

"But there are not a few who can write an intelligible letter, both in their own language and ours. . . . Many adults have learned to read who never went to school at all. One of my ablest Micmac correspondents went but three months. And there is living near Lawrencetown, Wilmot, N.S., an Indian, now over seventy years of age, who bears a remarkably good reputation, who learned to read after he was above forty years old, and he can read Micmac as well as I can, if not better."

A significant fact has been stated as to the value of missionary effort, that it cost the United States Government one million eight hundred and forty-eight thousand dollars to support two thousand two hundred Dakota Indians, during seven years of their savage life; but after they were Christianized, it cost only one hundred and twenty thousand dollars to support them, during the same length of time.

The late Hon. Hiram Price, Commissioner of United States Indian Affairs, stated that there was more drunkenness and crime among the two hundred thousand inhabitants of Washington, the capital of the Republic, than among the two hundred and fifty thousand Indians in the United States. He believed that no other method for the elevation of the Indians was to be compared with the labors of the Christian missionaries among them.

In 1862, Archdeacon McDonald went as a missionary

of the English Church into the Yukon country. His headquarters were at Fort Yukon, one mile within the Arctic Circle. Missionary expeditions were made down the river Yukon for hundreds of miles, visiting tribes of Indians who had never seen a missionary. Many of these were taught to sing the hymns and memorized translations of the Lord's Prayer and Ten Commandments; and large numbers accepted the truth of the Gospel, becoming, nominally, Christians. The language spoken by the Indians, from Fort Yukon to the Peel river, is the Tukudh; but there are many dialects of the same language spoken by the tribes in that vicinity. After ten years of earnest work, parts of the New Testament were translated and published, and now the New Testament in full. The English Church Prayer-Book, a hymn-book, and other books, have been prepared in the Tukudh tongue.

There are many devoted Christian Indians under the instruction of native Christian leaders, who cheerfully teach without any salary. On the Upper Yukon there are numerous bands of Indians who have never had the Gospel of Christ preached to them. A syllabary of the Tukudh language was prepared, consisting of five hundred syllables, and some of the Indians have learned it in two weeks, so that they could read intelligently.

Away in that northern land, many of the heathen Indians have been instructed by the Christian red men, and through their influence they have learned to read, sing hymns, and engage in the devotional exercises of the praying Indians. The Gospel is doing much good among these people, and the hearts of many have been made glad. Thousands of Indians have been baptized since the work began. Bishop Bompas superintends the vast diocese of the Mackenzie River district, where Archdeacon McDonald labors. The work is carried on among the Tukudh and Tinné Indians and the Esquimaux.

The Tinné Indians include Chippewayans, Yellow-Knives, Dog-Ribs, Big River, Slave, and Nahany or Mountain Indians. In the diocese of Moosonee, one thousand two hundred miles long and eight hundred wide, containing Indian tribes speaking six or seven different languages, Bishop Horden is zealously toiling to lead the Indians and Esquimaux to Christ.

Religious books have been prepared for the use of the native Christians, many of whom are striving to lead their heathen brethren into the light of the knowledge divine. At one time, while the Bishop was on a visit at Rupert's House, he met a man who asked to be baptized. Never having seen him before, he was astonished, and told him so. Then he asked the man whether or not he could read, and he answered in the affirmative. A book was brought, and the stranger read it fluently. The previous winter a band of Indians, of whom this Indian was one, met some Indians at Rupert's House who could read, pray and sing. The heathen Indians requested the Christian Indians to teach them, which they did, and when compelled to part through lack of food, they gave to them some of their religious books. The man was baptized, and a short time after the whole tribe was admitted by baptism into the Church.

Bishop Young is working hard in the diocese of Athabasca, and winning many of the red men for Christ. This diocese has an area of nearly three thousand square miles. Scattered over this vast diocese are found Indians belonging to the Beaver, Cree, Chippewayan and Slave tribes.

Toil, hardship and isolation deter not the faithful missionaries in their work of elevating the dwellers in their northern homes.

In 1840, Robert Terrill Rundle, of the Methodist Church, went to Edmonton and Rocky Mountain House to preach the Gospel to the Cree and Stony Indians. He labored assiduously for the salvation of these tribes, and rejoiced in seeing many led to Christ. The songs he taught the people in those early days are still remembered by them, and many a heart clings fondly to the memory of those distant years. This faithful man still lives in England, having become superannuated only one year ago. His name will endure in the geography of our western country, for Mount Rundle rears its lofty head in the vicinity of the railroad in the mountains.

Sinclair, Steinhauer, Woolsey and Brooking laid the foundations of Christian truth among the Indian tribes in that distant region, supplementing the labors of Evans and Rundle; and from that day thousands of Indians have heard the Gospel news, and rejoiced in its saving power. Many have died in the faith, testifying with their latest breath to the power of Christ to forgive sin.

The McDougalls, father and son, took up the mantles

of the departed missionaries, and the Crees, Stonies and Saulteaux heard anew the story of God's love to man. Song and story around the camp-fires were full of spiritual life and joy. The painted savage heard with astonishment the conquests of the Christ, and he acknowledged the Christian Master of Life as his Leader and Friend. Proud hearts were melted as the missionaries sang of Jesus' love, and the lodges in the land of the Northern Lights resounded with the shouts of Christian joy.

Time and space fail in giving to all the faithful toilers among the Crees, Saulteaux and Stonies their meed of praise. Travellers have mentioned their names with reverence, and the Indians treasure the memory of their labors in their hearts. Young, German, Ross, Langford and Semmens are only a few of the self-sacrificing spirits who carried the truth among the lodges, and followed the Indians over the lakes and into the forests, that they might win them for Christ.

Across the mountains into British Columbia the red men have gone, and there, too, the intrepid spirits have followed them. Duncan, of Metlakahtla, the English Church missionary, and Thomas Crosby, the energetic Methodist, have seen many of the Haidas, Tsimsheans, and other Indian tribes led to forsake their potlaches and heathen feasts and sacrifices for the nobler way of the Christian life. Not content with preaching to the Indians around Fort Simpson, and travelling in his canoe, Crosby aroused the missionary spirit in Eastern Canada, which nobly responded to his call; and the mission yacht, *Glad*

Tidings, was built and equipped, and now is speeding over the mighty Pacific, carrying the knowledge of Christ to distant tribes.

Crosby, Tate, Green, and many others, are striving to plant missions among the tribes along the coast and in the interior, that they may teach the Indians how to support themselves honestly and well, and enjoy the purity and blessedness of the Gospel of peace.

Tens of thousands during the past thirty years have heard with joy the wondrous story of the life of Christ, and been constrained by its influence to forsake their customs, and follow the nobler teachings of the Prince of Peace.

Longer would we linger on these joyous scenes, listening to the testimonies of medicine-men, chiefs, old women and children, who have felt the power of religious truth, and bowed with joy before the cross. The mighty hosts who have, during the past fifty years, heard with joy the truth preached in the lodges and wigwams scattered throughout the Dominion, are sufficient testimony to the value of missionary labor. The tomahawks and plumed feathers have been laid aside, the war-paint is seen no longer, and the wild war-whoop has been silenced forever in the lodges and camps of the red men, whose hearts have been touched by the Man of Nazareth. Only when the final day has come and all the ransomed have returned to the home of God, shall the wondrous news be fully told of the races and tribes of red men who, in simplicity of heart and life, followed the teachings of the Great Spirit in this Canada of ours.

THE CROSS IN THE CAMP.

Eagle Arrow and White Calf were listening attentively to the new teachings of the missionaries, and, while many others were eager listeners in the lodges, they seemed to grasp more intelligently the truths presented in the native tongue. The doctrines of Christianity and the customs of the white men contrasted strangely with the native religion of the red men. They gazed in astonishment when something peculiar struck their fancy, and sometimes laughed at the singular illustrations of religious truth. It was all new to them, and their minds had not been trained to look at these things from the Christian standpoint, so they had their own methods of interpretation, which savored of the camp and the Indians' mode of life and thought.

"Tell it over again; it all sounds new and strange to us, and we wish to do what the Great Sun tells us."

It was repeated, and their countenances changed with alternate sunshine and shadow. Unusual emotions filled the heart of the Christian teacher as he gazed upon the faces of these seekers after truth. Homeward they travelled, pondering over the truth. It was the theme of many an evening's conversation in the lodges, where aforetime love and war were the sole topics of discourse. Some approved and others dissented from the new doctrines. Still they spread, until all had heard in the camps the story of the Cross. But there came to the hearts of the Blood Indians serious temptations, which weakened their faith. They had gone to the white settlements, and witnessed the lives of the white men, and returned with grave doubts as to the power and purity of the new religion. Christianity was to them the religion of the white man, and they looked for its influence upon the lives of the white people. Then the missionary was confronted with a powerful argument against the Bible and the Christ. These red men said, "Your religion is not good for us, for it fails to reform the lives of the men who have read the Bible and been under your instruction since they were born." The medicine-men gained fresh courage for the conflict, but ultimately they learned that blasted were their hopes, for the Nazarene was destined to conquer, and win the red men for Himself. Steadily the truth is progressing, and the final conquest soon will follow. The tribes of red men who have bowed at the Cross have been led to glory in their new-found joy. The Great Teacher of life has touched their hearts, and aroused their sympathies on behalf of others. Through the influence of Christian teaching, the roving Sioux of the western prairies forsook the Indian song and dance, the practice of polygamy was rejected, and they became useful and industrious mechanics and tillers of the soil. The children of the camps are gathering into the schools, where they are being educated. Native teachers and ministers preach the Gospel of righteousness to their fellow-men.

J. L. Garvin, chief of the Choctaw Nation, said: "Thanks to an all-wise God, the blanket has been replaced by decent apparel; the tomahawk has been exchanged for the useful axe; the scalping-knife for the ploughshare; and the dismal tone of the warrior's whoop has mellowed into the sacred songs of Zion."

Here and there among the camps, John Eliot went as the social leader and civilizer of the Indians, with a burning zeal for the salvation of the souls of the red men; and, after twelve years of hard study, mastered their language. Fifty years he toiled on their behalf, leaving the Bible and a religious literature for the people. Half a century later, David Brainerd, with a holy inspiration, followed the tribes in the forests, breathing words of prayer and love. Salvation through the cross was the subject of his story, and the Indians in their wigwams wept and prayed as he spoke of the Christian's Master of Life. A few short years of holy toil, and the devoted missionary, at the early age of twenty-nine years, passed away in godly triumph, rejoicing in the harvest garnered from the wigwams of that forest land. Christ, among the lodges, has won many trophies from sin, superstition, degradation and woe.

THE LORD'S PRAYER

IN THE CREE SYLLABIC CHARACTERS.

ᑳᑎᐯᔨᐦᒋᑫᐟ ᐅᑕᔭᒥᐦᐊᐤᐃᐧᐣ

ᓄᑕᓈᐣ ᑭᐦᒋᑭᓯᑯᕽ ᐁᐊᔮᔨᐣ,
ᑭᑕᑭᐢᑌᔨᐦᑖᑲᐧᐣ ᑭᐃᐧᐦᐅᐃᐧᐣ;

ᑭᑐᑌᓈᐃᐧᐃᐧᐣ ᑭᑕᐃᐧᐅᒋᐦᒋᐸᔨᐤ;
ᐁᐃᑌᔨᐦᑕᒪ ᑕᐃᐧᐃᐦᑭᐣ ᐅᑕ ᐊᐢᑮᕽ
ᑲᐃᓯ ᐃᐦᑭᕽ ᑭᓯᑯᕽ.

ᒥᔦᓈᐣ ᐊᓄᐦᐨ ᑲᑭᓯᑲᐠ ᑫ ᐅᐦᒋ
ᐱᒪᑎᓯᔮᕽ.

ᐁᑲᐧᔭ ᐱᓯᐢᑫᔨᐦᑕ ᓂᒪᒋᑐ
ᑕᒍᐃᐧᓃᓈᓇ, ᑫ ᐃᓯ ᐁᑲ ᐱᓯᐢᑫ
ᔨᐦᑕᒍ ᑲᒪᒋᑐᑕᑯᐃᐧᔭᐠ;

ᒪᒥᐧᐊᓃᓂᓈᐣ ᑭᒋᐁᑲᒪᒋᑐᑕᒫᕽ;
ᐸᒋᑎᓴᐦᐊᒫᐃᐧᓈᐣ ᑲᒫᔭᑕᕽ:

ᑮᔭ ᑭᑐᑌᓈᐃᐧᐃᐧᐣ, ᒥᓇ
ᓲᐦᑳᑎᓯᐃᐧᐣ, ᒥᓇ ᑭᐦᒫᔨᐃᐧᐃᐧᐣ,
ᑲᑫ, ᒥᓇ ᑲᑫᐧ ᐁᒣᐣ.